Unconventional Partners

"America is the result (and this should be constantly present to the mind) of the two distinct elements . . . which in America have been admirably incorporated and combined with one another. I allude to the spirit of Religion and the spirit of Liberty."

Alexis de Tocqueville

Unconventional Partners

Religion and Liberal Culture in the United States

ROBERT BOOTH FOWLER

WILLIAM B. EERDMANS PUBLISHING COMPANY • GRAND RAPIDS

Copyright © 1989 by Wm. B. Eerdmans Publishing Co.
255 Jefferson Ave. SE, Grand Rapids, Mich. 49503
Printed in the United States of America

Library of Congress Cataloging-in-Publication Data

Fowler, Robert Booth, 1940-
  Unconventional partners.

  Bibliography: p. 162
  1. United States—Religion.   2. Religion and culture.
3. Liberalism—United States.   I. Title.
BL2525.F68   1988   291.1'71'0973   88-11251

ISBN 0-8028-0342-3

CONTENTS

PREFACE

OVER THE PAST TEN YEARS the world of political studies in the United States has seen a virtual revolution on the subject of religion and politics. The field has burgeoned with publications, organizations, and scholars actively involved. It has been wonderful to behold, and to participate in with many others. But after I had been away from research in the area for several years in the early 1980s, I came back to the field impressed by our need for the development of theory. A little distance had made it clear to me that much of our collective endeavor in this field operated apart from theory, except for very modest particularistic theories regarding public opinion, voting, attitude formation, and the like. Moreover, what theory we did use was often the child of other disciplines, especially the sociology of religion—a discipline that, to be frank, had not for some time been a source of much bold, broad-ranging theory (though there are now signs of change that are very exciting). Indeed, "theory" in the arena of religion and politics most often seemed to mean "normative theory." Important as normative theory is, a shortage of it, or at least of expressions of normativity, is hardly the problem in religion and politics. A shortage of empirical theory, however, is a problem.

My concern was the development of theories that might help digest the rapidly expanding amount of data we have—in my case, data regarding religion and politics in the United States (one must start somewhere). The assistance I seek focuses on the hope that theory development can not only help in explaining the considerable empirical materials we have, but can also serve as a stimulus for the generation of new and confirming (or disconfirming) materials. It could be a source of both explanation and hypotheses.

I make no assumption here that theory-building is more important than field research—far from it—but simply suggest that we in this field are clearly at the point where we need to let ourselves go and try theory creation. I take for granted that any such theories would necessarily have to meet a test of congruence with the data at hand even as they might fruitfully try to break out of the conventional perspectives that have gone before.

In this study, my goal was to develop a theory, suitably tentative and exploratory, to describe the relationship between our liberal society and religion, especially organized religion, in the United States. Aware of and respectful of several alternative theories, I sought to propose and argue for another, which to my mind more adequately explained the events and the data we have on religion and politics in the United States. Nothing about my theory is finished—not its conception, not the evidence it draws on, nothing. It is meant to stimulate rethinking of classic theories and of the entire relationship between religion and our liberal order—and thus to some extent the issue of religion and any culture.

One term I need to address immediately is "culture" because it is so central to my enterprise—while it is so beyond intellectual definition or agreed upon boundaries by now. "Almost anything human could be, and at some point has been, used as the basis for a definition of culture."[1] No single definition can possibly address all the controversies surrounding this deeply contested concept. Today a good definition must therefore be encompassing. Into this sea of dispute, if not despair, I propose to sail simply saying that by culture I mean widely shared beliefs and practices within a society; by American political culture I mean widely shared beliefs and practices in the United States that are integral to our public life.[2]

Along the way I have been helped by so many. Two people were especially important in this project's intellectual development. My friend, Charlie Anderson, who has cared for me in good times and bad, was essential. At the beginning he took my modest idea and both challenged it and augmented it. Kenneth Wald read my work in a much later stage, and his stimulating and invaluable critique helped make this a much better argument. Numerous other colleagues in the Political Science, Religion, and Politics group played roles as critics, commentators, and at times enthusiasts. Philip Abbott encouraged me to publish a first, brief statement of my thesis as "Religion and Liberalism in the United States,"

1. Paul Bohanan, "Rethinking Culture: A Project for Current Anthropologists," *Current Anthropology* 14 (October 1973): 358.
2. The literature warring over the meaning of culture is vast; a good introduction might include: Paul Bohanan, "Rethinking Culture: A Project for Current Anthropologists," *Current Anthropology* 14 (October 1973): 357-65; Richard Merelman, *Making Something of Ourselves: On Culture and Politics in the United States* (Berkeley: University of California Press, 1984); Marvin Harris, *Cultural Materialism: The Struggle for a Science of Culture* (New York: Random House, 1979); Clifford Beertz, *The Interpretation of Cultures: Selected Essays* (New York: Basic Books, 1973).

in *The Liberal Future in America: Essays in Renewal*, edited by Philip Abbott and Michael B. Levy (Westport, CT: Greenwood Press, 1985). I am grateful for their help, just as I am for my students in religion and politics who were sometimes more pointed though no less kind in their reflections. I am also grateful to Lori Schlinkert who had to type and re-type and did so for me with equally large amounts of patience and good cheer. A lot of people, in short, have assisted me on this journey. I accept the responsibility for the result, but I am immensely grateful for so many helping hands.

RELIGION
LIBERAL SOCIETY

CHAPTER ONE
Religion and Liberalism

DANIEL BELL HAS OBSERVED, "From the end of the nineteenth century to the middle of the twentieth century, almost every sociological thinker . . . expected religion to disappear by the onset of the twenty-first century. . . ."[1] It is now obvious that this has not taken place, especially in the United States, and that it gives no sign of taking place. Undeniably, some of the forms, influences, and expectations of religion have changed and will continue to, but religion persists.[2]

Both secularization and religion appear to ebb and flow in all cultures over history. But religion endures, and perhaps Stark and Bainbridge have it right in *The Future of Religion* (1985) when they argue that the permanence of religion as a human phenomenon is more likely to be the case than some inexorable process of secularization.[3] In any case, religion has not disappeared before the forces of secularization, especially in the United States. ~~IN SECULAR AMERICA~~

Here as well as elsewhere, religion is in fact often challenging the secular order. That challenge is in part an implicit acknowledgment of the forces of secularization; American religious activism depends on those opposing forces for its renewed energy.[4] But the presence and the very real energy of our strengthened, more self-confident and more political religion today justifies Peter Berger's suggestion that we have gone to some extent "From the Crisis of Religion to the Crisis of Secu-

1. Daniel Bell, "The Return of the Sacred? The Argument on the Future of Religion," *British Journal of Sociology* 28 (December 1977): 419-49.
2. Mary Douglas and Steven Tipton, eds., *Religion and America: Spirituality in a Secular Age* (Boston: Beacon, 1983), pp. 3-13.
3. Rodney Stark and William Sims Bainbridge, *The Future of Religion: Secularization, Revival and Cult Formation* (Berkeley: University of California Press, 1985), ch. 1.
4. See, for example, Theodore Caplow et al., *All Faithful People: Change and Continuity in Middletown's Religion* (Minneapolis: University of Minnesota Press, 1983), ch. 1.

larity."[5] Religion has unmistakably reentered the public consciousness, and in some places secular culture does seem under attack. Secularism as a necessary component and inevitable companion of the modern nation-state now appears problematic, a major shift from a few decades ago.[6]

That religion continues to be important in American lives—far more important, as Kenneth Wald notes, than politics[7]—is undeniable. More than half the adult population (56 percent) rates religion as very important to them. Close to 70 percent claim to be members of organized religious groups, and 40 percent claim to attend worship services weekly. To be sure, religious membership and worship attendance do not appear to be rising in the 1980s, though that fact conceals the variations within the whole—the slide of "mainstream" Protestantism as opposed to the vigor and growth of evangelicalism and fundamentalism (about one-third of the population identify with evangelicalism, less than one-quarter with "mainstream Protestantism"). It is also easy to demonstrate that knowledge levels about religion and the Bible are low, and indications that people's religious feelings influence their everyday ethics are, at the least, ambiguous.[8] PRIVATE/PUBLIC

Yet, while there are some signs that religion is no more than a superficial gloss, indicators of renewed and deeper interest also abound. Half the population claim that their religious interest has risen above what it was five years ago. Interest among youth is on the upswing; Bible study has risen; daily prayer is common. In addition, for the first time in over two decades, Americans believe that religion is of increasing importance in our society as a whole, a judgment that some of the recent manifold outbreaks of religion in politics have undoubtedly influenced.[9]

Most of these findings focus on "official" religion—recognized activities in the Judeo-Christian traditions usually connected in some sense with formal religious institutions. But there is also in the United States an extensive universe, typically diverse in its manifestations, that lies outside the traditional and established religious channels. It almost always

5. Peter L. Berger, "From the Crisis of Religion to the Crisis of Secularity," in *Religion and America*, pp. 14-24.

6. Two differing but in some ways converging views: Richard Merelman, *Making Something of Ourselves: On Culture and Politics in the United States* (Berkeley: University of California Press, 1984); Martin E. Marty, "Religion in America since Mid-Century," in *Religion and America*, pp. 276-78.

7. Kenneth D. Wald, *Religion and Politics in the United States* (New York: St. Martin's, 1986), p. 9.

8. *Religion in America: 50 Years, 1935–1985* (Gallup Report No. 236, May 1985), pp. 11-13, 22.

9. *Ibid.*, pp. 13, 16, 45.

serves to connect individuals more directly, more personally, with God or spirits than "modern" religious institutions usually do. Such religious expressions range from the long-documented evidence that many more typical Americans pray than ever enter a church all the way to a host of shadowy groups, never in surveys, who pursue demonstrable religious practices or are in fact religious groups. Witchcraft, spiritualism, devotionalism, Satanism, and the like are only some of the more obvious illustrations. Scholars have found such outcroppings of unofficial and often unacknowledged "popular religion" everywhere in America. It too has to be part of why there is such vigor in the religious impulse in America.[10]

In short, Peter Berger is correct when he comments, after reviewing the data, that "the majority of Americans are as furiously religious as ever—and very probably *more* religious than they were when de Tocqueville marveled at this quality of American life."[11] Noting that American religion is also considerably intertwined with our political life—and with increasing frequency—one can say that reflection on the relationship between religion and the American society is an appropriate endeavor. Indeed, reflection on the subject is an old American enterprise, as old as the first English settlements in the New World.[12] And the endurance of religion in people's lives, despite predictions of its demise, and its accelerating involvement in politics give a new stimulus to this longtime concern of America.

Two views have dominated reflection concerning the relationship between religion and American culture. One, drawn from Marx, Weber, and Durkheim, has been reinforced by de Tocqueville and H. Richard Niebuhr, among others, and has emphasized the *integration* of religion into our liberal society: sometimes it helps shape our society, often it reinforces our society, and almost always it reflects our social order. The other view, heard more and more today, suggests a quite different relationship, one of *challenge*. In this view, sometimes held by religious activists and often by those alarmed by assorted politicized religious groups, religion seems more and more at odds with our culture and its leaders and determined to challenge American society.

10. See Peter W. Williams, *Popular Religion in America: Symbolic Change and the Modernization Process in Historical Perspective* (Englewood Cliffs, NJ: Prentice-Hall, 1980).

11. Peter L. Berger, "Religion in Post-Protestant America," *Commentary*, May 1986, p. 44.

12. A good account of the interactions of church, state, and culture in the American colonies is found in Thomas J. Curry, *The First Freedoms* (New York: Oxford University Press, 1986).

Each of these analyses has its attractions. Each encompasses part of our history and our contemporary situation. Each deserves serious consideration—which it will receive here. But each is also flawed. Classical observers placed far too much emphasis on the interconnections between religion and our broader society. More recently, others have given too much attention to the signs that religion is a challenging alternative to our familiar world. Neither perspective goes deep enough, to discover how strange and unconventional the "integration" has been or how superficial the "challenge" is.

In this book I intend to propose another view, a case, I believe, that is crying out to be made: I argue that religion in America has been, and continues to be, an *alternative* to the liberal order, a *refuge* from our society and its pervasive values. Yet, by providing that space from our liberal order, it unintentionally *helps* the liberal world.

By *refuge* I mean a retreat in a religious sense, a place where one escapes liberal society or its costs and enters into another and, in its way, quieter realm. This situation might lead, of course, to conflicts with liberal America. Once in a while it has, and we do see some signs of this possibility today. Mostly, though, the path people have chosen has been retreat in the curious partial way religion and churches exist in American lives. The retreat is only temporary. It is not meant as a desperate escape, or even a general repudiation of liberal culture and liberal values. Religion is, rather, another realm that is valuable in its differentness, but loved—as liberal society is—only with a partial or ambivalent love. If refuge translates to support, religion supports through its passive role in a far more subtle fashion than is usually argued. Religion has not built modern America, nor does it cheer it on. Yet, by providing a temporary alternative, which fills needs that liberal culture cannot, it helps sustain our liberal order. It serves to fill up, so to speak, some of the inevitable but real fissures of American liberalism—by being a relief-giving and yet nonthreatening alternative.

By *liberalism* and our *liberal* society I mean three things in this study: 1) a commitment to skeptical reason, an affirmation of pragmatic intelligence, and an uneasiness about both abstract philosophical thinking and nonrational modes of knowledge; 2) enthusiasm in principle (and increasingly in practice) for tolerance not only in political terms but much more obviously in terms of lifestyle and social norms; 3) affirmation of the central importance of the individual and individual freedom.[13] By *lib-*

13. My colleague James Farr has been a source of stimulation and insight here, as in so many areas.

eral culture I mean not only these values of modern American liberalism but also its practices in our political order, our schools, our media, and the major institutions (except, to some extent, of course, religious institutions) of our society. Culture is not only ideas but practice, and in these institutions liberal values ordinarily reign, as many students of culture in our era have noted.[14]

That these values are widely held within our culture is a well-established fact.[15] That there is evidence of ambivalence among the population at large is equally well established. Americans do not fully love liberal skepticism and individualism. We tend to support the "right of choice" regarding abortion and yet modify it with considerable popular disapproval of abortion on demand. We voice great popular uneasiness about the absence of fixed "moral values" in schools and among public officials, and we do have a "second language" of community struggling to break out in American life.[16] Indeed, the very existence of this ambivalence is the ground on which my thesis about the role of religion in our liberal society is built. But ambivalence does not mean that the values are not there and supported. They are.

There are two ways in particular in which religion constitutes a temporary refuge from this mind-set in America. It is certainly a refuge from liberal skepticism and liberal individualism, our peculiar, relentless, and demanding moral ideals for humankind. As a refuge from skepticism and expansive, expanding tolerance, the church remains a place where absolute spiritual truths are still usually affirmed, a place where there are certainties, no matter how much they may evaporate when one considers

14. Two good sources here are Merelman, *Making Something of Ourselves,* and Daniel Bell, *The Cultural Contradictions of Capitalism* (New York: Basic Books, 1978).

15. The poll data back up this popular liberalism, of course, and they do so again and again. But I think one learns the most about it through such qualitative studies as Robert Bellah et al., *Habits of the Heart: Individualism and Commitment in American Life* (Berkeley: University of California Press, 1985); Jennifer Hochschild, *What's Fair? American Beliefs about Distributive Justice* (Cambridge: Harvard University Press, 1981); Merelman, *Making Something of Ourselves;* Richard Reeves, *American Journey* (New York: Simon and Schuster, 1982).

16. Two relevant examples: the long-established pattern of public opinion on abortion is succinctly summarized in Richard McBrien, *Caesar's Coin: Religion and Politics in America* (New York: Macmillan, 1987), p. 153; "The Class Conflict Over Abortion," *The Public Interest,* no. 52 (Summer, 1978). Merelman, *Making Something of Ourselves,* is an excellent source on the schools and the media.

them in terms of concrete morality or public policy. And for many religious people, they do not evaporate then.

This point can scarcely be overemphasized. It is no accident that conservative churches are growing. They provide the spiritually based certainties that modern liberalism—and a good deal of liberal religion—cannot offer. Similarly, the enduring strength of the Roman Catholic Church continues to turn on its institutional, doctrinal, and especially sacramental orthodoxies, despite Vatican II, guitar masses, and hip priests. On the other side, it is certainly equally unsurprising that "mainline" Protestant churches have failed to prosper in the age of skeptical liberalism. They provide ambivalent refuge from the imperatives of liberalism as Americans experience them. Indeed, to some degree they are its religious children.[17] The story a friend recounted recently of her disappointment when she enrolled her children in a "mainstream" Presbyterian church in Illinois is by now all too common. She sought some firm standards, but what she got was a youth minister as hip as hip culture outside. He allowed teenagers to rampage through the church on "retreats," and he even reported—almost bragged—about a teenage pregnancy that was "created" in the church sanctuary the year before.

Religion also can, and often does, offer a refuge from American liberalism's central ethic of the individual. In all our discussions of the "me decade" of the 1970s (which seems to be lasting far longer than a decade), or the broader concern with the individual that *is* liberalism today (however it is variously affirmed), or the celebration of the individual that is justly famous as the heart of the American political tradition, we often forget that there are other worlds, especially worlds of practice, in the United States. We also sometimes forget how attractive these worlds are to many citizens. I do not mean to equate religion with the long-trumpeted groupiness of American life. That can be neatly incorporated within American liberalism, and long has been: pluralism is liberalism's social ideal, or at least approved reality.[18] I do not even mean to connect

17. For data on relative church growth, see *Religion in America* (Gallup Report), p. 11; Dean Kelley, *Why Conservative Churches Are Growing* (New York: Harper and Row, 1972); Jeffrey Hadden, *The Gathering Storm in the Churches* (Garden City, NY: Doubleday, 1969); Andrew M. Greeley, *American Catholics since the Council: An Unauthorized Report* (Chicago: Thomas More, 1985), pp. 21-22; see also David Leege, ed., *Notre Dame Study of Parish Life*, a series of reports published in the 1980s. The complex subject of what has accounted for "mainline" problems is explored in much more depth in ch. 7 of this work.

18. Two good essays that deal with this theme are: Louis Hartz, *The Liberal Tradition in America* (New York: Harcourt, Brace and World, 1955);

religion with such mundane, but perhaps noteworthy, facts as that our marriage rate exceeds our much-touted divorce rate.

Religion goes well beyond these points in being a refuge from the self in at least two ways that are of great significance. It offers a refuge in its very affirmation of transcendence, though it is sometimes difficult for those who are not religious to understand just how important this fact can be to the believer. After all, faith in some kind of God is integral to any ordinary definition of religion and is so in American religion. The Christian God is invariably portrayed as one who is with the believer— "Lo, I am with you always"—and as the being who cares for every person no matter how desperate his or her life is, and, specifically in the New Testament, for the lonely, the widow, the orphan, and the poor. Moreover, Christianity obviously addresses the loneliness of death and potential nothingness, a realm where liberalism is utterly silent.

In this context one thinks of Freud's enlightened, liberal essay *The Future of an Illusion*.[19] Freud, the liberal skeptic who held religion to be an appalling error, was well aware of how belief in transcendence functions as a refuge, as a powerful consolation for people. It gives them an explanation for their suffering and provides a basis for hope. While Freud believed that we could and should do without such a crutch, he nonetheless acknowledged the pain of individual suffering that he felt was the root of religion. In this he was far more acute than many of today's secular liberals, for whom religion in America is a fossil that inexplicably endures despite the effects of the winds and rains of liberalism.

Perhaps more important in ordinary human terms is religion's role as a refuge from relentless individualism in its social, even communal, aspects on earth. This is partly a matter of religion as the community of believers, whether seen in international, national, denominational, or local church terms. Studies suggest the appeal of church in this sense for couples who begin creating their own would-be community when they enter child-bearing and child-rearing ages. These studies also establish the attractive power of particular churches that do provide such a satisfying social life. For many Christians and other religionists in America, the church more or less approximates the community they seek but too rarely find in liberal society.[20] One should note too that an important rea-

---

Herve Varenne, *Americans Together: Structured Diversity in a Midwestern Town* (New York: Columbia University Press, 1977).

19. Sigmund Freud, *The Future of an Illusion* (Garden City, NY: Doubleday, 1964).

20. Some of the complex dynamics are explored in Dean R. Hoge and David A. Roozen, eds., *Understanding Church Growth and Decline, 1950–1978*

son for defections from religion, one that is much more prevalent than religious skepticism, is the perceived failure of specific churches to be community-like. When they are not refuges in this community sense, they pay the price.[21]

In addition, there is no dismissing the widespread belief in our culture that religion is *for* the social and *about* the social. That is, regardless of whether religions do promote bonding among people, the expectation that they should remains strong. The idea persists that religion is about love above all else—and not just love of God—and that religious people and their houses of worship should manifest this love. Theologians and clerics may debate, but studies of popular attitudes toward churches demonstrate that people routinely expect religion to be about community, and they are often disappointed when they discover that churches are made up of quite ordinary people in a liberal culture that is at best ambivalent concerning this goal. The point is this: the culture has anointed the church as one of the "havens" from liberalism.

There is a substantial irony in the role religion plays for many Americans: providing them with a refuge from a skeptical and subjective liberalism that lacks transcendent, spiritual grounding, and addressing the needs for community in an America devoted to individual competition and self-reliance. The irony is that liberalism was not born apart from religion, specifically the Christian religion, nor did its classic expositors favor such a separation. Indeed, liberalism's "core values of individual liberty . . . and constitutionally protected rights have often been derived from Christian assumptions."[22] John Locke, surely the most important founding theorist of liberalism, "saw political life as requiring both reason and faith."[23] Reason did not lead to ultimate skepticism. Far from it. Instead, it was our means to learn the natural (moral) laws we ought to

---

(New York: Pilgrim, 1979); Kelley, *Why Conservative Churches Are Growing;* related here is the life-cycle view of modern church attendance patterns, for which see, for example, Greeley, *American Catholics since the Council,* pp. 74-75.

21. Three able books on the issue of why people leave (and join) churches are: John Kotre, *The View from the Border* (Chicago: Aldine, 1971); Dean R. Hoge, *Converts, Dropouts, Returnees: A Study of Religious Change among Catholics* (New York: Pilgrim, 1981); Edmund A. Rauff, *Why People Join the Church* (New York: Pilgrim, 1979).

22. Paul Sigmund, "Christianity, Ideology, and Political Philosophy," in *Essays on Christianity and Political Philosophy,* George W. Carey and James V. Schall, eds. (Lanham, MD: University Press of America, 1984), p. 85.

23. Eldon J. Eisenach, *Two Worlds of Liberalism: Religion and Politics in Hobbes, Locke, and Mill* (Chicago: University of Chicago Press, 1981), p. 85.

follow in life; and behind them lay the God and the Jesus in whom Locke had deep faith. If anything, Locke was skeptical of limitless reason. He judged that humans needed revelation as a complement to liberal reason in order to get them to live according to God's natural laws. Thus, while Locke celebrated individual freedom and tolerance, he made sense of them only in a world where reason could not uncover all truth and was not enough for living a good life. Integral to life were God and his laws, which were "not against reason but beyond reason."[24] They remained the ultimate truth and were essential for every society: liberal values and Christianity went together.[25]

While Immanuel Kant was less influential on Anglo-American liberal thought, he ranks with Locke as a giant in the development of liberalism. He too placed religion in a central position in his social thought. To be sure, Kant's rejection of reason's capacity to discover a transcendent God, let alone the precepts of Christianity, seems dramatically to separate religion from liberal reason in his scheme. But this was not Kant's aim. He was religiously committed, an individual whose deism somehow also admitted a personal God. And he believed that humans all possess knowledge of universal moral law that substantiates God's existence and is crucial for a satisfactory social order.[26]

David Hume, on the other hand, was an important influence on American thought during the late eighteenth century, along with others who were influenced by the Scottish Enlightenment of that age.[27] Hume was the thinker least sympathetic to religion among liberalism's classic exponents before the nineteenth century, though it goes too far to say that he was "the most notorious enemy of revealed religion in Europe after Voltaire."[28] To him, religion was a consolation for people's deep dis-

24. John Dunn, *Locke* (Oxford: Oxford University Press, 1984), p. 85.

25. For serious exploration of Locke, there is, of course, no substitute for reading him, especially in this context, John Locke, *Two Treatises of Government,* Thomas I. Cook, ed. (New York: Hafner, 1959); Locke, *A Letter concerning Toleration* (New York: Bobbs-Merrill, 1955); Locke, *The Reasonableness of Christianity* (Palo Alto, CA: Stanford University Press, 1958); see also Dunn, *Locke,* and Eisenach, *Two Worlds of Liberalism*.

26. Two good places to begin with Kant are Immanuel Kant, *Religion within the Limits of Reason Alone* (New York: Harper and Row, 1960), and Patrick Riley, *Kant's Political Philosophy* (Totowa, NJ: Rowman and Littlefield, 1983).

27. Garry Wills, *Inventing America: Jefferson's Declaration of Independence* (Garden City, NY: Doubleday, 1978); John Diggins, *The Lost Soul of American Politics: Virtue, Self-Interest, and the Foundations of Liberalism* (Chicago: University of Chicago Press, 1984).

28. Michael Ignatieff, *The Needs of Strangers* (New York: Penguin, 1986), p. 83.

satisfaction with themselves and others, dissatisfaction they lack the strength to accept otherwise. Moreover, Hume felt that religion had many sour social fruits, such as competing religions and warring churches. While Hume demonstrated that he could do without religion personally, he did not for a minute think societies could. Morality needed a transcendental—a religious—bulwark. Without it, social order could collapse and people would be dangerously adrift—a position de Tocqueville was to apply to America in the 1830s.[29]

John Stuart Mill, defender of liberal toleration and the individual, was the most important liberal theorist in the nineteenth century and he remains a much admired expositer of liberalism today. While Mill brushed aside traditional religion—and Christianity in particular—as irrational superstition, in his own life he learned about worlds other than his liberal world of tolerance and utilitarian rationality. He not only discovered the worlds of aesthetics and emotion, which he had not known as the child of his mentors, his father and Jeremy Bentham; he also came to appreciate the very practical task religion could perform in justifying and strengthening even the most "rational" morality. That Mill opted for a religion of humanity rather than religion as classically defined in the West does not alter his recognition of its social power for his liberal values. He did not propose that liberalism do without religion, nor did he expect that liberalism *could* do without it.[30]

Except for Locke—and even his case may be argued—none of the great European philosophical contributors to liberalism from the seventeenth through the nineteenth centuries was an orthodox Christian. And it is true enough on the face of it that liberalism "is not without its problems for the Christian," sometimes in its exaltation of property rights, at other times in its melioristic assumptions and implicit state worship.[31] But the classical liberal thinkers simply did not propose to separate religion from their liberal political and social thought. Indeed, for all of them religion was integral to liberalism, most commonly as a philosophi-

29. On Hume see David Hume, *The National History of Religion* (Oxford: Oxford University Press, 1976); Eisenach, *Two Worlds of Liberalism*, ch. 12; Ignatieff, *The Needs of Strangers*, pp. 95 and 97 and ch. 3.

30. John Stuart Mill, "The Utility of Religion," in M. Lerner, ed., *Essential Works of John Stuart Mill* (New York: Bantam, 1961), pp. 402-31; Mill, "Utilitarianism," in Marshall Cohen, ed., *The Philosophy of J. S. Mill* (New York: Modern Library, 1961), pp. 312-98; Mill, "Three Essays on Religion," in *The Philosophy of J. S. Mill*, pp. 443-524; Mill, "Autobiography," in *Essential Works of John Stuart Mill*, pp. 11-182; Eisenach, *Two Worlds of Liberalism*, chs. 14 and 16.

31. Sigmund, "Christianity, Ideology, and Political Philosophy," p. 86.

cal and/or practical basis that would maintain a cohesive moral standard, a grounding for their social order.

This linkage of classical liberalism with religion was also a close one in the American liberal tradition, both in theory and in practice. In chapter 4, I examine the hypothesis that, in fact, much of the American variant of liberalism derives from Protestant (Calvinist) Christianity.[32] Even in the later eighteenth century, when influential American intellectuals who were hardly conventional Christians emerged—Madison and Jefferson, for example—religion and a republican form of liberalism were closely connected. Christianity and liberalism were not, to be sure, dominant among some of America's Founding Fathers; but deist Enlightenment religion and liberalism were.[33] By the 1830s the interconnection of Christianity and liberalism in the larger culture was obvious to the French visitor Alexis de Tocqueville. Individual freedom, the search for equality, the wondrous group life of America—the entire restless, undisciplined culture was held together by religion. It was the unseen hand

32. See, for example, Sidney Mead, *The Lively Experiment* (New York: Harper and Row, 1963); William Lee Miller, "American Religion and American Political Attitudes," in *Religion in American Life*, vol. 2, James Ward Smith and A. Leland Jamison, eds. (Princeton: Princeton University Press, 1961), pp. 82-84; Wald, *Religion and Politics in the United States*, ch. 3; William Clebsch, *From Sacred to Profane: The Role of Religion in American History* (New York: Harper and Row, 1968), pp. 1-14; Franklin H. Littell, *From State Church to Pluralism: A Protestant Interpretation of Religion in American History* (Garden City, NY: Doubleday, 1962).

33. The literature on Jefferson and Madison is extensive even when it focuses on religion and politics or church and state. A few examples: Charles B. Sanford, *The Religious Life of Thomas Jefferson* (Charlottesville, VA: University of Virginia Press, 1984); Adrienne Koch and William Peden, eds., *The Life and Selected Writings of Jefferson* (New York: Random House, 1944), pp. 355-56, 639-40, 704, 717-19; Adrienne Koch, *Madison's "Advice to My Country"* (Princeton: Princeton University Press, 1966), ch. 1; Robert L. Cord, *The Separation of Church and State: Historical Fact and Current Fiction* (New York: Lambeth, 1982), pp. 20-35, 45-62, 121-29, 135-65, 219-29; Leo Pfeffer and Anson Phelps Stokes, *Church and State in the United States* (New York: Harper and Row, 1964); William Lee Miller, *The First Liberty: Religion and the American Republic* (New York: Knopf, 1986). Parts 1, 2, and 4 in Miller offer a view that is between Cord and Pfeffer and yet is both lively and interesting for all its middlingness. On the republican, liberal, and Christian influences of American political thought in the founding period, see James T. Kloppenberg, "The Virtues of Liberalism: Christianity, Republicanism, and Ethics in Early American Political Discourse," *Journal of American History,* June 1987, pp. 9-33.

providing the shared standards that imposed the limits so necessary for American culture's survival.[34]

Only in recent decades have many theorists of liberalism in the United States sundered the traditional connection between religion and liberalism. For many, modern directions of intellectual discovery have made it impossible to found liberal values on religious claims that are not sustainable by reason. For others, religion's sheer loss of fashion among liberal theorists and mainstream philosophical life in general has been decisive.

In the decades since World War II, there have been many directions in the search for a justification for liberal values—another story and a fascinating one—but there has been little interest in the traditional link to religion.[35] Only recently has renewed interest appeared, and it often comes in the guise of a critique of a liberalism which, it is now assumed, lacks any natural connection with religion, whatever its history.[36] Moreover, religion's other historic role for liberal thinkers from Hume to de Tocqueville—as a sustainer of common standards, or, in more grand language, a force for community—has only recently once again begun to attract some attention. Indeed, for decades liberal thought lost interest in the question of what holds American society together—until it became clear that perhaps it is no longer holding together. The revival of interest among American intellectuals in community and public good hardly leads directly to religion, but it makes it timely to raise the questions: What are the remaining connections between religion and American liberal culture? Can they be restored? Are they likely to be trans-

---

34. Alexis de Tocqueville, *Democracy in America* (New York: Vintage, 1957), vol. 2, book 1, ch. 5.

35. The business of justifying liberal values is a busy one and has been for the past forty years; see the analysis of this activity for the first half of the period in Robert Booth Fowler, *Believing Skeptics: American Political Intellectuals, 1945-1964* (Westport, CT: Greenwood, 1978), chs. 4 and 5. For some recent examples, see: John Rawls, *A Theory of Justice* (Cambridge: Harvard University Press, 1971); Don Herzog, *Without Foundations: Justification in Political Theory* (Ithaca, NY: Cornell University Press, 1985); Thomas A. Spragens, Jr., *The Irony of Liberal Reason* (Chicago: University of Chicago Press, 1981); Irving Kristol, *Reflections of a Neo-Conservative* (New York: Basic Books, 1983); Amy Gutmann, *Liberal Equality* (Cambridge: Cambridge University Press, 1980).

36. Two prominent examples of "liberals" (if this is quite the right word) interested in religion are Bell, *The Cultural Contradictions of Capitalism* and elsewhere, and, of course, Bellah et al., *Habits of the Heart*.

formed by a challenging religious energy? Or is their fate a steady and inexorable entropy?[37]

Because in differing ways and degrees so many subsequent observers have shared what I will call the "integration thesis," I give attention to it first. By the "integration thesis" I mean the idea that religion and America's liberal order are part of an intertwined whole, as they have been in our history, and thus that religion in America has served as a support for the established liberal order. Three versions will deserve treatment: 1) the hypothesis in its broadest form about the Western world, as articulated in the classic social theories of Marx and Weber and applied to the United States; 2) versions specifically developed for the situation in America, some concentrating on the theoretical links of religion and liberalism in the United States, others on the practical and historical connections (perhaps the greatest of them being de Tocqueville's); 3) the civil religion hypothesis, which holds that there is a civil religion in America that legitimates our liberal state and connects it closely with Christianity. This thesis was first well articulated in the contemporary period by Robert Bellah, and controversy continues to swirl around it, perhaps especially in this era of neoreligious patriotism.

Each of these versions of the integration idea has its plausibility, and none can be (or will be here) dismissed as simply wrong. This is not a subject for simple resolutions. But all integration theories have their limitations. They focus on a different America than we know now, one where religion and liberal society were, in fact, often closely integrated. Each version opts for integration as the reality in part because each tacitly assumes that the only alternative is opposition or challenge, of which they see little. None takes into account the possibility, which I propose, that support for a liberal state may come from religion not because it *is* well integrated into that society's norms and power but because it is *not*, and rather serves as a pressure-relieving escape from them.

The other accepted hypothesis, which contends that religion must be interpreted as a challenge to liberal America, has gained popularity in recent years. Proponents of this interpretation suggest that religion is shifting away from its integrative and conservative history, and more and

37. Renewed interest in the possibilities of religion as a means for holding together the American community may be found in Kristol, *Reflections of a Neo-Conservative,* and, from a different perspective, Bellah et al., *Habits of the Heart;* for a range of views on liberalism in a contemporary context see Michael J. Sandel, ed., *Liberalism and Its Critics* (New York: New York University Press, 1984).

more in America it champions dissent—often radical, challenging dissent. I will examine specific contemporary developments in the liberal Protestant, Catholic, conservative Protestant ("religious right"), and black church, among others, to explore the degree to which this fashionable perspective fits the evidence. Such an idea has its strengths. Religion *is* becoming much more political than was true in most—but not all—of our history. And there are those involved who do wish to challenge our liberal society radically. But this interpretation, frankly, builds on a weak foundation of empirical knowledge about religion in the United States. It overestimates the political influence and the unity of American religious groups, the taste for politics in American religion, and the attraction of radicalism even among activist religious elites.

CHAPTER TWO

A Refuge from Liberal Skepticism

AS THE TWENTIETH CENTURY HAS UNFOLDED, skepticism of truth—now even of scientific truth—has steadily expanded. We may know more, but it has led us to doubt more and believe less. As Jean Baudrillard has observed, "We are in a universe where there is more and more information, and less and less meaning."[1] This situation is particularly acute, of course, among Western intellectuals, including American intellectuals. But it has now—indeed, long since—ceased to be characteristic of them alone. The phenomenon is widespread, and it is naturally of the utmost relevance to religion, churches, and liberal culture in the United States.

Two kinds of skepticism are of particular significance. One is the skepticism of any ultimate meaning or truth—skepticism of God in religious terms. It has so clearly permeated American intellectual life that a religious definition of meaning, let alone an acknowledgment of the existence of God, has disappeared from ordinary intellectual discourse (outside the special precincts of theological seminaries and religious colleges). And while grand theory may be enjoying something of a revival in American intellectual life, there is no sign that new meaning systems have replaced religion—or, more precisely, Christianity.[2] One should note, however, that this kind of skepticism has not penetrated nearly so deeply into the American population at large. Religious belief remains as widespread as ever, and skepticism can only be inferred from the relative depth of belief, not its nonexistence.[3]

A second form of skepticism has cut deeper into the larger culture. This is a skepticism about what constitutes moral behavior. It has, especially in the realm of sexual mores, spread widely in the culture since the 1960s, creating both considerable popular confusion and pluralism on

1. Jean Baudrillard, *In the Shadow of the Silent Majorities. . . . Or the End of the Social and Other Essays* (New York: Semiotexts, 1983), p. 95.
2. Frederick Crews, "In the Big House of Theory," *New York Review of Books,* 29 May 1986, 36-42.
3. See *Religion in America: 50 Years, 1935–1985* (Gallup Report No. 236, May 1985).

the subject of appropriate standards for living. Unlike the first variety of skepticism, *moral* skepticism (and the resulting diverse moral practice) has not necessarily met opposition from religion in America. By no means have all churches posed a barrier to the advance of this "modern" movement. Indeed, some have eagerly embraced this cultural direction and even encouraged values relativism. Others, however, have resisted—and continue to resist now in an increasingly public fashion.

In a famous argument, Dean Kelley of the National Council of Churches maintained that the "conservative churches are growing" because they are "strict" in morality and foundation beliefs.[4] Given our study's hypothesis, we would expect this conservative growth, as people seek temporary refuge from the meaningless, morally permissive larger culture. This reaction may be called sensible by some and reactionary by others; but in any case its significance may be to identify religion's and the churches' role as increasingly important undergirdings for a liberal culture that more and more lacks confidence in any grounding or moral system.

In this chapter I will pursue the argument that skepticism about ultimate foundations and daily moral values is related to the strength of religion in our culture. The more the culture encourages skepticism, moral formlessness, and relativism, the more religion appeals to people as an alternative.

Religion as a Refuge from Liberal Skepticism

IN CONTEMPORARY AMERICA, intellectual and media elites are hardly notable for their religious interest (or church-going), and intellectual publications reflect the scant role religion and religious subjects play in intellectual discussions and debates (except for concern over vocal religious elements or movements in society).[5] Yet there is a discernible increase, in

4. Kelley, *Why Conservative Churches Are Growing* (New York: Harper and Row, 1972); Dean R. Hoge and David A. Roozen, eds., *Understanding Church Growth and Decline, 1950–1978* (New York: Pilgrim, 1979), p. 15.

5. The most exhaustive study is *The Connecticut Mutual Life Report on American Values in the '80s: The Impact of Belief* (Hartford: Connecticut Mutual Life Insurance Co., 1981); for TV/movie elite perspective, see Ben Stein, *The View From Sunset Blvd* (New York: Basic Books, 1979) and Lloyd Billingsley, "TV: Where the Girls Are Good Looking and the Good Guys Win," *Christianity Today*, 4 October 1984, pp. 36-41. It is somewhat difficult to measure the amount of discussion of religion in intellectual journals. Standards are missing. However, outside the admittedly large and vigorous ghetto of religious-intellectual publications, my view hardly could be controversial. Neither *The New York Review of Books* nor *The New Republic* would, for example, offer much by way of counterexample. A typical issue contains no discussion.

a minor key, of an arguably related theme: the consideration of modern liberals' difficulty in addressing ultimate meaning. There are no signs of a mad rush among intellectuals to embrace America's traditional religions, Christianity or Judaism; yet there are palpable ripples in contemporary intellectual life suggesting that ultimate skepticism has proved to be a limited meal. Skepticism has not lost its power, that seems clear; but its appeal is diminished. The alternatives to traditional religious definitions of ultimate meaning that have dominated the recent past—science, existentialism, pragmatism, among others—seem to have reduced charms. And the concern over the consequences of a society, or of liberalism in general, without ultimate meaning has manifestly mushroomed.

Reflecting the sweep of this uneasiness, the two examples I have chosen to illustrate this section, Daniel Bell and Michael Harrington, do not share a great deal besides a common concern for a more ultimate basis for living than contemporary liberalism provides. Their concern reflects a growing perception among many intellectuals that religion may be needed as a grounding for, not a replacement of, liberalism. They also share a perception that, as I would put it, religion operates for many as a refuge from liberal skepticism—a fact about which they are notably ambivalent. Daniel Bell, a social theorist of Jewish background, has spoken out frequently in recent years regarding what he takes to be the spiritual poverty of modern liberalism.[6] A professor at one of liberalism's intellectual centers, Harvard University, Bell charges that liberalism has no firm ground of being, leaving each person with only his or her own resources, whims, and anxieties. Part of Bell's unhappiness lies in what he perceives to be the resulting pragmatic costs. But another large element, one that transcends Bell's pragmatic concern, is really metaphysical and ontological: he wants a foundation, a God, if you will.

Bell suspects that his desire is shared by many others. A spiritual renewal may be ahead in America and elswhere. "The exhaustion of modernism, the aridity of communist life, the tedium of the unrestrained self and the meaninglessness of the monolithic chants, all indicate that a long era is coming to a close."[7] Ahead must lie a new religious consciousness, which Bell welcomes: "Will there be a return of the sacred, the rise of new religious modes? Of that I have no doubt. . . . It is a constitutive aspect of human experience because it is a response to the existential predicaments which are . . . of human nature."[8]

6. See Bell, *The Cultural Contradictions of Capitalism* (New York: Basic Books, 1978), for his most elaborate statement.
7. *Ibid.,* p. 448.
8. *Ibid.,* p. 442.

Michael Harrington, socialist intellectual and activist, strikes much the same note. He too sees the exhaustion of the traditional "religions" of America, the West, and the communist world. Indeed, while traditional religion lingers on in America (as opposed to the rest of the developed world), if slowly and surely declining, atheism really exercises power in public and private lives. It is, Harrington says, the "stark, hedonistic and thoughtless atheism which . . . is the real faith of contemporary Western society."[9] Meanwhile, the god of materialism has already failed in communist lands. "'Leninism' with its mummified, atheist God in Red Square and its theology, 'dialectical materialism,' hobbles on in a very weak condition."[10]

People hunger for something more. In Harrington's vision it will be a better faith, more grounded in ultimate reality and more devoted to enriching human lives, one that encourages a more just and genuinely democratic society. And while Harrington is less confident of the rebirth of a ("proper") religious sensibility than is Bell, he is just as sure that the time is now ripe.[11]

This so far modest intellectual revolt against skeptical liberalism's image of the good person as a nonspiritual being is, however, arguably just one more illustration of how American intellectuals proceed in partial isolation from the American population. For the evidence shows that religious belief has remained nearly universal among the American population. It is as strong now as it has ever been since public opinion surveys on the subject began in the 1930s: 95 percent of the population affirm belief in a God, 80 percent in the divinity of Christ.[12] Moreover, the most recent data establish that popular reliance on God is increasing. More than ever, people cite their trust in God as their ultimate guide in troubled times and with personal problems.[13]

This is not to say that Americans are an overwhelmingly religious people. Two-thirds claim to belong to a religious group, but fewer than half attend services on any given religious day.[14] Yet religious activity cannot be fully measured by church membership or worship attendance.

9. Michael Harrington, *The Politics at God's Funeral: The Spiritual Crisis of Western Civilization* (New York: Penguin, 1983), pp. 83, 187.

10. *Ibid.*, p. 54.

11. *Ibid.*, chs. 1 and 10.

12. See George Gallup, Jr., and David Poling, *The Search for America's Faith* (Nashville: Abingdon, 1980) and *Religion in America* (Gallup Report).

13. See the Gallup Organization, *The Spiritual Climate in America Today* (Princeton: Gallup, 1983).

14. Gallup and Poling, *The Search for America's Faith*, p. 80; *Religion in America* (Gallup Report), p. 16.

Many people who are religious, who pray, read their respective scriptures, and even belong to Bible study groups are not church members, as Gallup has found. This is one reason why there is little difference in the overall religious beliefs of those who attend church and those who do not.[15] In my terms, therefore, *refuge* does not require church attendance. It is always a state of mind and only sometimes a matter of place. And the state of mind today among Americans, on the whole, is definitely one in which a transcendent God exists and is often present.

Of course, there are gods and there are gods. Some are more clearly a contrast to liberal skepticism—the gods of the cults, for example.[16] But all of them are an alternative vision in at least some sense. And here studies of particular groups of believers and particular churches and denominations provide us with confirmation that religion actively serves as a refuge from liberal skepticism for a rising number of Americans. The National Council of Churches' Dean Kelley has argued in his pioneering work that religion for Americans is basically about meaning. It has other purposes, to be sure, but the heart of its attraction is to provide a sense of explanation and certainty in people's lives. It follows that churches and denominations emphasizing meaning and certainty are those that grow, Kelley's classic explanation for the decided emergence of evangelical and fundamentalist Protestantism as the larger branch of Protestantism in the post–World War II period. It also explains, he argues, why so-called mainstream churches, especially the Episcopal, United Church of Christ, and much of the United Methodist Church, lost so many members during the 1960s and, we may add, have not really grown since. As theological liberalism steadily took control of such mainstream denominations, they could no longer compete in aggregate terms with churches that offered answers rather than "explorations," "dialogues," and, ultimately, religious uncertainty. When they did not speak as effectively to people's need for absolute truth, relative decline followed.[17]

Some liberal Protestants—even some who claim to avoid the instant rejection of conservative Protestantism that is characteristic among the public voices of mainstream Protestants—can hardly conceal their contempt for the kind of religion Kelley sees growing. From their perspective, "the strictness principle seeks to create community by simplistic clarity and by the avoidance of the ambiguity that is at the heart of the human experience."[18] On the other side, intellectual opponents of re-

15. Gallup and Poling, *The Search for America's Faith*, pp. 79-80.
16. See ch. 9 in this work.
17. See Kelley, *Why Conservative Churches Are Growing*.
18. Robert A. Evans, "Recovering the Church's Transforming Middle:

ligious modernizers (skeptics, relativists, those who speak of ambiguity and paradox) invoke Kelley's principle—knowingly or not—as a fact of life and a normative good. For example, Irving Kristol, a Jew, notes unhappily: "It is ironic to watch the churches . . . surrender to the spirit of modernity at the very moment when modernity itself is undergoing a kind of spiritual collapse."[19] Kristol goes on to illustrate with specific reference to the Catholic church: "If I may speak bluntly about the Catholic church . . . it is traumatic for someone who wishes that church well to see it modernize itself at this moment. Young people do not want to hear that. . . . Young people, especially, are looking for religion so desperately that they are inventing new ones. They should not have to invent new ones, the old religions are pretty good. New ones are being invented because the churches capitulated to modernity. . . ."[20]

The new religions Kristol is thinking of would appear to be cults; yet it is not cults that have done best, but rather, as Kelley says, traditional groups who believe in and practice fixed standards. Indeed, there now exist many studies that are relevant to and update Kelley's argument. Some sustain his argument that religion appeals where it is about absolutes, and churches offering absolutes gain in numerical strength. Studies of individuals who convert to Protestant fundamentalism show that they look to fundamentalism as a means to resolve personal confusion and "tension," and, if it does that, they remain committed.[21] On the other side, as Wade Clark Roof's work suggests, liberal Protestantism continues to be hurt by its lack of clear identity: What does it really stand for? What is its anchor in skeptical America?[22]

More broadly, the extensive data on why people turn to religion in the United States underscore again and again the fact that personal needs

---

Theological Reflections on the Balance between Faithfulness and Effectiveness," in *Understanding Church Growth and Decline,* p. 305.

19. Kristol, *Reflections of a Neo-Conservative* (New York: Basic Books, 1983), p. 326.

20. *Ibid.*

21. James T. Richardson, Mary White Stewart, and Robert B. Simmonds, "Conversion to Fundamentalism," in *In Gods We Trust: New Patterns of Religious Pluralism in America,* ed. Thomas Robbins and Dick Anthony (New Brunswick, NJ: Transaction Books, 1981), pp. 127-39.

22. Roof, "America's Voluntary Establishment: Mainline Religion in Transition," and Edwin Scott Gaustad, "Did the Fundamentalists Win?" both in *Religion and America: Spirituality in a Secular Age,* ed. Mary Douglas and Steven Tipton (Boston: Beacon, 1983), pp. 130-49 and 169-78, respectively; and Wade Clark Roof and William McKinney, *American Mainline Religion: Its Changing Shape and Future* (New Brunswick, NJ: Rutgers University Press, 1987).

are first. Gallup and Poling and Rauff agree on this central finding about motivation. The personal concerns that matter include a sense of drifting and emptiness and a desire for spiritual truth and life that American liberal culture cannot "solve" because it provides no "way" to a "true" resolution.[23]

None of this should surprise anyone. Religion in Protestant America has always been very individual—as well as cultural, traditional, and communal. And, one must say, despite the flourishing theological business in all branches of American religion, it is individualistic as opposed to intellectual. The recent restudy of Middletown's vigorous religious life (people in Middletown, as with people throughout the United States, are unaware of Bell's and Harrington's pronouncements that God is dead and liberal skepticism rules) confirms that religion is highly individual and personal. It also confirms that, while it is no longer especially doctrinal, it still revolves around accepted metaphysical and ontological absolutes.[24]

This phenomenon is not only true of Christians in America. While the degree of the recent "return" to Judaism among American Jews is controversial, there is much less disagreement over its primary motivation. The search for meaning and identity appears to be the most common theme in the Jewish religious renewal in the United States. And this fact is hardly surprising given the "liberalization" of much of modern Judaism—and of American culture.[25]

As we have seen, the strength of this attraction to religion in our liberal society because it can provide meaning leads people to certain religious groups over others. But it has also led many of the 1960s generation back to the same churches they once left. Hoge has found, for example, that spiritual hunger is a major reason for Roman Catholics who return to the church of their youth.[26] Yet at the same time, spiritual hunger is a major reason people leave certain churches today. What Hoge found for Roman Catholics, Gallup and Poling confirmed for the entire population. Dissatisfaction with actual churches often derives from their

23. See Edmund A. Rauff, *Why People Join the Church* (New York: Pilgrim, 1979); Gallup and Poling, *The Search for America's Faith*, ch. 1.

24. Theodore Caplow et al., *All Faithful People: Change and Continuity in Middletown's Religion* (Minneapolis: University of Minnesota Press, 1983), p. 104, ch. 4.

25. For an interesting and controversial discussion of these issues, see Charles E. Silberman, *A Certain People: American Jews and Their Lives Today* (New York: Summit Books, 1985), p. 244, ch. 6.

26. See Dean R. Hoge, *Converts, Dropouts, Returnees: A Study of Religious Change among Catholics* (New York: Pilgrim, 1981).

perceived failures in witnessing to a deep spiritual reality rather than from the rejection of religion as a whole by the dissatisfied. This is especially true among youth. Indeed, a continuing complaint among both those who attend church and those who don't is the emptiness they claim they find all too often at church.[27]

In short, the refuge hypothesis is strong. People turn to religion—and often to and from specific churches—on the basis of how those churches provide a firm spiritual foundation for life. But this hypothesis is not to be accepted without limitations. Indeed, sociologists interested in the study of church growth and decline insist that the situation is much more complex than my view would suggest. For example, national data establish that while belief in God, Christ, and heaven and hell are as strong or stronger than ever, there is a steady drift *away from* absolutist positions regarding the Bible. Over the past twenty years, the literal interpretation of the Bible has, in fact, ceased to be the majority view.[28] Apparently, not all absolutist religious convictions appeal. The same decline may have taken place in the average frequency of prayer during the 1960s and 1970s,[29] but Gallup's findings more recently emphasize prayer's renewed appeal.[30]

There is considerable evidence that much of the decline in "liberal" mainstream churches in the 1960s and 1970s did not result from a mass exodus to stricter, more conservative religious groups. Many liberal Protestants quit their denominations, but not for fundamentalism.[31] Rather, the relative—and absolute—growth of conservative churches has probably had more to do with their members' birth rate (much higher than among higher-class mainstream Protestant denominations) than anything else.[32] Moreover, many students of religion agree that liberal groups lost—and continue to lose—a good number of the young adults (20-35 years old) raised in their denominations because they are simply no longer interested in religion, certainly organized religion, though they

27. Gallup and Poling, *The Search for America's Faith,* pp. 95-96, 33-34; see also Hoge, *Converts, Dropouts, Returnees.*

28. David A. Roozen and Jackson W. Carroll, "Recent Trends in Church Membership and Participation," in *Understanding Church Growth and Decline,* p. 37; see also Roof and McKinney, *American Mainline Religion.*

29. *Ibid.,* pp. 37-38.

30. *Religion in America* (Gallup Report), p. 45.

31. Dean R. Hoge and David A. Roozen, "Some Sociological Conclusions about Church Trends," in *Understanding Church Growth and Decline,* p. 329.

32. Dean R. Hoge, "A Test of Theories of Denominational Growth and Decline," in *Understanding Church Growth and Decline,* p. 197.

normally claim to believe in God and even to have spiritual interests of some sort.[33] It is not entirely clear whether liberal denominations suffer greater youth losses because of the class/educational level characteristic of their young people, because of the encouragement of skepticism and relativism often found within these denominations anyway, or for other reasons. Opinions differ, and the evidence is too mixed and too slight for us to be sure at this point. What we do know is that many young people now find meaning in themselves or assorted lifestyle enclaves, as Robert Bellah and his colleagues noted in *Habits of the Heart*, and so they feel no need for traditional religion or churches.[34]

As a result, the growth of churches offering absolute religious truth, at least during the 1960s and 1970s, may well have provided us with a distorted picture of the currents of popular belief. Such groups may have grown partly because they offered a refuge, certainly, but not because everyone sought such a refuge for his life. They may have grown for the opposite reason, that is, because much of the culture during those decades was not seriously interested in a religious world view, and those who were interested felt the need to rally to the colors.

The irony here, of course, is that one might have expected more theologically pluralist and openly liberal Protestant churches to have grown in response to the liberalized bent of American culture. That did not happen because a more liberal religious view is not the point for those who are not seeking meaning in religion or organized religion at all.[35] This view, of course, would dictate that intensely held religious beliefs are not really the crucial factor in church growth and decline. What count are the broader cultural developments whose particular effects will vary according to the institution (or religion). The issue really is whether or not religion is "a dependent variable."[36]

Even such skeptical analyses, however, have often produced evidence that underscores my thesis here: that religious conviction and practice are central to Catholic as well as Protestant church growth, if not the

33. William J. McKinney, Jr., "Performance of United Church of Christ Congregations in Massachusetts and in Pennsylvania," in *Understanding Church Growth and Decline*, ch. 10; Hoge and Roozen, "Some Sociological Conclusions," in *Understanding Church Growth and Decline*, pp. 329-33.

34. Robert Bellah et al., *Habits of the Heart: Individualism and Commitment in American Life* (Berkeley: University of California Press, 1985), pp. 72-73, 82.

35. See, for example, Hoge, "A Test of Theories," in *Understanding Church Growth and Decline*, p. 197.

36. Dean Kelley, "Commentary: Is Religion a Dependent Variable?" in *Understanding Church Growth and Decline*, ch. 15.

only factor.[37] Indeed, a most relevant and fascinating study of the United Church of Christ (UCC) in two large states in the East found that in this, the most theologically liberal denomination, one factor affecting individual church growth and decline was the theology enunciated at church. Even within this bosom of liberal religion, churches tending to offer strict definitions of meaning were likely to hold their own or grow in the face of general denominational decline.[38]

All this merely serves to restate in a more modest and more careful sense my basic point. In America many people go to church, or look to religion, to find and affirm a different realm than America's skeptical, "loose-bounded" liberal culture can provide. Where they find that alternative, they often stay; where they do not, they complain and sometimes leave, often to continue their quest on their own, sometimes to join another church or denomination more successful at providing them with meaning. For the growing numbers of those not in search of such meaning, or at least not in search of it through religion, what a given religious group offers does not really matter; they often just abandon the church.

Nothing in this argument suggests that those who turn to a "strict" church really intend to reject liberal culture in a wholesale way. Their objective appears to be to develop a temporary refuge where they may get their footing and return to the larger society so armed. In any case, this is what must happen. Few people can live within their strict church alone, or even create a tight world where only its values reign.

Religion and Values

RELIGION ALSO SERVES, often enough, as an island of secure *values* in the sea of liberal pluralism, relativism, and skepticism. Or, at the least this is what tens of millions who look to organized religion hope. This is where religion has the most obvious practical implications for life in our

37. For Roman Catholic parishioners' view of the purpose of parishes, see David C. Leege and Thomas A. Trozzolo, "Religious Values and Parish Participation: The Paradox of Individual Needs in a Communitarian Church," in *Notre Dame Study of Catholic Parish Life*, Report No. 4 (June 1985), pp. 1-8; on mainstream Protestants, see, for example, Hoge and Roozen, "Research on Factors Influencing Church Commitment," in *Understanding Church Growth and Decline*, pp. 56-57.

38. McKinney, "Performance of United Church of Christ Congregations," in *Understanding Church Growth and Decline*, pp. 224-47.

liberal society. It is one thing if modern liberalism offers no God or much sympathy for spiritual concerns; it is quite another if it cannot meet popular desire for secure values in life. And if religion functions to provide values that the culture does not, and yet does not challenge American liberalism, then religion is indeed an unintentional partner of the utmost significance for liberalism.   NATURE USES GRACE

We know that many classical liberals self-consciously depended on religion to provide what they judged liberalism could not do itself: the virtues and norms needed to ensure a secure ballast in a society so self-consciously devoted to individual liberty. They took it for granted that liberty could not exist without justified values to undergird and limit it. From a contemporary perspective, liberty has spread so deeply into all areas of culture that "loose-boundedness" (some critics might say "permissiveness") is the American normative reality. The question is, Is there any ballast left?

Daniel Bell and Michael Harrington clearly reflect this problem when they describe a society caught in a centrifugal whirl, where people are adrift, without common values, often without any values at all other than current fashion and equally unsatisfactory hedonistic self-indulgence. Harrington notes that in the resulting chaos, religion seems to have lost its power and no longer works to reinforce liberalism, much less support the egalitarian democratic ethics he favors. Bell reaches a similar conclusion. As a result, both yearn for the emergence of a secure, spiritual grounding for their respective values, which, however much they differ from each other, have nothing in common with anarchistic moral individualism. But how to achieve such a more communal morality is not clear to them. They agree that faith and ethics cannot be manufactured just because intellectuals proclaim they should be, or because their social utility seems so apparent.[39]

The argument of Robert Bellah and his associates in the recent widely discussed *Habits of the Heart* is related; it is more focused and perhaps richer and more complex. While much of it addresses the dialectic of individualism and community in the United States (and thus is appropriate for our next chapter), the questions of moral skepticism and moral individualism are also central. The authors of *Habits of the Heart* show that diversity and relativism in much ethical thinking and practice among the American people is undeniable; indeed, unlike Bell or Harrington, they offer intensive empirical research to substantiate this claim. This prevalence of ethical formlessness seems to follow from what they find

39. Bell, *The Cultural Contradictions of Capitalism*, pp. xxviii-ix, 276-77, 154-71; Harrington, *The Politics at God's Funeral*, pp. 199, 218, 35.

to be the absence of any transcendental, much less absolute, moral grounding among so many of the people they interviewed.[40]

Bellah and associates report that Americans view firm values, duties, and obligations with suspicion because "spontaneous interpersonal intimacy" is the ideal in our fluid moral universe.[41] And they note the rise of the therapeutic professionals and their ethic in particular as a sign of the times, reflecting a world where "self-actualized" people rather than a secure, certain moral world are the goal.[42]

The consequences of moral individualism and its close companion, skeptical rejection of uniform moral teachings and duties, alarm them as much as they do Bell and Harrington. But the accuracy of their view is debatable. It sounds suspiciously as though they are confusing California with all of the United States, just as Harrington's and Bell's somewhat similar analysis may reflect their coastal, intellectualist world more than it does the country at large. However, their diagnosis does gain support from students of American culture whose perspectives cannot possibly be judged narrow.[43] For Bellah and company, the consequence of the language—as they like to put it—of our moral relativism is disastrous. It prevents America from acting collectively as a nation. Indeed, this relativism makes it difficult to conceive of one's own efforts in the public realm, much less those of one's opponents, in any general or shared moral framework. There simply is scant "notion of a common language of moral discourse in which public debate can reach at least occasional consensus. . . ."[44]

In this light, the authors of *Habits of the Heart* well appreciate how some institutions in America—family, church, and small towns—serve as refuges. But they are doubtful about whether religion (and the churches) serve as a refuge from skepticism and relativism in moral life. They do not believe that there is as much popular desire for stable, shared moral values as other studies suggest. Instead, they insist that such a refuge behavior is really for the purposes of individual expression in an atmosphere of security, whether in church or in other institutions such as the family.[45]

Bellah and his colleagues sympathize with this popular desire. They even sympathize with those who desire to take refuge from the larger cul-

40. Bellah, *Habits of the Heart*, p. 82.

41. *Ibid.*, p. 85.

42. *Ibid.*, pp. 97-107.

43. For a perspective that is more broadly—though perhaps less scientifically—based, see Richard Reeves, *American Journey* (New York: Simon and Schuster, 1982).

44. Bellah, *Habits of the Heart*, pp. 133, 20-21.

45. *Ibid.*, pp. 236-37, ch. 9.

ture in religion or elsewhere. But their sympathies are sharply circum-scribed. They are swept up by their own agenda, their urgent belief that America needs a more public-spirited ethic and thus a religion that is oriented toward the whole—and toward improving the whole.[46] They maintain that religion can, and should, provide the antidote to ethical skepticism and confusion, albeit in a thoughtful, nonfanatical fashion; but it is our responsibility—ultimately a Christian responsibility—to do so in the world of public life and conflict, not in a private world of retreat.

Despite what Richard Merelman has called the "loose-bounded-ness" of current American culture,[47] lamented by an expanding number of cultural observers, religiously based moral systems are hardly dead in the United States. On the contrary. Though secular observers such as Merelman ignore religion, and Bellah and his associates do not really think that religion is the ethical grounding for most citizens' moral out-look, their conclusions can be doubted. For example, Gallup's findings, far broader and more truly empirical (if also less probing), challenge this judgment.[48] The substantial minority of the American population in-volved in organized religion are more likely to have clear and notably more "strict" positions on moral issues and to link them self-consciously with religious absolutes.

This is markedly true in regard to emphasis on the family and un-easiness or opposition to abortion, pornography, drug use, and casual sex. While the diversity in American religions, believers, and ethics is un-deniable, the overall association of relative moral conservatism and re-ligious commitment is not in doubt.[49]

Thus, while Bell, Bellah, Harrington, Merelman, and the like de-scribe an America flying apart, bursting at its disintegrated moral seams, they are actually describing only one America. They ignore another that is involved in the church and firm in its moral belief on many ethical is-sues. In this latter America, religion and the churches continue, on the

46. *Ibid.*, ch. 11.
47. The theme of Merelman's *Making Something of Ourselves: On Culture and Politics in the United States* (Berkeley: University of California Press, 1984).
48. See Gallup and Poling, *The Search for America's Faith*, chs. 1, 2, and 4, for their diffuse sense that moral attitudes and religious beliefs are deeply bound together, even if sometimes the process involves a self-conscious re-pudiation of *church* interpretations of the moral teachings of religious truth.
49. See, e.g., Corwin Smidt, "Evangelicals and the 1984 Election: Con-tinuity or Change?" paper presented at the annual meeting of the Society for the Scientific Study of Religion, 1985; and, more generally, Hoge, "National Contextual Factors Influencing Church Trends," in *Understanding Church Growth and Decline*, p. 105.

whole, to provide some boundaries for liberalism today just as they did 150 years ago, when de Tocqueville wrote *Democracy in America.*[50]

There is no doubt that this latter America dwells rather self-consciously within the morally individualistic and skeptical world that most American intellectuals and cultural observers know well. The secure base of shared values on which freedom flourished, as de Tocqueville saw America, has lost many of its adherents. The social results are obvious to Americans of all persuasions.[51] The current situation has specific consequences for particular religious groups more than for others. We must return to Dean Kelley's contention, this time in the context of moral permissiveness, that growing churches tend to be those more "strict" in ethical norms. The explanation lies in the concept of refuge. As society—especially its public opinion elites—moves away from moral rigorousness, those who desire a different America often seek refuge in "conservative" churches.[52] There is no question that evangelical Protestants are critical, usually highly critical, of permissiveness in American society; there is also no doubt that they are much more conservative on such "social questions" as abortion and sexual behavior than is the population at large.[53] The well-established attraction of organized religion for parents with children because they seek "good" moral influences for their children is an expression of the same impulse.[54]

50. See Bellah, *Habits of the Heart;* Caplow, *All Faithful People;* and *The Connecticut Mutual Life Report on American Values,* among many more sources here. The literature on this other, fashionable America is enormous.

51. The poll data, of course, is vast, but another approach that illuminates this trend is Reeves, *American Journey.*

52. Kelley, *Why Conservative Churches Are Growing,* pp. 121, 131; for an updated report (but not fundamentally different pattern), see *Religion in America* (Gallup Report), p. 11.

53. The evidence is extensive, but some few pieces are: J. Milton Yinger and Stephen J. Cutler, "The Moral Majority Viewed Sociologically," in *New Christian Politics,* ed. David G. Bromley and Anson Shupe (Macon, GA: Mercer University Press, 1984), pp. 69-90; James Davison Hunter, *American Evangelicalism: Conservative Religion and the Quandary of Modernity* (New Brunswick, NJ: Rutgers University Press, 1983); Bellah, *Habits of the Heart,* pp. 93-97; Franky Schaeffer, *Bad News For Modern Man: An Agenda for Christian Activism* (Westchester, IL: Crossway Books, 1984), chs. 1-4; see also Kelley, *Why Conservative Churches Are Growing.*

54. For the theory that children lead people back to church, see, e.g., Hoge and Roozen, "Research on Factors Influencing Church Commitment," in *Understanding Church Growth and Decline,* p. 52; for a more skeptical view, see David A. Roozen, "The Efficacy of Demographic Theories of Religious Change: Protestant Church Attendance, 1952-1968," in *Understanding Church Growth and Decline,* pp. 135-39.

But the evidence that religion appeals to people in the United States as a moral refuge is not unlimited. The world that Bell and Merelman describe is no intellectual fantasy. Even as Gallup and Poling found that the search for a firm grounding for values attracts people to religion, we know that there is a steady stream of people who reject or abandon churches they perceive as too strict.[55] The skepticism of fixed moral views that lies behind such a pattern, however, appears to be fairly localized within the larger population. It appeals mostly to elites—defined in educational and professional terms (though not business elites)—and to their eventual successors, affluent and well-educated youth.[56] Here is the stronghold of resistance to moral strictness and the center of popularity for liberal views on abortion, homosexuality, and the like.[57]

This is also a major factor in explaining the loss of membership and/or the absence of growth among middle-class, liberal Protestant churches, a phenomenon that strengthens my refuge hypothesis. Organized religion's unquestioned loss of appeal in our society among high-status younger people who favor a lifestyle premised on the de-emphasis of absolute moral values might seem to make a perfect fit between them and such liberal Protestant denominations as the United Church of Christ or the Episcopal Church.[58] Often it does so. But what we have observed regarding religious meaning and skepticism also holds with the related matter of moral absolutes. More and more often, the chosen alternative is to stay away from, or drop out of, organized religion altogether. There is thus this irony: it is the morally (and theologically) liberal churches that have suffered as sectors of the American population have liberalized their ethical views.[59]

55. E.g., Wade Clark Roof, "Alienation and Apostasy," *Society*, May-June 1978, pp. 41-45; Hoge and Roozen, "Research on Factors Influencing Church Commitment," in *Understanding Church Growth and Decline*, pp. 57-61.

56. This is the overwhelming conclusion of every study, the most thorough perhaps being *The Connecticut Mutual Life Report*.

57. See the following essays in *Understanding Church Growth and Decline*: Hoge and Roozen, "Some Sociological Conclusions about Church Trends," pp. 330-33; Hoge and Roozen, "Research on Factors Influencing Church Commitment," pp. 57-61; Hoge, "A Test of Theories," p. 197; Hoge, "National Contextual Factors Influencing Church Trends," pp. 120-21. See also Roof, "America's Voluntary Establishment," in *Religion and America*, pp. 130-49.

58. Roof, "Alienation and Apostasy"; Hoge and Roozen, "Some Sociological Conclusions about Church Trends," in *Understanding Church Growth and Decline*, p. 329.

59. Hoge and Roozen, "Some Sociological Conclusions about Church Trends," pp. 329-33; Roof, "America's Voluntary Establishment," in *Religion and America*, pp. 130-49.

Both sides of the debate over moral permissiveness in the United States, then, view at least organized religion with the same eyes. For both it is very much about clear moral standards, even though, except for fundamentalist Protestant schools, it is not clear where such standards are in place anymore in such religious institutions as religious schools.[60] Still, the religious and the nonreligious appear implicitly to acknowledge the role American religion plays in terms of moral norms; and both demonstrate that de Tocqueville's image of religion in the United States as being fundamentally about providing moral ballast is still very much alive.

Conclusion

MY ANALYSIS that religion operates in good part as a temporary refuge from liberal skepticism is related to familiar arguments about religion in every society and age that associate it with social-psychological needs. It is directly in the lineage of *The Future of an Illusion*, Freud's classic argument that religion is about comfort, comfort in the face of the suffering of life, above all the inescapable reality of death, and comfort in the face of the absence of obvious meaning in the cosmos as well as clear, certain guidance in life. Comfort is, by this view, what religion is all about.[61] Modern liberalism does not provide such comforts—and does not pretend to—and yet Americans seek them, many through religion.

In the hands of Freud and those who have agreed with him in our time, people who choose this "refuge" lack courage. At its best, choosing refuge underscores human weakness, and at its worst it suggests that involvement in religion is an act of self-delusion that tens of millions indulge in, a kind of self-medication for the pain and confusion of life. Curiously, there are many within the American religious community who are also uncomfortable with this approach to religion, especially if it becomes too much the vocation of a believing individual or a faithful church. This is religion, critics say, that is too much about comfort and too little about challenge. For them religion must not withdraw to security but go out and transform the world, or at least try to. It must bring the gospel of justice, peace, and healing—the gospel of faith—to fashion a changed world. Their voices are louder and louder in American religion today, and we will examine their messages and strengths in chapters six through eight.

Yet most people at present are not interested in or organized for re-

60. See the religion and education issue of *Daedalus*, Spring 1988.
61. See Sigmund Freud, *The Future of an Illusion* (Garden City, NY: Doubleday, 1964).

ligion as challenge. They seek its comforts, its refuge. They do not, on the whole, speak in psychological terms of needs or comfort. They speak in religious language—of faith and values. Religion is about them, believers say, and that is why they are religious or involved in religious groups.

CHAPTER THREE

Religion and the Escape from Liberal Individualism

MY SECOND CLAIM is that religion commonly functions as an alternative to liberal individualism, and people expect it to do so in American culture. My view is that even in America, religion (and its contrast with the rigors of liberal individualism) is popularly associated with "community" by the larger society. I use "alternative" to mean a compensation for liberalism, not a rejection of liberal individualism in all its expressions. The churches' function as community is an addition, one might say, to liberalism (and certainly does not deny for a moment the signs of individualism predictably also there). It provides a kind of "socializing" of normal liberalism for large numbers of Americans who are far from ready to repudiate their liberal values or institutions, but who nevertheless seek the community they so rarely find in liberal culture.

This view is not, of course, self-evident. It applies only to those who find in religion, especially organized religion, release for the contradictions in their lives between liberal individualism and the need for community; those who do not become consumed by the "community" dimension of their religion, for whom temporary refuge is not enough; and those for whom religion is not a fullscale retreat. This view does not describe those who seek to turn from liberal individualism by escaping it completely. They too affect society, but in a way that is not supportive in the long run—they withdraw their energy, loyalty, and talent. Thus we must do more than suggest a link between religion and a desire for "community." We must suggest why this connection promotes backhanded support for the society.[1]

Of course we must get clear what we are talking about when we discuss *liberal individualism,* a deceptively simple two-word phrase. Two sides of liberal individualism, much discussed today, are the *expressive* and *utilitarian* dimensions.[2] By *expressive individualism* I mean the celebration

1. Kenneth Wald's observations have been useful to me here.
2. See Richard J. Neuhaus, "Four American Individualisms," *Religion*

of freedom to do what a person wishes, the lifestyle freedom that has swept over large areas of American society since the 1960s. By *utilitarian individualism* I mean the ethic that judges actions in terms of the practical advantages a person gains from them, according to that individual's calculations. These two forms are close in some ways, though utilitarian individualism is more "rational" in a means/ends sense and often involves economic calculations. The latter has long been pervasive in liberal culture, while lifestyle individualism has developed much more recently.

Both expressive and utilitarian individualism make the individual and his or her subjective feelings or calculations sovereign. Both implicitly or explicitly affirm the goodness of a society without any shared moral standards. While both understand that people will have moral standards, they emphasize subjective morality and a great flexibility for everyone to develop personal norms. It follows that "tolerance" and "pluralism" are often favorite words in the vocabulary of people who celebrate liberal individualism—popular words, indeed, in our contemporary liberal society.[3]

The pervasiveness of individualism in America needs constant underlining. The evidence is indisputable that individualism and freedom are the values Americans treasure above all others. Often enough "the meaning of one's life for most Americans is to become one's own person, almost to give birth to oneself."[4] Nor is there much doubt about the power of individualism in our culture, of the commitment to "self-actualized" existence and its tension with ideas of duty, obligation, or community.[5]

This is even true to a considerable degree in the world of American religion, a realm where individualism is no stranger. After all, religion—and certainly organized religion—is far from neatly isolated from the larger culture. Much of American Protestantism had a large element of individualism in it from the start. Emphasis on an individual relationship with God, individual salvation, individual prayer, and a personal spiritual journey have long been a staple of religion in America. These ideas endure. Also relevant here is the decided pluralism among American religious groups and the continuing strength of the pointedly individualistic idea in Protestant and Jewish circles that each congregation is

---

and Society Report 2 (May 1985): 1-2; Robert Bellah et al., *Habits of the Heart: Individualism and Commitment in American Life* (Berkeley: University of California Press, 1985), chs. 1, 2, and 6.

3. Bellah, *Habits of the Heart,* p. 27.
4. *Ibid.,* pp. 82, vii-viii.
5. *Ibid.,* pp. 97-107.

sovereign.[6] And of course we must note the one-third or more of those Americans who believe they are at least modestly religious, but proclaim they have no need to pursue their spiritual goals in an institutional setting. For them religion is a private, distinctly individual affair.[7]

At the same time, religion, especially organized religion, is also a locus in the United States for a continuing yearning for community. By community I mean a condition of closeness among people that may have spiritual, social, or broader participatory dimensions, and in the case of religious community usually has all three. The longing for community in this sense is powerful, perhaps especially so in a liberal culture such as ours, where human relations are casual and spontaneous, utilitarian and affective rather than formal, binding, and long-term, and where interest groups are second nature but where it is hard to conceive of the public good.[8] Even the modern world of "helping" psychology, something of a competitor to religion and a stronghold of individualism, where community often seems defined in hollow fashion ("self-interested individuals join together to maximize individual good"), acknowledges the need for and importance of community.[9] No matter how much we perceive Americans to be speaking only the languages of individualism, students of American culture consistently find that the people retain what Robert Bellah calls a "second language," the language of community and commitment.[10]

What I want to suggest is that this often quiet second language is particularly connected with religion, especially organized religion in the United States. Here community is a legitimate idea and here Americans expect it to be. Granted there is some question how often churches are a locus for the urge toward community rather than an expression of assorted existing communities: local, class, or ethnic.[11] Even if this skepticism is sometimes well founded, however, it does not alter the evidence that people frequently look to religion and the churches to symbolize community. The issue is not the origins of the connection between organized religion and community, but the popular association of the two.

6. In developing the overall theory, I have been influenced by Herve Varenne, *Americans Together: Structured Diversity in a Midwestern Town* (New York: Columbia University Press, 1977).

7. George Gallup, Jr., and David Poling, *The Search for America's Faith* (Nashville: Abingdon, 1980), ch. 4.

8. Bellah, *Habits of the Heart*, pp. 206, 85, 191.

9. *Ibid.*, pp. 134-39.

10. *Ibid.*, p. 154.

11. John Wilson, *Religion in American Society: The Effective Presence* (Englewood Cliffs, NJ: Prentice-Hall, 1978); see his discussion of class and ethnicity in chs. 14 and 15.

FORMAL   BINDING   LONG TERM
SPONTANEOUS / UTILITARIAN / AFFECTIVE

Equally, it is a frequent error to place individualism and community at opposite and warring poles. There are many possibilities in terms of their relationship, depending on what "community" and "individualism" mean. In the United States the two often go together, as people express individualism in free and changing patterns of association with groups and communities; in the same way, people may participate in institutional religion in part for community reasons and yet self-consciously determine *not* to reject liberal individualism.[12] Again religion often serves as a temporary refuge, a compensation or counterbalance, and often an ambivalent one. But it is not, in most cases, a radical alternative. Religion hovers between the worlds of radical individualism and total community.[13]

In my discussion I am interested in four expressions of community within religion. The first part of my discussion explores community in spiritual and social senses. Later, I will concentrate on community expressed both in participating within organized religion and in connecting organized religion with the larger society.

The desire for spiritual community refers particularly to what is often called the search for a *community of believers,* the interest in finding a group of persons with whom one may share spiritual concerns, feelings, and rituals. This search very frequently leads people to church as they search for something deeper in life than individual lifestyles and "doing one's thing." It is not the only alternative available or used, but in America it is the most common. This quest for depth often takes the form of individual spiritual journeys, but its usual form involves joining a religious group or church to seek a community of shared belief.

Closely related is the urge toward *social community,* the fact that people join a church to find a congenial social circle, quite apart from an interest in "spiritual" community. These two cannot easily be separated because experience in churchly social communities strongly influences attitudes about the reality and appeal of larger communities of believers.

In any case, the data on the linkage of organized religion and community is overwhelming. *Religion* attracts those seeking transcendence from skeptical liberalism, but *church* is much more intimately connected with community. After all, more Americans belong to a church or synagogue (70 percent) than to any other private association, and by an immense margin.[14] Consider the evidence, for instance, regarding Catho-

12. The persistent, simple-minded assumption that individualism and the community are automatic opposites in theory and practice does not have any particular logic either theoretically or in experience.

13. Bellah, *Habits of the Heart,* pp. 236-37.

14. *Religion in America: 50 Years, 1935–1985* (Gallup Report No. 236, May 1985), p. 40.

lics. The Notre Dame Study of Parish Life has documented active Catholics' definition of their image of church as "the community of believers." Many Catholics look to the church for individual spiritual growth, but notably more think of it in terms of a "spiritual community." Indeed, given a range of possible images, 42 percent of active Catholics describe it in those words, more than any other view (though often in tandem with other views).[15]

The social dimension of community that Catholics seek in church is symbolized above all perhaps by the classic (and continuing) popularity of bingo at the church hall. No parish activity attracts more participation except mass itself. Bingo's social function is obvious, but the fact is that social activities in general are important "as a vitalizing force" in churches even as they satisfy the individual layperson's social needs.[16] Among Catholics, research suggests, attraction to church because of their need for community is strongly related to their evaluation of how well their family (especially through their Catholic mother) embodied community during their childhood. Where they perceive failure, it is quite common for them to reject church—and the model of church as community.[17] Gallup has found that the same is true for the entire population. When family and church are closely associated in one's upbringing, that is, when there is a strong sense of family and the family participates together as a community in church, children link church and community together and are likely to be church members as adults.[18]

Systematic interviewing of both Roman Catholic converts and returnees has confirmed the close link between the family community and the church as community. Why do people join the Roman Catholic Church? Why do they return after a period of alienation or lack of interest? The answers are overwhelmingly connected to marriage and family: for converts, marriage is crucial, often marriage to a Catholic. One study established that fully 83 percent converted for reasons of marriage and/or family. For returnees, the act of marriage, a turn from an individualistic

15. David C. Leege and Thomas A. Trozzolo, "Religious Values and Parish Participation: The Paradox of Individual Needs in a Communitarian Church," in *Notre Dame Study of Catholic Parish Life,* Report No. 4 (June 1985), pp. 1-8.

16. David C. Leege, "Parish Organizations: People's Needs, Parish Services, and Leadership," in *Notre Dame Study of Catholic Parish Life,* Report No. 8 (July 1986).

17. See Andrew Greeley and Mary Durkin, *Angry Catholic Women* (Chicago: Thomas More, 1984), for Greeley's usual argument on this subject.

18. The very close association of family, religion, home, and church receives Gallup's attention in *The Search for America's Faith,* ch. 2.

lifestyle to a more communal one, brings many into, or back to, the church.[19]

All of this applies to American churches generally, not just to Roman Catholicism, where both church doctrine and ethnic loyalties (somewhat diminished today except for the important Hispanic and Asian-American elements of the church) self-consciously promote community. Another significant illustration may be found in Jewish circles in the United States. While the current strength of Judaism in a religious sense is under intense debate, we know that Jews who "return" to Judaism strongly emphasize desire for community as an essential motivation.[20] And this movement toward Judaism attracts many Jews in a characteristic American fashion. Desire for community and desire for a more vibrant Judaism in one's life rarely leads to an all-or-nothing decision. Instead, individual Jews in individualistic America pick and choose in a spirit of freedom what and how much Judaism they want in their lives. These individuals are not rejecting liberalism, on the whole, but reaching out for an element of religious community to fill an important space in their lives.[21]

This discussion and that which follows, which argues that organized religion is intimately connected with the search for community in American life (and with our parallel ambivalence toward individualism), also draws on the extensive data we have on church growth (and decline). That literature is divided over the degree to which factors internal to a church or denomination are decisive in growth/decline as opposed to external factors (such as cultural and population trends).[22] Both are important. To isolate their respective interactive influences is all but impossible. No doubt the search for community and the tradition connecting churches and community have their roots largely (if, perhaps, not entirely) outside any given church. But how well religious groups address the need will influence their numbers because a crucial motivating factor leading people to any church, *indeed the most common factor,* is desire for more community—both in the family and in one's life in general. Churches and denominations that tap this association of religion and

19. Dean R. Hoge, *Converts, Dropouts, Returnees: A Study of Religious Change among Catholics* (New York: Pilgrim, 1981), p. 44.

20. See Charles E. Silberman, *A Certain People: American Jews and Their Lives Today* (New York: Summit Books, 1985); Arthur Hertzberg, "The Triumph of the Jews," *New York Review of Books,* 21 November 1985, pp. 18-22.

21. Silberman, *A Certain People,* pp. 250, 270, chs. 6, 7.

22. For a vigorous challenge to the neodeterminists who dismiss internal church factors, see Dean M. Kelley, "Commentary: Is Religion a Dependent Variable?" in *Understanding Church Growth and Decline, 1950–1978,* ed. Dean R. Hoge and David A. Roozen (New York: Pilgrim, 1979), pp. 338-39.

INTERNAL FACTORS - WITHIN
EXTERNAL   "   - WITHOUT

community are likely to grow.[23] They will more often than not attract those who have a fairly "traditional" lifestyle, a manifestation in practice of their commitment to community. Those who attend church and those who do not are little different in lifestyle. But the former are more often married, more likely to have children, and more likely to have more children than are those who do not go to church. Their behavior suggests that in many instances their drive for community is intense; without question, this drive propels tens of millions to church.[24]

Though the connection between children and church involvement is a controversial subject, there is no doubt that the arrival of children in a family is often crucial to forming church ties. Just as adolescents' departure from church is a routine move on their road to self-reliance and the affirmation of American individualism, so an interest in church among young couples with new children reflects a reborn interest in community. A definite life cycle rhythm is at work in American organized religion.[25] Since church is associated with family, often through an individual's own past, it is part of a package of family-community values. It is also assumed to be a family-promoting institution. Parents are commonly in favor of church as a place for their kids. In our terms, they see it as an alternative not to life in liberal America but to the unchecked dominance of liberal individualism and relativism.[26]

One final illustration of the interaction of church, religion, and community is the neighborhood factor. It is rarely discussed but decidedly important. Studies of church growth and decline indicate very clearly that the degree to which a neighborhood is a community and the degree to which a church is located within that psychological concept may affect a church's fate enormously. The point is a sensible one. A strong neighborhood community will assist neighborhood churches—if those churches become part of that community. If they stand aloof, or if

23. See, e.g., Edmund A. Rauff, *Why People Join the Church* (New York: Pilgrim, 1979); Gallup and Poling, *The Search for America's Faith*.

24. As well illustrated in Theodore Caplow et al., *All Faithful People: Change and Continuity in Middletown's Religion* (Minneapolis: University of Minnesota Press, 1983).

25. Bellah, *Habits of the Heart*, p. 62.

26. There is no shortage of skepticism concerning the theory that having children increases participation in organized religion. For example, for liberal Protestants, David A. Roozen, "The Efficacy of Demographic Theories of Religious Change: Protestant Church Attendance, 1952–1968," in *Understanding Church Growth and Decline,* pp. 135-36; for a contrary view regarding Roman Catholics, see Jay Dolan and David C. Leege, "A Profile of American Catholic Parishes and Parishioners: 1820s to the 1980s," in *Notre Dame Study of Catholic Parish Life,* Report No. 2 (February 1985), p. 6.

RLIGION

CHURCH △ COMMUNITY

the neighborhood exists in name only, neighborhood churches can get into trouble quickly.[27]

Many churches have found themselves facing death when their neighborhood world collapsed or changed decisively, and with it the attitudes toward the church. They illustrate the skeptics' suspicion that churches are very much the creatures of these cultural communities. But churches are far from helpless in these circumstances, however long the odds may look. They can be models of community in places where there is none—and revive themselves in the process. In fact, if my hypothesis is correct, we would expect only churches that do model community, at least to some extent, to flourish. If they reflect a sense of a community of believers, encourage family life, and reach out to their neighborhood, they address the needs that bring people to church more than anything else does. People will likely see them as more than a vague form of entertainment, an image that does not help churches, because they cannot really compete with other more exciting or more restful forms of entertainment available on Sunday morning.[28]

There is no evidence that how well a church satisfies the interest in community has the slightest thing to do with the grand declarations on the subject of community by the church's denominational leaders or headquarters staff. The relevant testing ground is, as always, concrete experience, in this case the actual life of local churches rather than abstract moral or political pronouncements. This is one important reason why denominations not noted for their strong foundation beliefs, vigorous evangelism, or firm morality do continue to retain large memberships. Wherever one goes in religious precincts in America, people often belong to their local church, parish, or synagogue more significantly than they do to their particular denomination—or in some cases even their specific religion. Whatever the image of a denomination, a local church of that denomination with a reputation for addressing community needs will attract members. And there are numerous such churches in every denomination.[29]

Another way to approach this subject is to explore how important the *failure* to find community is in explaining why people leave organized religion. If people do regularly drift away in disappointment when churches display a dearth of community, social and spiritual, this would

27. Douglas A. Walrath, "Social Change and Local Churches: 1951–1975," in *Understanding Church Growth and Decline,* pp. 248-69.

28. Dean Kelley, *Why Conservative Churches Are Growing* (New York: Harper and Row, 1972), p. 92.

29. See David C. Leege, "The Parish as Community: Developing Community and Commitment," in *Notre Dame Study of Catholic Parish Life,* Report No. 10 (March 1987).

BELIEF

MORALITY △ EVANGELISM

tend to suggest that many people do look to churches, as the concrete institutions of religion, to model community. At least there is a good deal of confirming evidence that how well institutional religion models community counts with people. Gallup has noted the critical stance of many youths toward how well churches and religious people (self-defined) live up to their professed values. This includes how well Christians embody a loving community at church—and elsewhere in their lives.[30] That some of these younger people are frankly not interested in church, or perhaps any other community, while they pursue their expressive individualism may be ironic.[31] But it does not change the fact that young people do judge the consistency of the religious world especially on its commitment to communal values, however unrealistic that may be and whether or not their judgment matters.

A quite mundane but relevant piece of evidence is the lay reaction to how much conflict exists at church. Conflict at church or synagogue is very unpopular; and the perception of intrachurch tension leads directly to membership declines.[32] This is entirely predictable, given my hypothesis. People do not go to church for the excitement of conflict. They go in good part for community, which is defined as harmony with the universe and fellowship with others. People commonly perceive conflict at church as a statement that the institution has failed in a basic way, that it cannot fulfill a basic need that led them there in the first place. Quite frequent "jokes" among involved laity about conflicts and political disagreements at churches only confirm the point. The jokes invariably imply both criticism and disappointment over the existence of conflict. The model is that at church harmony should reign.

We can also draw on data from intermarriage (marriage to someone from another religion or another major branch of a religion) and its effect on one's connections with organized religion. Andrew Greeley notes that intermarriage is a leading explanation for religious "disaffection." What this evidence shows for our discussion is that in the interest of community (family oneness), people will leave a given church or religion; indeed, they are more likely to disaffiliate for this reason than for any other.[33] This

30. Gallup and Poling, *The Search for America's Faith,* ch. 1 and p. 88.

31. Hoge, "National Contextual Factors Influencing Church Trends"; and "A Test of Theories of Denominational Growth and Decline," in *Understanding Church Growth and Decline.*

32. Hoge and Roozen, "Some Sociological Conclusions about Church Trends," in *Understanding Church Growth and Decline,* pp. 324-25; Wade Clark Roof, Dean R. Hoge, John E. Dyble, and C. Kirk Hadonay, "Factors Producing Growth or Decline in United Presbyterian Congregations," in *Understanding Church Growth and Decline,* p. 221.

33. See, e.g., Hoge's argument in *Converts, Dropouts, Returnees.*

is what we would expect, because it underscores that people are community-seeking souls who assess the organized religion they encounter in good part on its ability to speak to this need.

Another factor encouraging people to drop out of organized religion also accents its linkage with community: this is the family "strain" theory. People who have had a turbulent family life as children, or have considerable tension with their original family today, frequently view their family's church, if they had any—indeed, any kind of organized religion—with either ambivalence or hostility. From another side, this repeats what we already know: the close association in America between church and family documents again that "communities" associated with the family will pay a price when the family does not model the community people expect from it.[34]

Mostly, though, organized religion benefits from the popular perception that it is a place where community is affirmed, if not fully practiced. People look for community in religious activity. Often—very often—they find enough of it to satisfy them. Of course we must be careful not to exaggerate the part religion, especially organized religion, plays as a source for the alternative value of community in liberal America. Community can be, and is, pursued in many places in America. Bellah and his colleagues in *Habits of the Heart* want to withhold the word *community* from the numerous lifestyle groupings that are everywhere in America but are somehow too limited, shifting, and superficial.[35] Varenne is equally uncomfortable about using the word *community* for American group life because community is secondary to Americans' concern with liberty, and, in an anthropological sense, our group life is composed of associations with extremely loose boundaries.[36]

There is, however, something slightly purist at work here. Many "lifestyle enclaves" may not fulfill the ideal kind of community that some intellectuals define and yearn for. But the neighborhood bar, soccer club, PTA, bridge club, or what have you—even if built around somewhat fluid circles of friends—are the outlets many people find in their search for community, outlets they enjoy.[37] Sometimes a religious group is part

---

34. Andrew Greeley argues this in several places, including in "Religious Musical Chairs," *In Gods We Trust: New Patterns of Religious Pluralism in America,* ed. Thomas Robbins and Dick Anthony (New Brunswick, NJ: Transaction Books, 1981), pp. 101-26.

35. Bellah, *Habits of the Heart,* pp. 72-73.

36. Varenne, *Americans Together,* explores the kind of prevalent "community," chs. 4 and 7.

37. This view of fluid, multiple social interest groups as Americans' life is based on Varenne's *Americans Together,* a very stimulating essay, and on Bel-

of this picture, sometimes not. For those for whom it is not, the reasons are several, as we have seen. For some, church is not a place to seek community: their experience has taught them lessons about the failures of churches as real-world institutions committed to community only in principle. For others, especially younger middle- and upper-middle-class Americans, interest in community is modest at best; and their attraction to organized religion as a refuge from liberal individualism is often equally modest. Such Americans, as we know, are likely to be non-ambivalent participants in liberal culture, individuals of a utilitarian and/or expressive kind. But while their numbers rose sharply in the 1960s and 1970s, and liberal Protestantism in particular suffered the consequences, their attitude hardly characterizes the American population as a whole.[38]

The definition of community I have used so far emphasizes community in the sense of sharing and closeness in both spiritual and social dimensions. I have suggested extensive data supporting the idea that people think about organized religion as a place of community and in many cases go there to experience community, or at least to experience a respite from the individualism of the larger liberal society. So much of this association of religion and community is perceptual: it refers to feelings. What community means as a result varies enormously from person to person, including their behavior.

Perhaps this is why, when one explores two other dimensions of community's interface with American religion, the actual record is mixed. This is so when one looks at actual lay involvement in organized religion—not the symbolic connection of church and community but the actual evidence that people take part. The record is equally mixed when one looks at the church's expression of community through active witness to the outside world. In both instances evidence of commitment is surprisingly modest.

Participation in organized religion, beyond the three-quarters or so of the population who claim membership in a religious group, is hard to document. There is evidence on the most obvious measure: attendance at worship services. The data here, while self-reported, are extensive and the patterns plausible. Evangelical and fundamentalist Christians are much the most active in this modest sense. The strong majority

---

lah, *Habits of the Heart,* pp. 71-75, from which the term "lifestyle enclaves" comes.

38. Wade Clark Roof, "America's Voluntary Establishment: Mainline Religion in Transition," in *Religion and America: Spirituality in a Secular Age,* ed. Mary Douglas and Steven Tipton (Boston: Beacon, 1983), pp. 130-149.

SPIRITUAL
SOCIAL   UTILITARIAN

are in church at least once a week and often more. Since Vatican II, Catholic attendance at mass has fallen; still, most Catholics appear at mass in a given month, and a sizable minority attend every week. The lowest attendance occurs among liberal or mainstream Protestants, the majority of whose members do not attend in a given month. Attendance at services is not emphasized among non-Orthodox Jews, so that the rare appearance of Jews at synagogue except on High Holy Days means little.[39]

Of course, participating in one way or another guarantees nothing, including a sense of community. Indeed, participation can damage a strong sense of spiritual community by bringing one in conflict with other church members. But participation does often lead to an increased sense of community for an individual and for a religious body. That is why success in generating a sense of community in a local church or parish correlates importantly with opportunities for participation. Only open, active churches allow community to grow; those that are ruled by one person or by a small group will not be centers of participatory-based community. Nor, data show, will those where that elusive trait "caring" is not manifest. This too makes sense. Opportunities for participation will not necessarily breed community unless participants find among themselves people who care about others. But where caring and opportunity abound, the ideal of community that people seek in religion will actually exist in specific local churches.[40]

However, formal religious services are hardly the sole activity for any religious group. There are numerous other opportunities for participation in organized religion in America, one might say numerous opportunities for creating or participating in community at church. Indeed, the chances for going beyond community as a spiritual ideal have long been extensive at churches and synagogues. Organizations abound. Women's groups, men's groups, Scripture study, social action, charity, church governance, music, youth, and education—the list is long and the opportunities are there. Moreover, many churches today self-consciously keep their buildings occupied and busy for many hours, seven days a week, often renting or lending space to day-care groups, social action agencies, youth organizations, and so forth. Often these groups are connected

OTHERS - COMMUNITY
SELF - INDIVIDUAL

39. *Religion in America* (Gallup Report), pp. 42, 11; Dolan and Leege, "A Profile of American Catholic Parishes and Parishioners," p. 6.

40. David C. Leege and Thomas A. Trozzolo, "Participation in Catholic Parish Life: Religious Rites and Parish Activities in the 1980s," in *Notre Dame Study of Catholic Parish Life,* Report No. 3 (April 1983), p. 6.

with the parish, and parishioners are welcomed or even urged to participate in them.

But the fact is that, given the opportunities, actual participation is
small. It appears closely correlated with people's overall attitudes toward
their religion and the churches' general cohesiveness, as one might expect. Thus in evangelical and fundamentalist churches, most members
are involved beyond merely attending; among Catholics, about half
claim to be; among liberal Protestants, far fewer than half are.

The most extensive data we have on any one group come from the
superb Notre Dame Study of Catholic Parish Life. This contemporary
study found that of the half or so Roman Catholics active beyond attending mass, the largest group (26 percent) participate in church social-
recreational groups and activities; almost as many are active in the church
liturgies as readers, choir members, and the like; more than 10 percent
work in church educational programs (including evangelism efforts,
helping to run the parish, etc.).[41]

If we do not use religious measures of participation, which are low,
Jewish patterns of involvement are impressive. To be sure, 25 percent of
American Jews have no connection with organized Judaism. But the vast
majority are at least occasionally involved in the considerable range of
Jewish organizations, 10 percent or so intensely, another third actively,
the rest more infrequently.[42]

The amount of activity or participation—of real or potential community—in an organizational sense *within* religious groups is vast compared to the degree of interconnection with the *outside* world. Practice
indicates that community with the outside world continues to be low on
people's agenda—even in this day of supposedly politicized religion.
Granted, most organized religious groups have one or more forms of
outreach to the larger community, thus making some effort to build
paths of community beyond their walls. But a great proportion of this
outreach concentrates on the larger community of the religious denomination to which the churches belong. A typical Catholic church, for example, makes many efforts in a year to connect with local, national, and
even international communities. But it does so mostly in terms of help
in local Catholic schools or the apostolate to the (usually Catholic) hand-
icapped or the Sisters or Brothers of something or other in Africa or
Guatemala. Moreover, even including the often remarkable outreach
programs of the Knights of Columbus, the actual numbers of active laity

41. *Ibid.*
42. Daniel Elazar, *Community and Polity: The Organizational Dynamics of
American Jewry* (Philadelphia: Jewish Publication Society, 1976), pp. 70-77.

are very small. This pattern is repeated by many Jewish synagogues insofar as a great deal of their outreach is directed toward Israel; and certainly by many conservative Protestant groups, whose tension toward the outside world beyond the "born again" is evident.[43]

Lay opposition to community outreach, if outreach means involvement in social-political causes or groups, has been and continues firm. The more the clergy or denominational leaders become involved in such causes, and the more they bring their commitment home to the church, the more lay resistance tends to rise.[44] Among clergy, opinion is more mixed and may, in fact, be increasingly favorable toward engagement with the larger community on social and political issues.[45] But it is simply undeniable that few people join an organized religion or go to church to get involved in social-political action. This is not the kind of community involvement they are after. Some people do become busy in charitable activities such as community meal programs, community pantries, and the like—though the number is still small in proportional terms. Community in this broader sense of a relationship between the faithful and the larger company of God's people is a regular but quite small part of almost all organized religious groups' activities.

Looking at both participation in internal church activities and in those reaching out to the larger society, one is tempted to ask if all the talk of "community" by members of organized religion is meaningless—and with it my theory that this is a powerful force attracting people to organized religion. After all, as we have seen, the lay interest is small. But the question is not especially relevant, I think, to the fact that only modest numbers of people *reach out* from their religious community to the larger community. These numbers are predictably small, given my hypothesis that people go to church in large part to escape—for a time—the larger liberal culture. That participation *inside* religious "communities" is higher is equally predictable. But that the appeal of this inside kind of activity as an expression of community commitment is not larger

43. Leege and Trozzolo, "Religious Values and Parish Participation," p. 5, presents the Catholic data, the best we have on any branch of American religion.

44. For summaries of the data, see A. James Reichley, *Religion in American Public Life* (Washington, DC: Brookings, 1985), ch. 6; Robert Booth Fowler, *Religion and Politics in America* (Metuchen, NJ: Scarecrow Press, 1985), ch. 4.

45. Consider, for instance, the signs of a historic shift toward this kind of activity among the clergy of the Southern Baptist Convention: James Guth, "Southern Baptist Clergy: Vanguard of the Christian Right?," in *The New Christian Right: Mobilization and Legitimization,* ed. Robert C. Liebman and Robert Wuthnow (New York: Aldine de Gruyter, 1983), ch. 6.

may be surprising. Perhaps it is surprising, but only if one assumes that church is somehow the center of life for most members rather than a temporary refuge; only if one forgets other community options that abound in our individualistic society; and only if one downplays community defined as feelings of unity or as formal membership and insists on evidence of extensive other involvement.

One should remember that virtually every organized religious group is a hive of activity—and not just on the Sabbath. Thus they may be a minority, but many members of every organized religion are very active. Whether they are obtaining, or encouraging, the community they seek as a result of this activity is another question.[46]

Conclusion

WE MUST CONCEDE that we do not yet have a perfect set of evidence that establishes directly that religion serves as a kind of escape hatch from excessive cultural liberal individualism, a place where one can find the idea of community, if not always its practice. But I think the pieces of evidence I have put together—the studies on joining and leaving organized religions, the evidence about participation, the conception of religion in terms of community, and the like—should be read in an interpretive fashion to mean just that. The evidence suggests close association between organized religion and community in one and usually more senses—in a spiritual, social, participatory, or an interactive sense with the larger society.

The point is that religion, organized religion especially, operates as an alternative to the liberal individualism which is basic to our culture. That contrast does not work out to religion's disadvantage on the whole. Nor, it is my thesis, to liberal society's, though showing the connection of religion and community is not quite the same thing as establishing the rest of the loop.[47] It is not the same thing as establishing that the consequence is unintended support for liberal culture.

There are other interpretive possibilities. We could read the interest in community as a statement of nonsupport for liberal culture. As I observed earlier, this might take several forms. It could, for instance, reflect nonsupport through the growth of a religious subculture that is intensely sympathetic to "community" and hostile to the larger American culture

46. While we have good data on Jewish and Roman Catholic participation levels beyond attendance, much more information is needed regarding Protestant churches here. Also needed is systematic data on the connections between participation (and kinds of participation) and perceived community.
47. As Kenneth Wald has pointed out to me.

PERCEIVED COMMUNITY
PARTICIPATION

and trying to change it in radical ways. Or it could reflect nonsupport through the people who enter religious culture for the purpose of permanent escape from individualism.

The major case against these possibilities is simply that Americans (including religious Americans) do not reject liberal individualism, as we have noted. They do not ordinarily see religion and liberal culture as mortal enemies at war in society or in their own souls. That they rarely see such a war means it does not exist for them. Church and culture, though partly about different values, fit together.

It is not my contention that this fit is self-consciously understood by the large part of the population that is both community-oriented (reorganized religion) and committed to liberal individualism. And it is true enough that there are self-consciously religious people who do propose to sweep away liberal individualism in our culture just as there are those who want to retreat into a religious world where liberal individualism can be kept at bay. But our data about lay attitudes toward political involvement by organized religion, as well as the evidence of the laity's nonradical issue views, suggest that the number of such activists is very small.[48]

There may be a case for arguing that the number of those who seek to escape liberal culture by entering separatist religious settings is growing, not so much in the insignificant numbers of the "cults" as in the substantial numbers involved in the Christian school movement among fundamentalists.[49] Still, all the evidence at hand suggests that for the average churchgoer there is no yearn to have community replace individualism.[50] Apparently Americans do believe they can (or should) have it all. As long as this holds true, then organized religion will continue to serve, as I suggest it does, as an indirect supporter of a liberal culture it must necessarily view ambivalently.

48. For a succinct discussion of issue views, see Kenneth Wald, *Religion and Politics in the United States* (New York: St. Martin's, 1986), ch. 4.

49. Christian schools, of course, come in many different forms. See the following: John C. Carper and Thomas C. Hunt, eds., *Religious Schooling in America* (Birmingham: Religious Education, 1984); John C. Carper and Neal E. Devins, "The State and the Christian Day School," in *Religion and the State: Essays in Honor of Leo Pfeffer*, ed. James E. Wood, Jr. (Waco, TX: Baylor University Press, 1985), pp. 211-32; Alan Peshkin, *God's Choice: The Total World of the Christian School* (Chicago: University of Chicago Press, 1986).

50. Even if Christianity were somehow to push forward the idea of community into the larger American society, would it come in a form which underscored individualism? This is the query and suspicion of Bellah in *Habits of the Heart*, pp. 232, 236.

CHAPTER FOUR

Alternative Views: Integration

THE ARGUMENT OF THIS BOOK is that religion in America is "integrated" into liberal culture only in the sense that it has supported the culture, albeit unintentionally, by providing a temporary *refuge* from that liberal culture. It fills in some of the gaps people perceive in liberal society, but it can do so only because many citizens believe that it offers somewhat different ideals and practices than liberal society can, which, as it turns out, is a controversial perception. Indeed, this perception of difference is much of what attracts people to religion or, at least, to church and synagogue. This separateness, or perceived separateness, is a far cry from the classic view of religion and culture. The classic view has been that religion has been quite directly integrated into established cultures in the West, and has not been (nor is) different or separate from them, and that this is even truer of most churches and other religious institutions. Such has been the staple of sociological theory about religion and culture since the nineteenth century.

This chapter and the next will challenge the conventional tight integration theory, at least as applied to the United States. Sometimes this theory comes echoing the theories of Max Weber and Karl Marx: their integrationist theses frequently reappear in discussions on religion and politics in America, though usually free of the elaborate theoretical baggage and turgid Germanic prose that weighed down these masters. Alexis de Tocqueville's *Democracy in America* represents another form of the integration thesis. The next chapter will address his ideas regarding religion and liberal culture in the United States, along with other approaches rooted more specifically in the American experience.

All these approaches agree, or may be used to argue, that organized religion has rarely existed in much tension with our broader culture. They contend that religion has played a major role in developing our culture or in providing some of crucial raw materials for our culture, *or* that it has been a creature of our culture and as such has actively helped sustain the culture. All these approaches suggest that a close relationship was only to be expected. Religion, and especially the institu-

48

tions of religion, could only rarely be separate from a culture. This has been the experience of history in world terms and in America as well.

Today there is increasing dissatisfaction with this view, which is only to be welcomed. "Most sociological discussion of the political role of religion is not merely misleading, but pernicious. The standard view . . . is that the religion sustains the political status quo. . . . Clearly, such claims apply at best to only some religions and only in special social circumstances."[1] This increasing sophistication opens the door to a new range of possible theories, above all to a sense that in different times and places the arrangements between religion, culture, and politics may escape the time-worn formula of mutual embrace or opposition—the traditional dialectic. But such has not been—or become—convention.

How tightly integration exists today in the United States is the issue. Obviously, the classical theorists of sociology cannot address our question directly; but there is little doubt what a reading of Marx or Weber would lead us to expect. We can best approach this question by developing a more theoretical and historical background, which will give us the necessary grounding and perspective on this subject. It will also introduce the terms of the dispute in the American context, much of which is a fight over the past—that is, over who understands the past. This is true because so often the argument assumes that those who most fully understand the place of religion in our culture's past can lead us to make wise decisions on their proper relationship today.

Max Weber

NO ONE HAS EXPLORED THE CONNECTIONS between religion and culture more deeply than has Max Weber. It is with his insights that we must begin the journey into the paradigm of close integration between religion and culture. Weber's standing has soared in recent years. Interest in the life of this brilliant social theorist has attracted some of the attention.[2] More often, though, Weber's theory has held center stage. Fortunately, some of the work dealing with Weber's theory has moved beyond the academic industry that was long consumed with faulting

---

1. Rodney Stark and William Sims Bainbridge, *The Future of Religion: Secularization, Revival and Cult Formation* (Berkeley: University of California Press, 1985), p. 522.

2. E.g., see Arthur Mitzman's stimulating *The Iron Cage: An Historical Interpretation of Max Weber* (New York: Knopf, 1970); an excellent briefer treatment is H. H. Gerth and C. Wright Mills, "A Biographical View," in *From Max Weber*, ed. H. H. Gerth and C. Wright Mills (New York: Oxford University Press, 1958), pp. 3-31.

Weber's conception of the relationship of religion and society and has turned to a broader and less polemical, if not uncritical, estimate of his contribution.[3]

For us, it is Weber's renowned theory of the relationship between capitalism and Protestantism that is most relevant.[4] Weber's thesis, of course, was that in Europe, particular Protestant values—the idea of a calling to serve God, the importance of asceticism and hard work, the worth of each individual—exercised enormous influence in fashioning (as distinguished from being the *cause* of)[5] capitalism and its culture. This suggests a theory of the integration of religion and society whose relevance to the United States as a Protestant land and then as a Protestant capitalist country is apparent.

Weber's is an analysis of considerable complexity that is far more guarded and surrounded by qualifiers than ordinary vulgar misrepresentations of it suggest.[6] Nonetheless, its major outlines are clear enough. In its broadest construction, Weber's theory contends that religion is—or can be—of immense power in influencing the culture and institutions of society and thus is indeed ordinarily integrated with its surrounding social order. And it is in this form that Weber has, in effect, been brought to America to explore the subject of religion and liberal culture.

To proceed with Weber's contribution for our purposes we need to explore his theory more, which, since he did not deal with American society, will lead us away from America temporarily. Weber is concerned with reflecting on the role of a particular kind of Protestantism, Calvinism, or, in a perhaps slightly broader formulation, "ascetic Protestantism." He is interested in general Calvinist ideas, as he understands them, not Calvinist institutions or the detailed pronouncements of John Calvin.[7] In short, Weber's interest lies in the somewhat imprecise world of Calvinist Protestant ideas and their influence on the spirit of modern capitalism. It is equally important to be precise about Weber's focus re-

3. For an example, see Gordon Marshall, *In Search of the Spirit of Capitalism: An Essay on Max Weber's Protestant Ethic Thesis* (New York: Columbia University Press, 1982).

4. Especially in, of course, Max Weber, *The Protestant Ethic and the Spirit of Capitalism* (New York: Scribner's, 1958).

5. See Stanislav Andreski, "Method and Substantive Theory in Max Weber," in *The Protestant Ethic and Modernization: A Comparative View*, ed. S. N. Eisenstadt (New York: Basic Books, 1968), pp. 46-63.

6. See Ephraim Fischoff, "The Protestant Ethic and the Spirit of Capitalism: The History of a Controversy," in *The Protestant Ethic and Modernization*, pp. 67-86; see Weber, *The Protestant Ethic and the Spirit of Capitalism*, pp. 91-92, for an example of such cautious qualifying.

7. Marshall, *In Search of the Spirit of Capitalism*, p. 85.

garding capitalism. He argues that it is the "spirit" and values of modern capitalism, not the institution or the overall system of capitalism, whose origins lie in Calvinism.[8] Thus Weber does not argue that Calvinism caused or created modern capitalism but that it stimulated the formation of its spirit, which was necessary in turn—though not sufficient—for the emergence of capitalism as a system.[9] Nor, it should be stated, is it Weber's view that Calvinism was fundamentally a covering ideology for capitalism or the spirit of capitalism. Weber well appreciated that Calvinism was first and foremost a religious movement and that any other dimension or effect of it was, at most, secondary.[10]

This is not to suggest that Weber did not respect the power of economic arrangements in molding human life and history. He did. But he consistently shied away from any suggestions that economic determinants could operate as a single factor, cause, or explanation—a conclusion he applied to Calvinism in particular and the Reformation in general.[11] Weber rejected such reductive thinking because it would underestimate the strength of religion and would consider the world in too simple and linear a fashion. The world was much too dynamic for that approach.[12]

Weber insists, of course, that when he reflects on "the spirit of modern capitalism" he is employing an ideal type, a partial and exaggerated picture of the mental world of actual modern capitalists.[13] This approach, which some of his disciples also used regarding "Calvinism," allowed Weber to present an understanding of the "spirit of capitalism" that he found plausible. But it could not be verified. Even at the time it was highly debatable and has grown more so since.[14]

To be sure, such abstract category creation is integral to the fashioning of broad theory. And Weber's use of such ideal types does not affect his major claims for the purposes of this study: that "Calvinism" greatly influenced "the spirit of capitalism" and through it the basic order of Western society; and, contrary to Marx, that capitalist society was more the child of religion than religion was the child of capitalism.

The secondary literature on Weber's *Protestant Ethic and the Spirit of Capitalism* knows no limit, and a good deal of it is skeptical. Every

8. *Ibid.,* pp. 17-18.
9. *Ibid.,* p. 56.
10. Herbert Luthy, "Once Again: Calvinism and Capitalism," in *The Protestant Ethic and Modernization,* pp. 87-108.
11. E.g., Weber, *The Protestant Ethic and the Spirit of Capitalism,* pp. 75, 91-92.
12. John Wilson, *Religion in American Society: The Effective Presence* (Englewood Cliffs, NJ: Prentice-Hall, 1978), p. 4.
13. Marshall, *In Search of the Spirit of Capitalism,* p. 51.
14. *Ibid.,* pp. 115-16.

claim Weber made, and every claim that some interpreter has asserted he made, has drawn criticism.[15] Perhaps the favorite mode of reflection on Weber's thesis has been to apply it to other countries and in other locales, some far from Europe, places such as Sri Lanka.[16] Perhaps the most attention has been devoted to the plausibility of Weber's hypothesis in Britain. This is only reasonable since the spirit of capitalism flourished there first (and has declined there along with Protestantism in the twentieth century). Michael Walzer's cogent analysis, for example, insists that Calvinism in its British form cannot plausibly be tied to an emerging capitalist bourgeoisie class: Calvinism was concerned with godliness and piety, not economic gain. Moreover, Puritanism was an ideology of suspicion, not one that could build an order on capitalist contracts, which are founded on trust.[17]

The particulars of Weber's "Calvinism," especially the ideas of a "calling," material asceticism, and hard work,[18] have each attracted attention from scholars of American colonial culture, especially of Calvinist New England, sometimes with sufficient acknowledgment of Weber's creative pioneering, sometimes not.[19] But in terms of an analysis of the United States as a whole, Weber's specific integration of Calvinism and the spirit of capitalism has been less significant than his general demonstration that religion's influence in a culture cannot be ignored or underestimated. Many have followed in his train in the United States in the sense that they have insisted that significant portions of American culture, quite beyond the spirit of capitalism, have their origins at least in part in religious values, indeed in Protestant and often Calvinist values.[20]

15. A good summary of the debate is in S. N. Eisenstadt, "The Protestant Ethic Thesis in an Analytical and Comparative Framework," in *The Protestant Ethic and Modernization,* pp. 3-45.

16. Michael Ames, "Ideological and Social Change in Ceylon," in *The Protestant Ethic and Modernization,* pp. 271-88.

17. Michael Walzer, "Puritism as a Revolutionary Ideology," in *The Protestant Ethic and Modernization,* pp. 109-34; see also Charles George and Katherine George, "Protestantism and Capitalism in Pre-Revolutionary England," in *The Protestant Ethic and Modernization,* pp. 155-76.

18. E.g., Weber, *The Protestant Ethic and the Spirit of Capitalism,* pp. 121, 180; see also Marshall, *In Search of the Spirit of Capitalism,* ch. 4.

19. See Larzer Ziff, *Puritanism in America* (New York: Viking, 1973), ch. 1; Louis B. Wright, *The Cultural Life of the American Colonies: 1607–1763* (New York: Harper and Row, 1957; 1962), p. 24; Edmund S. Morgan, ed. *Puritan Political Ideas* (Indianapolis: Bobbs-Merrill, 1965), pp. xiii-xxv, xxxv-xlvi; Perry Miller, *Nature's Nation* (Cambridge: Harvard University Press, 1967), ch. 3.

20. See, for instance, James Ward Smith and A. Leland Jamison, eds., *Religion in American Life,* vol. 4 (Princeton: Princeton University Press, 1961),

In point of fact, most of these theories have been homegrown, apparently unaware of Weber's or other grand theories about religion and Western society. In most of them, religion fits so well into our liberal culture because the culture's roots are so firmly located in American Calvinism and the colonial era. Implicit is the notion that religion's direct influence on liberal culture in America is a thing of the past, something exercised long ago. Such analyses routinely ignore or dismiss the possible significance of today's religion. But this does not really matter. These integrationist theories insist that, regardless of just when it happened, religion did fuse with American culture and society and remains there today, even if it has metamorphosed into secularized forms and values; the original integration is still very much alive.[21]

There are qualified versions of these theories. But most generalize freely. They sweep across American culture and history as they propound their version of the connections between religion and society. They get a good deal more specific, however, when they identify what religious values helped mold our culture (though to an always undetermined degree) and what religions continue to reinforce them today, even though the political culture is the main contemporary transmitter. Candidates are almost as numerous as their partisans. We will look at four of those values in our culture whose origins are most often said to lie in our religious history: *pluralism, individualism, liberal moralism,* and, of course, *suspicion of government and politics.* There are others that deserve consideration, such as education and the weak but existent "communal" side of American life, both intimately linked, one might argue, to the "stubborn congregationalism of American religion."[22] But the four I have selected receive the most attention.

The contribution of American religious experience to our liberal *pluralism* receives (and merits) the most analysis. However, we must be cautious about what we say here. We are discussing America's political

p. 608; Sidney Mead, *The Lively Experiment* (New York: Harper and Row, 1963); William Lee Miller, "American Religion and American Political Attitudes," in *Religion in American Life,* vol. 2, ed. James Ward Smith and A. Leland Jamison (Princeton: Princeton University Press, 1961); William Clebsch, *From Sacred to Profane: The Role of Religion in American History* (New York: Harper and Row, 1968), pp. 1-14; and Franklin H. Littell, *From State Church to Pluralism: A Protestant Interpretation of Religion in American History* (Garden City, NY: Doubleday, 1962).

21. Kenneth Wald, *Religion and Politics in the United States* (New York: St. Martin's, 1986), pp. 55-57.

22. Clebsch, *From Sacred to Profane,* p. 75 and ch. 4. The following discussion is a greatly revised and expanded version of Robert Booth Fowler, *Religion and Politics in America* (Metuchen, NJ: Scarecrow Press, 1985), pp. 27-31.

and group pluralism—diversity in political opinion, multiple interest groups, and the practice of group bargaining—rather than moral diversity or relativism. The latter may have originated in part from other forms of pluralism at a much later period, but it was hardly a legacy of early American religion, even unintentionally.

The influence of religion on our group/political pluralism in America is at best debatable. Religious life in the colonies was characterized by diversity, and "the localism and laicism of American religion" remain noteworthy even today.[23] Sidney Mead accurately describes the churches in America as traditionally sectarian, confident of their light and extremely doubtful of others", which was not at all the gospel of liberal compatibility amidst vague diversity that sometimes obtains today.[24] This was obvious in the struggle within the vast panorama that was Christianity in eighteenth- and nineteenth-century America. Protestants warred with fellow Protestants over proper liturgy, control of the church, the role of baptism, and much more; Protestants attacked Roman Catholics, while both Protestants and Catholics waged war against new religions such as Mormonism. And few were loving in the struggle.[25] This was a kind of pluralism, but a pluralism forged by necessity, not by choice. It appears to make the "complicity of religion with pluralism" undeniable at least through the nineteenth century.[26] Pluralism or sectarianism there was, and today there undoubtedly remains remarkable religious diversity in the United States. The host of different religious folk in the beginning included Congregationalists, Episcopalians, Roman Catholics, Baptists, Methodists; later additions were Lutherans (of many varieties), the Disciples of Christ, the results of numerous Baptist and Methodist schisms, the black denominations, the Jews, the Christian Scientists, the Mormons, and the list goes on.

But how did this affect American culture? This is where speculative argument takes over. One view contends that religious diversity offered a pluralistic model to politics that seemed natural, reasonable, and beneficial. The tendency of members of one ethno-religious group or another to live together and often to vote as a unit, particularly in nineteenth-century America, did ensure a transfer of pluralism from religion to politics. From another side, though, perhaps this view has the process reversed. Perhaps our religious pluralism is more the creation of

23. Clebsch, *From Sacred to Profane*, p. 75.

24. Mead, *The Lively Experiment*, chs. 2 and 7.

25. E.g., Walter Brownlow Posey, *Religious Strife on the Southern Frontier* (Baton Rouge: Louisiana State University Press, 1965); Edwin Scott Gaustad, *Dissent in American Religion* (Chicago: University of Chicago Press, 1973).

26. Clebsch, *From Sacred to Profane*, p. 216.

eighteenth-century Enlightenment liberalism embodied in the First Amendment and our political system. While they have their limits, as polygamous Mormons learned, liberal, pluralist political ideas may well have had more to do with encouraging and sustaining religious pluralism than the other way around. Images of chickens and eggs come to mind. Perhaps the truth is that religious diversity and liberal conviction worked to the same end. But we don't know, and this idea too remains imprecise, an uneasy speculation.[27]

It is more comfortable to move on and note that *individualism* is a second feature of American liberalism that religion encouraged, as some students maintain. There is no doubt that Protestantism in the United States has been individualistic in its focus on individual salvation, resistance to mediators between the individual and God, and devotion to the doctrine of the priesthood of all believers. Thus it is no surprise that many historians contend that religious individualism played a part in encouraging individualism in our culture, at least as an article of vague faith. But again, has this been a cause or an effect of our Protestant individualism? The case can be argued both ways. Even if it is more an effect, it is not clear what the degree of Protestant influence has been—whether, for example, it was more important than the British Whig tradition or Enlightenment views supporting individualism. There undoubtedly was some melding of forces in achieving and maintaining this aspect of American political culture, but what "credit," if any, one should give to religious elements is elusive and likely to remain so.[28]

Another quite frequently argued theory is that the *moralism* characteristic of our society derives from early religious roots. One interesting version emphasizes American religion's integral role in reconciling the

27. On religious diversity in America, past and present, see Littel, *From State Church to Pluralism;* Mead, *The Lively Experiment;* Martin E. Marty, *Righteous Empire: The Protestant Experience in America* (New York: Dial Press, 1970), chs. 3, 7, 11, 13, 17, and 23; Andrew Greeley, *The Denominational Society* (Glenview, IL: Scott, Foresman, 1972), chs. 4, 5, and 8; Martin Marty, *A Nation of Behavers* (Chicago: University of Chicago Press, 1976), chs. 3-8. Sydney E. Ahlstrom, *A Religious History of the American People,* 2 vols. (Garden City, NY: Doubleday, 1975), is perhaps the most comprehensive discussion of religion in American history and thus of the reality of pluralism in religion, in society, and in their interactions.

28. E.g., see Richard Merelman, *Making Something of Ourselves* (Berkeley: University of California Press, 1984), pp. 7-8; H. Richard Niebuhr, "The Protestant Movement and Democracy in the United States," in *Religion in American Life,* pp. 28-32, 36, 51-59, 70. An extremely interesting discussion of "the self" and the Puritans is in Sacvan Bercovitch, *The Puritan Origins of the American Self* (New Haven: Yale University Press, 1975), ch. 1.

individual and society in American history. This is a perspective reminiscent of de Tocqueville (see chapter 5). In this view, American religion has tended to encourage a flexible, responsive morality able to adjust as time and culture change.[29] The more common version is that the dominant moral attitude in politics is absolutist and self-righteous and that it originates in Protestant religious moralism, a tendency to see issues in terms of absolutes and to insist that people conform to such absolutes. Obviously, politics in America today teems with such moralism, for example, the disputes over abortion or Central American policy. And the list of moralistic crusades connected with religion in our political history is long, from antislavery to Prohibition to prayer in the schools.

That there has often been disagreement about God's truth when it comes to particular issues, and that being virtuous has often degenerated into having proper manners, does not mean that religiously based moralism has not been sincere or real in its effects. It has been important in nurturing our continuing moralistic political culture even in an age of supposed skepticism. But to what degree is, once again, another question.[30]

America's characteristic moralism is one part of an explanation for the hostility toward and *suspicion of politics* and politicians that is basic to American liberalism. If politics must realize the will of God—should be "God's Hammer," but is not (the view of many American Calvinists)— or if it is necessarily a sinful, earthly institution, or both, then government and politics will seem unattractive. This will be especially true, perhaps, of the deals and compromises of liberal politics. This legacy from a religious past may well have contributed to the established American belief that politics and government deserve suspicion. Surveys consistently reveal that people are convinced that ordinary politicians are often dishonest, that politics is dirty, that it is often immoral, and that politics and government should stay out of people's lives or else do what is "right." And religious forces continue to encourage these beliefs every day. It does not matter whether it is Jerry Falwell or William Sloan Coffin, Jr., in the pulpit; their characteristic suspicion of ordinary politics and liberal government is the same.[31]

29. Clebsch, *From Sacred to Profane*, ch. 5.

30. A most developed argument (as applied to politics) is William Lee Miller, "American Religion and American Political Attitudes," in vol. 2 of *Religion in American Life*, pp. 81-118; Perry Miller, "The Puritan Way of Life," in *Puritanism in Early America*, ed. George M. Waller (Boston: D. C. Heath, 1950), pp. 16-22; Clebsch, *From Sacred to Profane*, ch. 5; Littell, *From State Church to Pluralism*, pp. 120-25, 163-64, 5-12, 17, 52-57, 65-72; Mead, *The Lively Experiment*, pp. 22-27.

31. Two effective illustrations of religious distrust toward government

The thesis that the integration of religion and culture in the United States is a product of the metamorphosis in secular directions of selected values from early religious experience in America is not so much right or wrong as it is speculative. We just don't know how much this integrationist view explains the intriguing parallels between many American political values and colonial Puritanism. It is also impossible to expect that we could ever answer this question, though it continues to be a question well worth asking.

Another problem with this approach is that it is both backward looking and static at the same time. Its implicit assumption is that religion is unimportant or even dead today as a major cultural influence, that the integration had spent its force at the latest by the middle of the nineteenth century, and that since that time the relationship between religion and liberal culture has been static. Rarely does one find the perception articulated that religion and liberalism had a dynamic and complex relationship throughout American history and do so today.[32]

Finally, it is at least arguable that the integrationist approach exaggerates the coherence over time of both religious and liberal norms in the American experience. It is at this last point of uneasiness that the work of Daniel Elazar is relevant. He argues that conventional discussions of our culture do not get us very far because they exaggerate our nation's homogeneity. He urges us to recognize that in our country culture is still diverse, indeed in some of its parts more diverse than ever. Thus in some places religion has had—and continues to have—more, as well as different, influence than in others. In a Weberian spirit, Elazar identifies three "pure" culture types appropriate to the United States: 1) Moralistic culture is the old Protestant disposition to use politics to create the good society. We can see its sway among many "liberals," secular and religious (especially liberal Protestants and Roman Catholics). 2) Individualistic culture predominates where religious influence has declined or has never been strong. California and the non-Mormon West are good examples. 3) Traditionalist culture is highly religious and conservative, appreciative of established verities and traditions both national and local, perhaps especially local. Its greatest strength is in much of the South.[33]

---

and politics are William Sloan Coffin, Jr., *Once to Every Man* (New York: Atheneum, 1977), and Jerry Falwell, *Listen America* (Garden City, NY: Doubleday, 1980).

32. See Elazar and McLoughlin below for examples of two scholars whose work reflects this critique.

33. Daniel Elazar, "The American Cultural Mix," in *The Ecology of American Political Culture*, ed. Daniel J. Elazar and Joseph Zikmund (New York: Crowell, 1975), pp. 13-42.

There is much to be said for Elazar's approach. He offers a fairly rich picture of American cultural diversity and recognizes that in many regions more than one model is present. There is evidence to support his thesis, for example, that by many measures the South is more traditionalist than the country as a whole. But, overall, Elazar's is a hypothesis and nothing more. Substantial evidence may be developed that would sustain it. At the moment, however, it remains only a heuristic hypothesis whose plausibility is unclear and whose chief benefit for our purposes is the caution it encourages about sweeping cultural claims concerning the United States as a whole.[34]

Another difficulty with Elazar's hypothesis is that it remains unclear at this stage what the proposed relationship is between religion and culture. How important is religion (and its values) or its absence to the evaluation of the several cultural styles Elazar says exist in the United States? More broadly, Elazar's understandable concern with contemporary culture has so far left unaddressed significant issues about the origin and history of the subcultures he proposes.

From another angle one might note the diversity of religions, certainly organized religions, in our culture, and wonder if that would also undermine the image of a neat integration of religion and culture in the United States. After all, our society hardly presents a homogenous pattern of Christian values, organization, theology, and the rest, not to speak of the increasingly visible presence of other world religions and of "alternative" religions on America's shores. The picture may have grown too complicated now for any simple integration model, though such reservations do not deter in the least advocates of the integration theory. On the contrary. For them, "religious diversity in the context of genuine pluralism enhances rather than destroys social integration."[35] They insist that it does so because it provides so many routes to influence, reconciliation, and socialization for religious groups while preventing the appearance of any situations of stark tension between religion and culture, church and state.

Perhaps the most ambitious single attempt to relate religion and the American experience over time is William G. McLoughlin's *Revivals, Awakening and Reform: An Essay on Religion and Social Change in America, 1607-1977*. McLoughlin's creativity lies in his attempt to formulate a sophisticated theory of the dynamic and continuing interrelationships

34. An early effort to test Elazar raised major doubts from a quantitative view: Timothy D. Schiltz and R. Lee Rainey, "The Geographic Distribution of Elazar's Political Subcultures among the Mass Population: A Research Note," *Western Political Quarterly* 31 (1978): 410-15.

35. Wilson, *Religion in American Society,* pp. 273-74.

between liberal culture and religion in the United States. In doing so, he avoids offering a static list of characteristics that somehow migrated from religion into liberal politics and remained there forever. McLoughlin's theory is that there have been five periods of religious awakening in American history: 1610–1640, 1730–1760, 1800–1830, 1890–1920, and 1960–1990(?). He contends that each has had a decisive influence on American culture: each led to alterations in our religious temperament and belief that in turn led to basic changes in our liberal political and cultural order, changes that have significantly determined American society.[36]

McLoughlin's strongest case is his detailed consideration of the interaction of religion and culture in the seventeenth and eighteenth centuries. He is convincing when he shows the impact of the Great Awakening (1720–1760) as it affected the liberal ideas of the revolutionary age; and he is equally convincing when he shows the influence of the second Great Awakening (1800–1830): the belief in America's chosenness; the development of civil religion; commitment to perfectionism and individual reformation; the democratic faith in the individual; and the urge to reform humankind. Yet even here—and notably in his brief considerations on later religious transformations—McLoughlin's evidence needs bolstering. McLoughlin is better at suggesting intellectual links than he is at mobilizing data. And when he turns to the current "transformation, 1960–1990(?)," McLoughlin is disappointing, offering little more than personal ideology and dubious predictions. This is frustrating since it is here that we could benefit most from his insights. For him, the middle decades of the twentieth century offer signs of another crisis in religion and in liberal ideology that may be summed up as the failure of liberalism, liberal religion, and liberal politics.

For McLoughlin, the first response was that of the 1950s: the alleged rush to traditional religion, Billy Graham, and the rest. Then America shunted aside traditionalism in religion and politics in the 1960s as the "death of God," *The Secular City*, the cults, and so forth swept into religion at exactly the same time that the New Left swept into politics. Finally, McLoughlin views the 1970s as the age of drift. The long-run solution, he predicts (and hopes), will be a new religion and a new polity that will be some form of Judeo-Christian democratic socialism.

He may be right, but I wonder. McLoughlin ignores the alternative that conservative religion and a more conservative politics are the future in liberal America. Ours is, after all, the day of evangelicalism in religion

36. William G. McLoughlin, *Revivals, Awakening, and Reform: An Essay on Religion and Social Change in America, 1607–1977* (Chicago: University of Chicago Press, 1978).

and conservatism in politics. But perhaps this is not quite the point. Where McLoughlin is on the mark is his recognition that both religion and liberalism in America must be seen as a dynamic process. This recognition requires us to do more than search for roots and then rest; it urges us, rather, to go on to ask what the influences of religion are now as well as what they were in the past in American culture and how they speak to each other.

From one angle, McLoughlin may seem very removed from Weber, and by the light of his motivation or the substance of analysis, he is. From another angle, though, McLoughlin faithfully pursues the Weberian model. The spirit of culture has been to a marked degree the creature of religion and religious change in the United States. Religion has in this sense mattered enormously, and it is no simple puppet of economic or other "material" forces. McLoughlin represents the best illustration of Weber's hypothesis at work on American shores, displaying its theoretical strengths.

Karl Marx

QUITE ANOTHER MOOD, of course, characterizes Karl Marx. Marx did not dismiss the power of religion or of churches and religious institutions; but he hardly saw them as a substantially independent social force. They were powerful not as a source of culture and society but as *agents* of those who built and dominated societies and cultures, ordinarily used as conservative forces to prop up the existing orders.

Yet in Marx's hands religion was rarely as completely integrated into a culture as in the ordinary Weberian version, where in time religious norms metamorphose and become the secular culture, or become all but indistinguishable from it. In Marx's analysis, religion is identifiable in its several manifestations and thus, he hoped, all the easier to eradicate as a direct or indirect rationalizer of regimes whose historical justification had passed. Beyond his heartfelt expressions of hostility, Marx actually had little to say about religion. Nor did Marx, in contrast to Max Weber, have any elaborate theory of religion and society. Yet it is quite possible to derive a theory or theories of religion and society from Marx's writings. His earlier writings are especially fruitful (though not without their problematic side).

Marx objected ultimately to religion because he believed—with no trace of self-doubt—that all religions are false. He was an atheist who took for granted, in the Enlightenment fashion, that no religions could meet any tests of rational investigation and thus are all false, concerned only with an "imaginary world."[37] Religion was for him, moreover, profoundly unhealthy for individuals because it is inevitably a form of "estrangement," a separation of a person from himself or herself.[38] This is true, Marx was certain, because religion was simply a human creation: "Man makes religion. . . . Religion is indeed man's self-consciousness and self-awareness so long as he has not found himself. . . ."[39] This necessarily meant an unhealthy separation of one part of oneself from the whole, since "the more man puts into God, the less he retains in himself."[40]

In political terms, however, Marx's main objection lay outside his definition of the rational or whole person. His complaint was that religion was at best a passive means by which people escaped their historical duty to revolutionize the world and was at worst an active agent scheming to prevent radical change in the world. Either way, it functioned in the service of the dominant productive forces of an age—in Marx's time, of capitalism and capitalists. It was thus absolutely necessary, the young Marx declared, that revolutionaries struggle to break the religious power over individuals and society; this was the crucial first step to serious change. "The abolition of religion as the *illusory* happiness of men, is a demand for their *real* happiness. . . . The criticism of religion is, therefore, the embryonic *criticism of this vale of tears* of which religion is the halo."[41] The "criticism of religion is the premise of all criticism."[42] Even when religion does not squelch all conflict, it continues to mystify reality: it hides "real divisions by substituting unreal ones."[43]

After his early writings, Marx did not pay much attention to religion either in its philosophical dimension or as a social force—as organized religion. He hardly mentions religion in his masterwork, *Capital.* And in his more programmatic *Critique of the Gotha Program,* religion is worth little more attention than his confident dismissal of its possibility

37. Karl Marx, "Theses on Feuerbach," in *The Marx-Engels Reader,* ed. Robert C. Tucker (2d ed., New York: Norton, 1978), p. 144.

38. Karl Marx, "Economic and Philosophic Manuscripts of 1844," in *Marx-Engels Reader,* p. 85.

39. Karl Marx, "Contribution to the Critique of Hegel's *Philosophy of Right:* Introduction," in *Marx-Engels Reader,* p. 53; Karl Marx, "The German Ideology," in *Marx-Engels Reader,* pp. 154-55; Marx, "Theses on Feuerbach," p. 145.

40. Marx, "Economic and Philosophic Manuscripts of 1844," p. 72.

41. Marx, "Critique of Hegel's *Philosophy of Right,*" p. 54.

42. *Ibid.,* p. 53.

43. Wilson, *Religion in American Society,* p. 277.

in his historical ideal.[44] It appears to be no longer the first impediment, much less a serious impediment, to revolution. Economic and class structures have crowded out religion—as they crowded out virtually all aspects of culture for Marx—in explaining and changing society. Religion has become just part of the cultural superstructure. He no longer took it seriously because it was not much of a threat; it did not work effectively as a conservative agent.

In any event, whenever Marx considered religion, he always placed it firmly in a secondary position, created rather than a creator, operating to retard revolution, indeed often used to that end by those in power.[45] This familiar "Marxist" view has had enormous impact on the analysis of the role of religion—and organized religion—in human societies. While frequently stripped of all other connections with Marx, the cliché that religion is a conservative social force has retained its casual analytic popularity, though no one could begin to analyze either the history of religion or contemporary world religion and be very confident of the predictive force of this proposition. Even less plausible is the Marxist notion that religion serves as the handmaiden of capitalist forces. The experience of the contemporary Iranian revolution is an instructive caveat here.

For us, of course, the relevant question is, how helpful is the Marxist analysis in the context of American religion and society? Marx himself cannot directly help us. By the time he turned to commentary about the United States, his interest in the religious dimensions of life had slipped away. He made scant comments on either religion or churches in the America of the mid-nineteenth century. Some studies, however, have advanced theories about religion and culture that are ultimately derived from Marx. One group has explored the deprivation theory: that religion is especially attractive to the poor or "dispossessed" in America. For them, the theory goes, religion is the substitute for a decent material life and stands in the way of their mobilization to alter their economic condition.

While deprivation is a tricky concept to define, research has repeatedly shown that church membership, attendance, or participation simply does not correlate with the degree of economic well-being. Nor at present is there a case for the thesis in terms of religious belief, though among younger people belief, while still the norm, is softest among the most highly educated—the affluent of the future. Moreover, studies exploring

44. Karl Marx, in "Critique of the Gotha Program," in *Marx-Engels Reader*, p. 540, suggests just how little religion and religious freedom were important to him and his ideal society.

45. Marshall, *In Search of the Spirit of Capitalism*, pp. 140-57.

those highly disconnected from the dominant social world around them—Marx's and other people's "alienated"—find that alienation does not correlate particularly with religious concern or involvement.[46]

Less popular and less influential has been an examination of the impact of religion through the lens of the "conflict theory," whose most celebrated progenitor was Marx. That is, observers have lavished so much attention on integration theories (and Marx's contribution to them) that religion's potential in the area of social conflict has not been much studied in the United States. This appears to have happened because, until recently, religious-cultural consensus was the reality, or assumed to be the reality. Points where religious division had served to "intensify conflict, sharpen hatreds, and promote disharmony" in the history of the United States were largely passed over.[47]

If one focuses more historically and concentrates on the specific issues of religious integration into American culture, most of the classic discussions are not explicitly in the tradition of Marx. The relationship of religion and capitalism, in particular, has not been a major concern, though the larger implication, that religion in America has normally been protective of the ongoing order, has been a focus. But there have been some exceptions among sociologists of religion. One leading text, for example, articulates this familiar view in familiar language: "In the main, the churches function to legitimate the dominant economic values and conduct in society"; our "economic hierarchy also receives direct legitimation from the religious system"; and "much" of the "weak clan consciousness" in America "is due to the religious factor in social life." None of this interpretation implies, of course, power for these values themselves, or even for the churches as they "legitimate dominant political and economic values." One must remember that this view holds that these are the values of, and the churches are controlled by, "the upper and middle classes." Economic interests rule; theology, values, and the churches follow and serve, just as Marx insisted.[48]

In addition, there have been socialist interpreters who have seen religion as a willing or eager servant of capitalism. But in the past, as today, left-wing analysts of America have pretty much ignored religion and any religious dimension in human lives, except for ritualistic attacks on it.[49]

---

46. Dean R. Hoge and David A. Roozen, "Research on Factors Influencing Church Commitment," in *Understanding Church Growth and Decline, 1950–1978,* ed. Dean R. Hoge and David A. Roozen (New York: Pilgrim, 1979), esp. pp. 51-52.

47. Wilson, *Religion in American Society,* pp. 274-76.

48. *Ibid.,* pp. 235, 363-64, 355; see esp. ch. 16.

49. Aileen Kraditor explores both socialist historians/theorists and so-

However, Marx's more general point, that religion has rarely been an independent variable in history and that it is usually tied to the larger society and its dominant elements, has often been portrayed as the story of religion in America. H. Richard Niebuhr's *Christ and Culture* ably makes the argument in principle—and regarding the United States.[50] It is staple fare today both in the hands of those inside and outside organized religion for whom God and country are an indissoluble pair, and in the hands of those who are most determined that religion should challenge our liberal order.[51]

The idea is that we have integration of church and the larger society in bountiful amounts, and that integration goes one way: from society to religion. Church follows culture and almost always is conservative, reactive, and nonprophetic. As John Wilson argues, the very pervasiveness of religion in America and its simultaneous "vacuity" demonstrate how much society has captured religion and how much its elites use it for both personal status and to justify the status quo.[52] Sydney Ahlstrom argues that the very status and nature of theology in the United States is largely a creature of American culture. There is little theology in the first place, which reflects the limited ideological spectrum and the relative absence of social conflict in our culture. What theology there is reflects the pluralism of denominations and the limited kinds of pluralism in our society.[53]

Let us first consider the revolutionary and nation-founding period in the late eighteenth century. There were serious disagreements among

---

cialist leaders/activists in the American context. The former tended to ignore religion, the latter either to denounce it or expect it to disappear. See Aileen S. Kraditor, *The Radical Persuasion, 1890–1917* (Baton Rouge: Louisiana State University Press, 1981), ch. 2, pp. 273-75, 313-16. The absence of treatment of religion is notable in such different but stimulating modern treatments as Herbert Marcuse, *One-Dimensional Man* (Boston: Beacon, 1964) and Mark E. Kann, *The American Left: Failures and Fortunes* (New York: Praeger, 1982). Peter Clecak, *Crooked Paths: Reflections on Socialism, Conservatism, and the Welfare State* (New York: Harper and Row, 1977) is an example of contemporary revisionist socialist thought that is sensitive to the issue of religion and the Left in America; see pp. 108-20.

50. H. Richard Niebuhr, *Christ and Culture* (New York: Harper and Row, 1951), ch. 3; H. Richard Niebuhr, *The Social Sources of Denominationalism* (1929; New York: Meridian, 1960).

51. For illustration, see John W. Whitehead, *The Second American Revolution* (Elgin, IL: David C. Cook, 1982); Coffin, *Once to Every Man*.

52. Wilson, *Religion in American Society,* pp. 420-21.

53. See Sydney E. Ahlstrom, "Theology in America: A Historical Survey," in *Religion in American Life,* vol. 1, ed. James Ward Smith and A. Leland Jamison (Princeton: Princeton University Press, 1961), pp. 232-321.

American public elites, including Jefferson, Madison, Adams, and Hamilton, over the relationship between church and state. There have been disputes just as strong about the Founding Fathers' disagreements among subsequent commentators, especially in our age.[54] Yet, overall, there was much less dissension regarding the proper place of religion in the larger society then than there is now. Almost all of the Founders expected religion to assist the American experiment, consolidating and conserving American values and the nascent national institutions. Religion's place was modest but supportive. It followed that they did not expect religion in any form to challenge the emerging liberal order, despite the revolutionary experience, where religious forces were hardly the inevitable handmaidens of conservatism.[55] Mostly, religion was to be a private and family matter. No wonder the Founders had little interest in, much less urgency about, the issue of state aid to religion. Religion in social terms was integrative and modestly valuable, but hardly central. And, of course, no link had been proposed between religion and a capitalism not yet born.

That position became far more widespread in popular American culture during the nineteenth century, from McGuffey Readers to the popular novels of Horatio Alger, where God and America often became fused. In that setting—and especially after the Civil War—it was easy for critics to suggest that religion was quite important in our liberal culture, that it was all too integrated, functioning as an important and compliant prop supporting the ongoing order.

This criticism, so often echoed since, involves an element of myth and ideological special pleading as well as truth. It ignores a plainly mixed record. There has been a fair amount of religious-based activism that has been far from merely reflexive conservatism in American history. Consider the religiously inspired abolitionists before the Civil War, the

54. For some differing views and interpretations, see A. James Reichley, *Religion in American Public Life* (Washington, DC: Brookings, 1985), chs. 3-5; Robert L. Cord, *Separation of Church and State: Historical Fact and Current Fiction* (New York: Lambeth, 1982); Leo Pfeffer's classic argument in *Church, State and Freedom* (Boston: Beacon, 1953); and Whitehead, *The Second American Revolution*, chs. 2, 3, 6, and 8. The *Journal of Church and State* is also a continuing source of arguments sharply tilted toward religious separation.

55. Except for important elements of the Anglican Church in America, support for the American Revolution was common among American churches and clergy; see Ahlstrom, *A Religious History*, vol. 1, ch. 23; for a broader consideration of religion and the American revolution, see Alan Heimert, *Religion and the American Mind: From the Great Awakening to the Revolution* (Cambridge: Harvard University Press, 1966), pp. 1-24, 604-5, and chs. 4 and 5.

Social Gospel reformers during the Progressive Era, Martin Luther King, Jr., and his churchly allies in the 1960s, and religious antinuclear crusaders today.[56] But one must still grant that the empirical record nonetheless tends strongly to demonstrate the reality that in the past most of America's religious culture was in comfortable coexistence with the American social, political, and economic order. Indeed, the relationship often has really been one of eager, even slavish, support.[57]

Today controversies abound, but on balance there is little tension between organized religion in the United States and the state. We need only to compare our recent record with the conflict that existed in the Shah's Iran, or that exists in Ireland, Poland, or Nicaragua. Nor has the church in any of its forms produced significant ideologies to counter liberalism. Some divisions of Christianity have manifested more ambivalence than most, for example, the Jehovah Witnesses, some fundamentalists, or the "sanctuary movement." If anything, though, the trend has been toward more integration of religion into liberal society, revealed in part by today's very characteristic engagement of organized religion with American politics.

Sometimes the connection with the established order is perfectly apparent and frankly affirmed. It is in what poll data have established, if one prefers that approach. Clergy and churchgoers of all religious persuasions report generally strong support for the American political order. It is no surprise, then, that no major religious denominations have attacked our political system in any basic way. In the pews and even at national headquarters we have no serious religious opposition to speak of. There are dissatisfactions here and there with one or another policy, and there are particular churches where dissent runs deep among small

56. The literature on the assorted radical moments in American religious history is enormous; as always, Ahlstrom's *A Religious History* is a good guide to both the literature and the history (see vol. 2, chs. 39-41, 47, 51-52, 62-63).

57. H. Richard Niebuhr developed this theme most extensively in its classical form; see, for example, Niebuhr, "The Protestant Movement and Democracy in the United States," in *Religion in American Life,* vol. 1, pp. 65-71; see William Lee Miller, "American Religion and American Political Attitudes," p. 81. Two modern studies that are very stimulating here are Clebsch, *From Sacred to Profane;* and John Murray Cuddihy, *No Offense: Civil Religion and Protestant Taste* (New York: Seabury, 1978); Ahlstrom's *A Religious History,* vol. 2, describes a somewhat mixed pattern in the 1865–1918 period when churches were mainly clearly apologetic for capitalism; Mead draws the connection tighter in *The Lively Experiment,* pp. 88-157.

groups of elites. But they are curiosities, mere asterisks in the data, often to their considerable frustration.[58]

This does not necessarily mean that nationalistic support is intensely cultivated at church. "America the Beautiful" is not sung every Sunday, and "The Star-Spangled Banner" is rarely heard at church. It is a mistake to see most forms of religion or the churches—clergy or laity—as bent on sustaining the liberal order in a highly self-conscious way. This does happen, and real opposition is rare; but ordinarily the process operates differently, if no less potently. Perhaps the most significant support for liberal society, one should recognize, comes when organized religion ignores it, as it often does.

For those who read the headlines—even those who are involved in studying politics but have little contact with religion in America—organized religion can seem very political today. Catholic bishops make the news denouncing the nuclear arms race or abortion; the National Council of Churches speaks out on race; the Liberty Federation endorses prayer in public schools, a strong defense policy, support for capitalism, a ban on pornography, and so much more; Jewish interest groups insist on ever more aid for Israel; and the lobbying goes on and on. Yet the reality in the pews, the sermons, and the church organizations is different, as students of religion know. There politics is rarely heard and rarely discussed.

This is not merely a matter of what the surveys show; it is a matter of what one experiences. In a perfect illustration I have called on before,[59] I remember standing with a crowd on a recent Palm Sunday in front of a large "socially conscious" church for the blessing of palms when a drunk came up and cursed the faithful as hypocrites. He shouted that they did not care about his kind. A perceptible shock swept through the faithful for a few seconds. A young man or two gave the drunk some money, he

58. The classic of the "conservative" reality is Jeffrey K. Hadden, *The Gathering Storm in the Churches* (Garden City, NY: Doubleday, 1969); one of the best discussions of some aspects of this issue is Charles Y. Glock, Benjamin B. Ringer, and Earl R. Babbot, *To Comfort and to Challenge: A Dilemma of the Contemporary Church* (Berkeley: University of California Press, 1967); a celebrated argument here is Marshall Frady, *Billy Graham: A Parable of American Righteousness* (Boston: Little, Brown, 1979); the best summation of current, relevant attitudes is Reichley, *Religion in American Public Life*, pp. 299-302, 269-82, 319-31.

59. Robert Booth Fowler, "Religion and Liberalism in the United States," in *The Liberal Future in America: Essays in Renewal*, ed. Philip Abbott and Michael Levy (Westport, CT: Greenwood Press, 1985), p. 96.

left, and the crowd of people turned to sharing the blessed palms. As quickly as it had come, politics was far away again. The relief was obvious.

While Marx's own observations cannot be much of a guide to the relationship of religion and American society, his (and others') broad thesis that religion serves established institutions and values is not without its plausibility when applied to the United States. The record is increasingly complicated, as proponents of the "challenge hypothesis" argue (in chapters 6-8).

The crucial matter at issue, though, is the basis of religion's "service." For Marx, as for many of the American versions, religious elements in society serve the larger culture by sharing and reinforcing its goals and values. As I have argued, however, it is the opposite view that is more plausible. At issue is not integration: there is no neat integration of religion into our larger culture (just as there is certainly no self-conscious alienation from it either). Yet religion remains another place in American culture. It is not devoted to celebrating individualism or capitalism or America. Integrationists are wrong about that. Religion is about other values and another place. It is thus that it serves liberal society, because it often leaves liberal society alone and sometimes provides relief from its philosophical and personal poverties.

CHAPTER FIVE

Integration (II)

WHILE SOME OF THE THEORIES ARGUING that religion and our liberal society are highly integrated have followed in the footsteps of such grand theorists as Weber and Marx, others derive their analysis quite self-consciously from the American experience itself. This does not make them more plausible, but it makes the distance between origin and current status shorter and their language and claims more accessible. In this context two theories, both of major importance, require attention. One is de Tocqueville's classic understanding of religion and society in the United States. The other is the civil religion thesis.

De Tocqueville

DE TOCQUEVILLE'S VIEW is undoubtedly the most intriguing of all theories describing the integration of the American liberal order and religion. Propounded in his classic of the 1830s, *Democracy in America,* his idea is elegant in its simplicity. According to him, there was nothing especially mysterious or particularly complex about why religion and our liberal order went together. They were integrated because religion provided liberalism and its American children what they had to have to function successfully as a social order: social and personal discipline. Liberalism itself could not provide such restraint. But in the midst of clashing groups, selfish wills, and all the other innumerable divisions in America, religion could and did provide a shared consensus. It allowed society to stay on the even keel essential for any social order to endure.[1]

Religion's special contribution was the restraining morality badly needed in a land where individual material gain was the consuming passion for so many citizens. It was, so to speak, a brake on American egoism, in practice much the most effective one. Even for those whose thirst for gain it hardly slackened, it restricted *how* their scramble for

1. Alexis de Tocqueville, *Democracy in America* (New York: Vintage, 1957), vol. 2. bk. 1, ch. 5.

wealth proceeded. "Men cannot be cured of the love of riches, but they may be persuaded to enrich themselves by none but honest means."[2]

Religion had the same role for individuals that it had for society as a whole: it provided individual Americans with psychological ballast. People who lacked a shared religious grounding were vulnerable. Thus "fixed ideas about God . . . are indispensable to the daily practice of men's lives." Without them people could never be free, since the practice of freedom required the psychological blessing of inner security. Citizens without such security often found life's uncertainty and confusion too great to bear; they were likely to turn society upside down as they sought to find "a master" to rule them and provide them with the security they could not find within. The authoritarian result was hardly appealing to de Tocqueville. No wonder he concluded of the American: "I am inclined to think that if faith be wanting in him, he must be subject, and if he be free, he must believe."[3]

The similarity between de Tocqueville's analysis and Erich Fromm's discussion of the United States more than a hundred years later is striking. Fromm, like de Tocqueville, was convinced that freedom could prove too heavy a burden for Americans unless they had substantial psychological strength, and that an "escape from freedom" into conformity or despotism was a constant danger. The difference was that Fromm, as a post-Freudian radical liberal, wanted nothing to do with de Tocqueville's sense that fixed moral norms based on transcendence could provide the needed psychological ballast for Americans. Such ideas were, to him, just other escapes from freedom.[4] De Tocqueville was hardly unaware of the apparent paradox that freedom was possible only when it had its accepted limits, only when it was far from the ideal in an anarchist's dreams. But to him this was simply the social reality: consensual limits protected freedom wherever it flourished. He simply did not think freedom was an abstraction.

Beyond its stabilizing role, de Tocqueville did not want religion to intrude greatly into American society, much less dominate it. Providing ballast was one thing; becoming the center of society was another. After all, de Tocqueville was no devotee of any religious truth or of any religion's ethical rules. His approach to religion largely concerned how it functioned in terms of society, more properly as another expression of the nineteenth-century grand social theory, though his angle of vision was restricted mostly to the United States and France.

2. *Ibid.*, p. 27.
3. *Ibid.*, pp. 21-23.
4. Erich Fromm, *Escape from Freedom* (New York: Avon, 1965).

The problem with de Tocqueville's theory is not its plausibility. His hypothesis is plausible, applicable to much of the American story long after his departure. In its sociological and somewhat pessimistic cast, it suggests that what many of the Founding Fathers also hoped for from religion came true. It did help provide a shared basis for community for the republican experiment. The problem is, rather, that liberalism has changed since his commentary. It has broken free of religion as a restraint, not merely in the voice of liberal theorists but in the practice of American liberal culture. De Tocqueville saw a pluralistic but united culture in which religion was an essential integrating factor. That world may well have existed in America then, but no longer.[5]

To be sure, for many individuals and millions of families, a religion-backed traditional morality is very much alive. But in our culture as a whole there is no evidence today that religion is the source of a shared morality of much breadth or that religion preserves our culture by restraining it through that moral consensus. Indeed, its absence in these Tocquevillean senses is exactly why intellectuals such as Daniel Bell perceive such a crisis in liberal culture. If their analysis does not incorporate the way in which religion and American liberal order remain connected as silent partners, nonetheless their alarm at the absence of an obvious and powerful cohesive agent in our increasingly centrifugal America is in Tocquevillean terms eminently reasonable.

This alarm has been sounded by more and more intellectuals, who articulate their sense that we need more community—in life, in spirit, in values—community that some conclude, as de Tocqueville did, we once had. One recent and stimulating illustration is Alasdair MacIntyre's *After Virtue: A Study in Moral Theory*. Schooled in the Western intellectual tradition as a whole, MacIntyre speaks in its generous idioms and draws eclectically from its rich traditions of thought. But there can be little doubt that his mind is very much on the United States. Like so many other intellectuals today, MacIntyre is taken with the image of crisis, proposing that we have a crisis of belief and life that is expressed in what he assumes is the current collapse of community in theory and practice. As he looks at Western history, he locates the crisis as the outcome of a slow

5. Demonstrating religion's role in cultural integration before the middle twentieth century is probably even less easy than demonstrating the culture's separation from classical restraints. Limited poll data from the past makes the challenge of forming each case through popular attitude studies impossible. Many theoretical studies, all of which have their empirical base, are relevant, but I think Richard Reeves' *American Journey* (New York: Simon and Schuster, 1982) may give the best sense of the case for the plausibility of de Tocqueville's analysis long past his time and the reality that the culture has now changed.

decay of religious faith and norms. Equally crucial, he insists, has been the collision of liberal ideas. Skepticism and individualism eventually led to Nietzsche's egoism and to human alienation in the twentieth-century West. The consequences are all around us. We are stuck without faith and community, and we face a bleak future in the "coming ages of barbarism and darkness."

MacIntyre argues that manufacturing hope by resurrecting conventional liberal answers, such as pragmatic utilitarianism or even the noble Kantian liberalism, is foolish. It is obvious to him that any "rational secular account of the nature and status of morality" has unquestionably "failed." Indeed, MacIntyre suggests that it had already failed by the end of the nineteenth century, though only now is the dreadful consequence inescapably before us.[6] MacIntyre's proposals for a recovery have nothing to do with religion either; he is too "modern" for that. Or perhaps not. For they involve a quaint and utopian affirmation of the vision of Aristotle, an Aristotle whom MacIntyre gently and selectively interprets as an exponent of what he seeks in the modern world: local community, shared virtues, an emphasis on character, an affirmation of common justice, and the like.[7]

Richard John Neuhaus, especially in *The Naked Public Square,* is much more obviously oriented to a perceived crisis of community and faith in the United States. Neuhaus, a Lutheran minister increasingly involved in public intellectual debates, warmly appreciates MacIntyre's argument. Indeed, his and MacIntyre's have much in common, though Neuhaus is explicitly committed to religion and scarcely interested in the possibilities Aristotle offers for contemporary America. Neuhaus argues that religion has always been deeply woven into American culture and American public life and that even secular, liberal separatists cannot avoid this unmistakable fact about American history. He specifically agrees with de Tocqueville's argument that religion has been an essential and integral underpinning of our liberal order—public and private—and that it continued to be for at least a century after de Tocqueville's era.

Today, however, Neuhaus observes (and complains), we are discarding this past. Like Christians on the right, from whom he separates himself on other matters, Neuhaus blames secular elites for driving religion out of public life, out of what he calls "the public square." They and their allies, those who "would exclude religion and religious-grounded values from the conduct of public business," according to him,

6. Alasdair MacIntyre, *After Virtue: A Study in Moral Theory* (Notre Dame, IN: University of Notre Dame Press, 1981), pp. 244-45, 238.
7. *Ibid.,* chs. 16 and 18.

operate under "the ideology of secularism" and falsely maintain that "America is a secular society." The consequences have been sad. Above all, we have lost our traditional "sacred canopy" for "the American experiment." The American liberal order is now bereft of a religious grounding. Gone with that are our past "language of communal meaning," our common "public ethic," our "sense of shared responsibility"—all of which ultimately derived from our religious background. We are "naked" and on our own.[8]

Neuhaus is convinced that our society cannot endure without this religiously based ethic. Our liberal order *requires* religion (in our culture's case, Christianity) because religion has provided the ethical and communal glue from the beginning. It was integral to our society's history and spirit. Neuhaus believes that his proof is found in what has happened as it has slipped away: the social disintegration he sees all around; the present crisis of faith and community; our exaltation of individual selfishness and limitless moral pluralism; and the chaos that has so closely and painfully followed on their heels. More and more, liberal pluralism yields "indifference to normative truth, an agreement to count all opinions about morality as equal (equal 'interests to be accommodated') because we are all agreed there is no truth . . . the result is the debasement of our public life by the exclusion of the idea—and consequently of the practice—of virtue."[9]

The public square, Neuhaus insists, is inevitably concerned with new occupants: selfish interests, the will to power, and secularism. The expulsion of religion from public life does not mean that the square remains naked; rather, what is left becomes "a vacuum begging to be filled." This spectacle of the egoistic new occupants undermines any other shared ethic and specifically the legitimacy of our state, Neuhaus maintains. It also directly threatens our democratic system of government, which depends on such an ethic.[10] This is a conclusion others share. Can one, they ask, have a democratic government at all if it does not rest on a shared set of values that religion has traditionally provided America?[11]

Of course, Neuhaus's worry reaches beyond his concern for the moral foundations of the United States or the legitimacy of American

8. Richard John Neuhaus, *The Naked Public Square: Religion and Democracy in America* (Grand Rapids: Eerdmans, 1984), pp. vii, 22, 60, 61, 21, 64.

9. *Ibid.*, pp. 111-12.

10. *Ibid.*, pp. 80, 59, 21, 64

11. See A. James Reichley, *Religion in American Public Life* (Washington, DC: Brookings, 1985), ch. 7; Sidney Mead, *The Lively Experiment* (New York: Harper and Row, 1963), ch. 5.

democratic government. It is unfortunate for more than these powerful, but pragmatic, reasons; it is ultimately sad because, for Neuhaus, God and religion teach the truth of community, common love, and concern. To see both popular belief in them and their power in society decline is to see truth denied. It is to see God denied.[12] — IS THE RESULT OF

A final and worthy expression of the uneasy mood that reaches out beyond intellectual opinion to a broader, popular America may be found once again in Bellah's *Habits of the Heart.* Here too the conclusion is, as we have seen, that community has largely fallen before individualism. Individualism may come in several forms in contemporary America: the individualism of the overt egoist is not the same as the individualism of the therapeutic ethic (which attracts so much attention in the "California" of *Habits of the Heart*), but neither has much to do with community. Nor can the authors of *Habits of the Heart* find, it follows, any evidence of a common, powerful religious ethic encouraging social communality. Religion is just another piece of America, not hostile to but hardly integral to the American liberal order. In their book, de Tocqueville's world is quite gone, and Bellah and his colleagues fear for the America that is left.[13]

Each version differs from the next, but not in the analysis that religion's place in de Tocqueville's America is only a memory today. Religion's overt and central service to—its integration with—our liberal state is over. Of course, few doubt that American intellectuals are happy with this result, though a chorus of criticism is on the rise. Indeed, some are concerned to urge that vigilance remain the watchword to keep things this way.[14] And, after all, the public at large routinely endorses the principle of the separation of church and state while bemoaning the end of prayers in school and approving of church tax exemptions, as well as other features of establishment that flourish in practice.[15]

12. Neuhaus, *The Naked Public Square,* p. 64.

13. Robert Bellah et al., *Habits of the Heart: Individualism and Commitment in American Life* (Berkeley: University of California Press, 1985), pp. 246-49, 275-95.

14. Among the leading separatist groups today are the American Civil Liberties Union, People for the American Way, Americans United, Common Cause, and the American Jewish Committee. The *Journal of Church and State* articulates this sentiment for Christian scholarly circles.

15. For one well-documented case study, see Paul J. Weber and Dennis A. Gilbert, *Private Churches and Public Money: Church-Government Fiscal Relations* (Westport, CT: Greenwood, 1981). For broader discussions, see Robert Cord, *Separation of Church and State: Historical Fact and Current Fiction* (New York: Lambert Press, 1982) and Leo Pfeffer, *Church, State and Freedom* (rev. ed.; Boston: Beacon, 1967). The debate over the evidence and the record, past and pres-

A sense of loss and the judgment that crisis is the consequence is the mood of Bell, Neuhaus, and the rest, a new mood among a diverse portion of intellectuals in modern America. It is, of course, a perspective astonishingly different from the outlook of the great minds of the twentieth-century European world who are arguably in the liberal tradition, such as Freud or Camus. One is struck by how often they are contemptuous of the value of religion and convinced that it should be dispensed with. Freud really felt that religious belief is a denial of civilized liberal individualism.[16] In his famous discussion with the priest in *The Plague*, Camus pointedly insists that he wants no God who lets innocent children die.[17] The same animus is not really present in post–1945 American liberal thought. But on the whole, religion is simply absent from the work of theorists from Robert Dahl to John Rawls. The message is clear: liberalism need not be tied to religion, indeed should not be.[18]

Not that liberal theorists ordinarily perceived religion to be a challenge to liberalism; but they took for granted its fundamental irrelevance or incompatibility with liberalism. Obviously, religious thinker-activists such as Reinhold Niebuhr and Martin Luther King, Jr., gained a great deal of their acceptance in spite of their "puzzling" religiosity.

Religion's strength, especially its historical strength as an integrative force for individuals and for American society (de Tocqueville's lessons), suddenly seems obvious to an increasing number of American intellectuals. Yet the Owl of Minerva has fled. For the Bells and Harringtons and MacIntyres, each for different reasons, there is no possibility of a "return" to religion, even were it desirable. Thus we are left with crisis and must walk down other roads toward solutions—if there are any other roads. De Tocqueville's world is dead. Religion's service as an integrative underpinning of America is dead, and with it the moral, communal anchor for American liberalism. Those who are more sympathetic to religion and its prospects, such as Bellah or Neuhaus, nonetheless share the common sense of its diminished public power. For them too the Owl of Minerva may have fled.

---

ent, is endless. For an overview, see Robert Booth Fowler, *Religion and Politics in America* (Metuchen, NJ: Scarecrow Press, 1985), chs. 9-11.

16. Sigmund Freud, *The Future of an Illusion* (Garden City, NY: Doubleday, 1964).

17. Albert Camus, *The Plague* (New York: Alfred A. Knopf, 1960), pp. 205-11.

18. Their claim was, on the whole, that they were "skeptical." Robert Booth Fowler, *Believing Skeptics: American Political Intellectuals, 1945–1964* (Westport, CT: Greenwood, 1978); see John Rawls, *A Theory of Justice* (Cambridge: Harvard University Press, 1971).

American Civil Religion

THE SECOND IMPORTANT THEORY of integration set specifically in the American context is the American civil religion thesis.[19] According to this notion, there exists in the United States a kind of national faith that functions as the central integrating feature of our liberal society. This civil religion is composed of elements drawn in large measure from American Christianity, powerful evidence of the integration of religion and our culture. The idea is that American Christianity has substantially changed into an American civil religion and thus is inseparable from our liberal order, which the civil religion justifies.

While the civil religion idea does not attract as much attention today among observers of religion at work in America as it did just a few years ago, it can scarcely be ignored. After all, this has been the age of Reagan, an obvious believer in civil religion. Since the civil religion thesis holds that religion has been decisive in providing the civil faith that upholds our liberal society, the integrative role assigned to Christianity is enormous. Discussions about specific values and their integrative role—for instance, religious individualism and liberal individualism—pale beside it. If the Christian religion has provided the ingredients of the rationale for our liberal order, then it could not, in fact, be more integrated into our culture.

On one level, indeed, perhaps Protestantism itself was the civil religion of the United States for much of our history. It furnished the shared values and, on the whole, the explicit justification for liberal America as God's special and blessed creation. Religion may have been technically separated from the state; but this was, in fact, irrelevant. Protestantism was so integrated into society that it was absurd to suggest that it was—or could be—separated from any major aspect of it.[20]

In a famous article first published in the 1960s, Robert Bellah emerged as the modern pioneer of the idea of a "civil religion," and he has continued to be a fertile contributor to the ongoing discussion.[21] Bellah contends that public life in the United States operates under a given religious framework that, while not explicitly Christian, clearly employs many of the traditional Christian categories now transferred to the secu-

19. The following discussion is taken in part from Fowler, *Religion and Politics in America,* pp. 31-40.

20. Peter L. Berger, "Religion in Post-Protestant America," *Commentary,* May 1986, p. 44.

21. Robert N. Bellah, "Civil Religion in America," reprinted in *American Civil Religion,* ed. Russell Richey and Donald Jones (New York: Harper and Row, 1974), pp. 21-44.

lar world. He has pursued this theme in several books, notably *Beyond Belief* and *The Broken Covenant*.[22] A significant example of Bellah's theme is the Puritan notion that America is special and that Americans have a special mission in world history. Presidents and other significant public figures have articulated such a mission in Bellah's central source, major public documents, and they have commonly claimed that this mission has derived quite specifically from God. Lincoln was an especially poignant and sensitive exponent of the link between God and American destiny—albeit in ways, as he said in his Second Inaugural, we could not know. John F. Kennedy, a hundred years later, preferred the same public affirmations and thus continued to give life to civil religion, the religion of God-blessed America.

Needless to say, Richard Nixon used civil religion for all it was worth during his presidency. He constantly invoked God, affirming his closeness to the American experience. He also declared our essential innocence as part of God's blessing. Nixon's easy proclaiming of these things was a study in contrast with Lincoln, who thought God's relationship with the United States was complex and ultimately mysterious. While this difference is a commentary on Nixon, Bellah argues that the essential point remains. Both invoked the tradition of civil religion, and both were believers.

This does not surprise Bellah; in fact, it is only to be expected. He insists that civil religion is a universal. All countries and all people have had such a faith. What is unique about it in the United States is its form, derived from the particular cast of American Christianity. This explains its tendency to assume the specialness of America, and our right as innocents to do—collectively, though, not individually—as we will in the world.

While one might point out that Lincoln lived in the past and Nixon was a mere manipulator of the civil religion metaphor, Bellah maintains that civil religion endures on the American scene. It did not disappear after Nixon, and it did not disappear after the assaults on the United States during the New Left period. To be sure, Bellah recognizes that the blows of the 1960s and 1970s had their effects. In conventional terms, American civil religion looked like "an empty and broken shell."[23] But Bellah is quite confident that it will endure, though in a changed form,

22. Robert Bellah, *Beyond Belief* (New York: Harper and Row, 1970); Bellah, *The Broken Covenant: American Civil Religion in Time of Trial* (New York: Seabury, 1975).
23. See Bellah, *The Broken Covenant*, p. 142; Bellah, "Civil Religion in America," in *American Civil Religion*, pp. 21-44.

into the future. It did endure in the age of Ronald Reagan, had indeed made a considerable recovery. And while Bellah might wish that its form had altered more than it has (and less than he expected), he acknowledges the need for civil religion or something like it. America, he has consistently argued, needs ties that bind.[24]

The work Bellah has done in delineating the civil religion idea is by no means the only or the first articulation of the threads that led to the full-scale consideration of civil religion. Within the field of the history of religion, the most admired writer on the subject has been Sidney Mead, especially in *The Lively Experiment*. More than Bellah, Mead tells the story of civil religion in its historical perspective, developing the idea's sway in historical events and popular sentiments. According to Mead, a sense of a civil religion expanded steadily in our nation's early history and became firmly entrenched by the time of the Civil War. Since the Civil War there have really been two religions in the United States: one is expressed in the various Christian denominations, and the other is the American national faith, a stepchild of American Christianity.

American national religion assumes, in both Mead's and Bellah's versions, that somehow this nation is called to be the agent of the divine. It urges Americans to be a community of people searching to discover and live God's ordained life. Yet at the same time it respects individual, intellectual, and political pluralism. Mead emphasizes democratic aspects of the American faith more than Bellah does, a faith in people and their self-government on earth (rather than the specific forms of our democratic system). However, Mead contends with Bellah that the origins, the forms, and the confidence of our civil faith lie in our Christianity, especially American Protestantism. But more than Bellah, Mead has been interested in the relationship between the two forms of religion he identifies in our country; he believes that they have often been intertwined and mutually supportive. At the concrete level of institutions and culture, Christianity has taken second place. Our supposed separation of church and state has not saved the nation's churches from dominance by the liberal culture and political order around them, with which they are all too integrated. Throughout much of our history the churches "found themselves as completely identified with nationalism and their country's political and economic systems as had ever been known in Christendom."[25]

24. Bellah, *The Broken Covenant*, ch. 6.
25. Mead, *The Lively Experiment*, pp. 88, 157, and chs. 5 and 8; Sidney Mead, *The Nation with the Soul of a Church* (New York: Harper and Row, 1975).

An example of the continuing use of the civil religion mode of analysis is Marshall Frady's remarkable study *Billy Graham,* the best modern argument for the deep interweaving of the liberal state and Christianity in America. *Billy Graham* is a product of the disillusioned 1960s, but it insists that the events of those years did not derail widespread faith in a God-blessed America. To be sure, Frady notes that Graham claims to reject civil religion and strongly support the separation of church and state; but while Frady believes the sincerity of such claims, he does not think they are accurate. According to Frady, Graham revealed his loyalty to civil religion through his aggressive role as a servant and companion of American presidents, beginning with Eisenhower and not easing until after the embarrassing denouncement of his friend Richard Nixon. This constituted a public linkage of America and Christianity in a way that apparently presented no problems at all for Graham. Graham also revealed his loyalties when he reacted with fright toward those who appeared to challenge the American social order, including Vietnam War protesters, Martin Luther King, Jr., and others in the civil rights struggles of the 1960s. Vietnam was especially important. Graham supported that war until it was almost over, and he still does not regret that stance. Frady concludes that he still believes in continuing American innocence at home and abroad and does not hesitate to lend his name to sanctify it.[26]

No one can seriously deny that the current situation is more complicated than it seemed even to Frady studying America through Billy Graham, who by the later 1970s had genuinely left behind his support of a civil religion. The language of civil religion is alive in our culture—very much so. While it may not be popular in elite intellectual circles—including elite religious leaders and teachers—it is a mainstay of important elements of our society.[27] It is repeatedly invoked not just at the White House but by many other political leaders; moreover, it is, despite denials, an obvious staple of the discourse of Christian conservatives.[28]

In every instance its integrative aspects are clearly etched. Whatever

26. Marshall Frady, *Billy Graham: A Parable of American Righteousness* (Boston: Little, Brown, 1979), pp. 240, 214-16, 232-36, 412-19, 430. Graham has changed a lot in recent years. For another discussion, see Robert Booth Fowler, *A New Engagement: Evangelical Political Thought, 1966–1976* (Grand Rapids: Eerdmans, 1982), ch. 3.

27. For two thoughtful discussions by religious intellectuals, see Andrew Greeley, *The Denominational Society* (Glenview, IL: Scott, Foresman, 1972), ch. 7; and Martin Marty, *A Nation of Behavers* (Chicago: University of Chicago Press, 1976).

28. E.g., see Jerry Falwell, *Listen America* (Garden City, NY: Doubleday, 1980).

version of civil religion one encounters, each is the same in that its substance draws far more heavily on American Christianity, especially nineteenth-century Protestantism, than anything else. While it is not accurate to describe civil religion as a creation of this Christianity, it is accurate to say that Christianity in the United States was integral to its creation. At the least, it provided much of the language in which civil religion has been articulated.[29] In this sense, religion and culture became integrated. Moreover, since analysts commonly argue that the civil religion functions to legitimate our liberal order, the larger effects of the integration reflected in the civil religion are important.

Few voices proclaim the existence of a civil religion without qualification. In fact, there is a good deal of skepticism about the idea of an American civil religion and about it as an illustration of the integration of religion into our liberal state. Martin Marty, the leading historian of religion in the United States, complains that civil religion as normally conceived is a "loose construction": it seems to mean almost anything and everything. It is also impossible to test empirically. Even when it is articulated lucidly and plausibly, Marty thinks that civil religion is too simplistic. Analysis tends to pick out only one aspect of civil religion (often its conservative, legitimating side), and the result is embarrassing in its sparse insight.[30]

John Wilson goes the entire distance to a full-scale repudiation of the civil religion concept and its hypothesis about the interactive influence of religion and our liberal polity. In *Public Religion in American Culture,* Wilson maintains that no one can find a civil religion in America. Rituals and dogmas are everywhere in our politics, but their demonstrated, coherent linkage to religion is absent. What the rituals and dogmas signify has changed over time, suggesting that they are less a set of timeless truths rooted in American religion than they are particular images reflecting specific times and circumstances. Thus our political rituals and dogmas are a little like the proverbial eel: whenever one reaches out for them, they take a different form, direction, and place. Moreover, while an eel can somehow be located, civil religion cannot be.[31]

Civil religion is, Wilson suspects, more to be understood in terms of its creators than of the thing itself. Wilson sees it as an artifact of an

29. John Wilson, *Religion in American Society: The Effective Presence* (Englewood Cliffs, NJ: Prentice-Hall, 1978), p. 176.

30. Martin Marty, "Two Kinds of Civil Religion," in *American Civil Religion,* p. 142.

31. John Wilson, *Public Religion in American Culture* (Philadelphia: Temple University Press, 1979).

uncertain age, an intellectual creation by and for those who seek some port in the sea of uncertainty. Other skeptics share this judgment, George Armstrong Kelly for one. Its origins lie in the academy, he argues, rather than the larger reality of American culture, and its purposes are to minister to academic disenchantment and find new footing for the spiritually uneasy in an age of intellectual skepticism.[32]

Skeptics are correct in worrying about quick assumptions that we have a civil religion, that there is evidence to back up what is largely a heuristic theory perhaps, or that its existence would demonstrate that religion is deeply integrated into our culture. Yet to dismiss the idea would be to take a large leap. Whether there is anything out there systematic enough to be called a religion is one thing; on the other hand, it is true enough that nation and God, for instance, have been and still are routinely tied together in the central public language of our nation, just as Bellah and others suggest. It is equally true that mission and idealism surround ordinary conceptions of our nation's self-image at home and abroad. It is hardly absurd to suggest that this is directly connected with our Protestant tradition, though to establish that definitively is quite another matter.

A more salient objection to the civil religion idea is that even if America has some vague civil "religion," and even if much of its content came from Protestant Christianity, what does this have to do with religion and our culture today? It may illustrate an important, if somewhat imprecise, integration achieved in the past, but it does not establish that such a relationship is at work today—except as a historical memory. Again, there is some rather amorphous evidence of the popular confusion of God's will and national destiny; but most of the evidence runs in quite another direction. The evidence is that the person in the pew does not see religion and nation/politics/culture with the same eye.[33] Unquestionably, this *disconnection* has never been more sharply emphasized than it is today by leaders and theologians in all realms of American religion, very much including conservative Protestantism. Indeed, the chasm draws so much attention today that when one eye does look at the nation and culture, it is with a critical stare.[34]

RELIGION

NATION / POLITICS / CULTURE

32. George Armstrong Kelly, *Politics and Religious Consciousness in America* (New Brunswick, NJ: Transaction Books, 1984), ch. 7.

33. This, of course, is my argument. The evidence is in chapters two and three.

34. See chapters 6, 7, and 8 for detailed discussions of leadership criticism in terms of specific religious groups.

Conclusion

INTEGRATION THEORIES about religion and American society deserve serious attention. Perhaps there is something like a civil religion still alive in the United States, though the relevant questions are how well it illustrates integration and how important it is. Similarly, there is a case to be made for de Tocqueville's theory of historical integration and society in America. But it applies today as a theory to illuminate more the past than contemporary America.

The interest in a dynamic theory of integration between colonial Protestant ideas and American liberalism whose results linger on today also merits attention, though the extent of its contemporary legacy is as unexplored as it may be unexplorable. There is also, of course, the thesis that American religion and its churches have mainly defended the established social and political order. While far too simplistic, this view describes much of the history of religion and culture in America in the nineteenth and twentieth centuries. However, it fits best with the realities of 25 or 125 years ago than it does today.

Almost all integrationist arguments dwell on historical evidence (or at least on historical theory; actual evidence is too often skimpy) or on the current record. The problem with historical arguments is obvious: they may or may not be accurate for some other day in United States history, but they do not amount to a case for today. The limitation of those that take account of the current absence, on the whole, of challenge to the liberal order is that they assume its alternative is strong support. In truth, finding that support is more and more difficult in the increasingly stormy relations between religion and contemporary culture in the United States. Cardinal Spellman is dead, and Billy Graham has left behind his uncritically patriotic religion.

People do not go to church to indicate support for America, or liberalism, or American institutions. They may have at one time, at least in part, but they do so no longer. Of course, the *result* of involvement in religion can still be support for the United States order, intentions aside. Similarly, the absence of evidence that people go to church to indicate support for our liberal order does *not* constitute evidence they go there in the alternative spirit of challenge. There are more than two possibilities, though it is to the challenge hypothesis we now turn.

CHAPTER SIX

The Challenge of Liberal Protestantism and the Roman Catholic Church

IT IS QUITE POSSIBLE TODAY to argue that religion in the United States, far from affirming liberal culture, is on a collision course with it. Whatever the disputed history of the integration of "Christ and culture" in America, the present seems to offer more fertile ground for a thesis of challenge. One can hardly ignore the National Council of Churches' frequent attacks on U.S. foreign policy, the National Conference of Catholic Bishops' dissent from U.S. economic and abortion policies, and the emergence of Protestant "conservatives," whose agenda is mostly about change in our culture—often drastic change. These dissenters and others hardly speak in a single voice. But everywhere, religion in America suddenly appears dissatisfied with the nation around it and inclined to voice the vocabulary of change and challenge.

In any event, this is a common image, particularly in the secular media and sometimes among religious activists. My argument, which will proceed by exploring the degree of challenge posed to America's liberal order by major religious groups, acknowledges the increased challenge from among religious leaders in the United States. That is a fact beyond denial. Whether it is descriptive of the mood of most religious people, however, is another question. Equally in doubt is the depth of challenge involved, as well as the effectiveness of the challengers. While the rhetoric of religious challenge is both substantial and growing, its reality is easily exaggerated.

To maintain some analytic clarity in what is necessarily a somewhat imprecise subject, it is essential to reflect on what would constitute a "challenge" to our liberal order from any part of American religion. Obviously, there is not, nor could there be, general agreement on such standards. I can only indicate what I mean by "challenge." It is a strong word in my view. It involves three components. To challenge American society

83

a group must actively oppose the basic liberal values of the culture and propose an alternative social/political ideology. It must do the same in relation to many, perhaps most, basic institutions. Finally, it must go beyond words to serious and effective (though effective need not mean successful) action. Without this third dimension "challenge" is little more than rhetoric. Such rhetoric may have psychological value or group competitive uses, but it does not indicate real challenge of the American order. Neither, of course, do policy disputes, even policy disputes articulated in hyperbolic and angry language, radical attacks on this or that particular institution, or ill-tempered denunciations of political leaders.

It follows that there is a great deal of room for churches, denominations, or other religious groups to take stances which while they are not real challenges to American society, we could not possibly describe as conservative in contemporary political language. There are not two categories, "conservative" and "challenge." Rather, there is a spectrum from conservative to challenge when we consider the substances of religious groups' ideology, policy, or practice. But while this is true, I insist that only where real challenge, as I have defined it, is present, may we say that religion does not support the existent liberal order at the most basic level. Only then does religion *consciously* and *determinedly* present itself as a radical alternative to liberalism.[1]

Mainline Protestantism

ONE ARENA in which hard-charging, change-oriented religion appears to be the order of the day is mainstream Protestantism. This realm includes the United Methodist Church, the United Church of Christ, the Episcopal Church, the American Baptists, and other denominations, as well as the broader National Council of Churches, which liberal Protestants have always dominated. Again and again, challenge is the topic and tone of the official published organs of these bodies, and memories of any era of uncritical integration with the larger culture are increasingly remote.

It is striking how sharply the political attitudes of mainstream Protestant clergy and leaders have changed in the past fifty—or even thirty—years. They were once very conservative, whatever the issues of the day, and strongly Republican in their voting habits. Even during the popular heyday of the New Deal, Protestant clergy were overwhelmingly opposed to Roosevelt and his policies, even more than were Protestants as

1. Kenneth Wald has noted to me that the matter is one of degree. Also see his *Religion and Politics in the United States* (New York: St. Martin's, 1986), pp. 240-48, for a succinct introduction to the "mainline" Protestants and politics.

a whole.[2] They remained so throughout the 1950s. They had little need to organize politically; their attitudes, except on economic issues, dominated the country. The groups that did organize often existed for the purpose of watching or blocking the Catholic Church in Washington.[3] During these decades, liberal activists were few in number and modest in influence within established Protestantism. Sometimes children of the Social Gospel movement of a half-century earlier, sometimes disciples of Reinhold Niebuhr, they thought in ways that are again out of favor today in more radical denominational offices.[4]

This situation changed drastically in the 1960s. The civil rights movement was the crucial first step: it activated many liberal Protestant clergy and denominational offices, turning them toward political advocacy and action. Moreover, it did so in a context in which mainstream laity, while trailing behind in enthusiasm—especially regarding direct clerical participation—were often supportive of the goals of civil rights for blacks, if not the activism associated with it. Equally significant, though in a different fashion, was the painful, divisive struggle over the Vietnam War in the late 1960s and early 1970s. By the late 1960s most mainstream clergy shied away from support for the war and wanted the United States to get out of its involvement rapidly. This opinion was *eventually* shared by their laity, and the population at large, but not in the late 1960s.[6] This gap between clergy and laity (about which more later) was part of a distancing process for many liberal, often younger Protestant clergy and clergy leaders, not only from their laity but also from the politics and government of the United States as a whole. Into this vacuum of political attachment has come liberation theology in the 1970s and 1980s. Developed by Latin and South American Catholics,

2. A. James Reichley, *Religion in American Public Life* (Washington, DC: Brookings, 1985), p. 226; note that the data Reichley draws on exaggerate Protestant support for the New Deal; he includes Southern (often evangelical/fundamentalist) Protestants who were often pro–New Deal in his data for "Protestants" and "Protestant clergy" for the period. On "mainstream" Protestants in general, see Wade Clark Roof and William McKinney, *American Mainline Religion: Its Changing Shape and Future* (New Brunswick, NJ: Rutgers University Press, 1987).

3. Reichley, *Religion in American Public Life*, pp. 228-29, 244-46.

4. For a brief introduction to the Niebuhrian and Social Gospel strains, see Robert Booth Fowler, *Religion and Politics in America* (Metuchen, NJ: Scarecrow Press, 1985), pp. 77-86, 145-54; Reichley, *Religion in American Public Life*, pp. 225-28.

5. For agreeing syntheses, see Fowler, *Religion and Politics in America*, pp. 154-63, 296-98; Reichley, *Religion in American Public Life*, pp. 246-50.

6. Reichley, *Religion in American Public Life*, pp. 250-54.

drawing on Marxist as well as Christian themes to emphasize the importance of radical action to aid the poor and the oppressed, liberation theology has many sides and dimensions. It has not been easy to establish its influence among leaders of mainstream Protestantism and in the theological schools that educate mainstream clergy. But in the 1980s signs of influence at liberal Protestant denominational leadership levels, among church social action agencies, and at the National Council of Churches are numerous. Ironically, they are more prominent there than they are in the Roman Catholic Church in America.[7]

Whether it is explained by the civil rights and Vietnam struggles, liberation theology, or something else, a substantial portion of mainstream Protestant clergy—and particularly clerical leaders—are strong participants in what is called the "peace with justice" movement, sympathetic to change in the political and economic structure of the United States—and the world. Surveys of clergy in such denominations as the Presbyterian, Lutheran, and Methodist establish their interest in, and to varying degrees support for, the "peace with justice" ethic.[8] This usually includes emphasis on world peace through rapid—and frequently unilateral—disarmament, coupled with dismissal of the deterrence theory. Equally integral is the rejection of capitalist and state socialist economic systems and the support for a reorientation of economic life toward the problems of the poor, hungry, homeless, and unemployed.[9]

The work of several social scientists has now confirmed that such views are dominant at the denominational and lobbying offices of major Protestant groups, to no one's surprise.[10] This is especially true of the

7. David Black, "Religion: A Witness to Theology's Changing Face," *The Virginian-Pilot and the Ledger-Star,* 5 July 1986; Reichley's discussion is interesting, *Religion in American Public Life,* pp. 256-67. Some basic works, among a vast number, on liberation theology are: Gustavo Gutiérrez, *A Theology of Liberation* (Maryknoll, NY: Orbis, 1973); José Míguez Bonino, *Doing Theology in a Revolutionary Situation* (Philadelphia: Fortress, 1975); Rosino Bibellini, ed., *Frontiers of Theology in Latin America* (Maryknoll, NY: Orbis, 1979); Sergio Torres and John Eagleson, eds., *The Challenge of Basic Christian Communities* (Maryknoll, NY: Orbis, 1981); Dom Helder Camara, *Spiral of Violence* (London: Sheed and Ward, 1971); Robert McAfee Brown, *Theology in a New Key: Responding to Liberation Themes* (Philadelphia: Westminster, 1978).

8. Reichley, *Religion in American Public Life,* pp. 269-73.

9. "Peace with Justice Week," *Religion and Society Report,* December 1985, pp. 5-7.

10. Allan Hertzke shared with me the confirming results of his 1985 interviews with liberal Protestant lobbyists in Washington; see Allan Hertzke, *Representing God in Washington: The Role of Religious Lobbies in the American Polity* (Knoxville: University of Tennessee Press, 1988); Reichley's more

United Methodist Church, the Episcopal Church, and the United Church of Christ. Above all, the National Council of Churches and its staff, heavily influenced by the liberal Protestant political agenda, reflect this orientation. That its current general secretary, Arie R. Brouwer of the Reformed Church in America, is sympathetic to an evangelical religious viewpoint has not diminished the orientation of the NCC's activism. Brouwer is also a zealous supporter of an activist peace and justice view, now traditional and expected among his fellow liberal Protestant elites.[11]

Indeed, activism is evident everywhere one looks in contemporary mainstream Protestantism. In recent years liberal Protestant leaders and organizations have been in the forefront in one highly publicized cause after another: opposition to President Reagan's Central American policy; support for "free choice" in regard to abortion; the nuclear freeze; opposition to the escalating military budget; criticism of tightening limitations on our welfare system; the sanctuary movement. It is clearly impossible to portray official liberal Protestant churches as routine apologists for American liberal culture—or even as subtle backhand defenders of it. The facts are as unmistakable as they may be surprising: a new day is here, and we may no longer fairly describe this Protestantism as somehow integrated neatly within our social order.

On the other hand, it would be erroneous to take it as a serious challenge to our liberal society either, though a few both inside and outside mainstream Protestantism have made this mistake. Such a judgment lacks perspective. Even the most activist Protestant elites are not, on the whole, very radical. It was one thing to denounce Ronald Reagan or his policies at home and abroad; it is quite another to formulate serious theoretical critiques of American culture and institutions and to act on them. There is little of the latter in mainstream Protestantism. Mostly, its activist leaders appear to parallel—too closely, critics from several arenas say—the left wing of the Democratic party. And this is hardly a universe concerned with radical change.

Granted, when compared with some of their conservative laity, these activists may seem radical. Moreover, sensational media coverage such as the 1983 attacks on the World Council of Churches and the National Council of Churches in *Reader's Digest* and on CBS's "60 Minutes" have encouraged the radical image. So have such overheated, but not lightweight, exposés of the politics of naiveté and self-hatred in "advanced" liberal Protestant circles as Edmund and Julia Robb's *The*

---

limited work agrees with Hertzke's findings, *Religion in American Public Life*, pp. 275-78.

11. Linda-Marie Delloff, "In Spirituality and in Service: The NCC," *Christian Century*, 29 May 1985.

Betrayal of the Church.[12] But just how radical is it to oppose U.S. intervention in Central America or to fault the U.S. government's alleged lack of attention to the homeless?

Perhaps this account underestimates the more radical implications of liberation theology at work among liberal Protestant elites. There is a good deal of "prophetic" religion going on in these circles today: calls for an immediate world economic transformation resulting in an egalitarian, communitarian order are common, as are proclamations of the urgency of unilateral disarmament, world government, and brotherhood and sisterhood among all people.[13] This "real" agenda is far more challenging to American institutions than the National Council of Churches and such groups' predictable left-liberal policy agenda even suggests. But the neo-pacifist, neo-socialist rhetoric that these groups often couch in biblical language does not seem to be meant very seriously if action is the final test. And as these groups move increasingly into organized politics, their "prophetic" rhetoric may well cool, will have to cool if they want to have actual policy influence. At the moment, we have to rest with the observation that social issue activists in control of policy within mainstream Protestantism are far more "liberal" than the Reagan administration—or, indeed, the average American—but that is as far as one should go.

Challenge there is, then, from liberal Protestantism, more challenge than most histories of Protestantism would ever lead us to expect at any time. But while this shift to challenge is historic, its actual radicalness is open to question. Moreover, liberal Protestantism's challenge is undercut by a lack of effectiveness in the political process (though this focus admittedly omits such possible measures of effectiveness as education or

12. On the 1983 controversy, see, e.g., Rael Jean Isaac, "Do You Know Where Your Church Offerings Go?" *Reader's Digest,* January 1983, pp. 120-25; National Council of Churches, "Response to *Reader's Digest* Article," 1983; "*Reader's Digest* Article Called Half Truths, Hearsay," *Dimensions: The Wisconsin United Methodist Newspaper,* February 1983, p. 1; Richard Ostling, "Warring over Where Donations Go," *Time,* 28 March 1983; Edmund W. Robb and Julia Robb, *The Betrayal of the Church: Apostasy and Renewal in the Mainline Denominations* (Westchester, IL: Crossway Books, 1986).

13. For some samples of "radical" Protestantism in perspective, see Jervis Anderson, "Standing out There on the Issues: Bishop Paul Moore, Jr.," *New Yorker,* 28 April 1986, pp. 41-95; Richard N. Ostling, "Opting for the Browning Version: The Episcopal Church Picks an Activist Liberal as Its Leader," *Time,* 23 September 1985; "Peace with Justice Week," *Religion and Society Report,* December 1985, pp. 5-7; "Methodists Refuse to 'Wallow in Doom,'" *Religion and Society Report,* July 1986, pp. 2-6; any of the writings of Robert McAfee Brown, e.g., *Theology in a New Key;* William Sloan Coffin, Jr., *Once To Every Man* (New York: Atheneum, 1977).

witness through nonviolent action). This judgment is the standard one today. The radicalness of liberal Protestant social agencies may be wildly exaggerated sometimes, but their effectiveness in current political wars rarely is. Liberal Protestant activists, on the whole, have a reputation as paper tigers in the political process, a reputation that hurts because it can become a self-fulfilling prophecy.[14]

It is true enough that Protestant lobby groups were leaders in the modern movement of organized religion to participate in Washington politics. The Methodists appeared in strength first. By 1923 they had erected the Methodist Building, a continuing headquarters for mainstream Protestant groups. Though the Methodists were atypical, after World War II most other Protestant groups began their first steps toward establishing a regular lobbying presence in Washington. In 1946 the Northern Presbyterian and the Baptist voices were established; by 1948 the Lutheran voices; and after 1950 the National Council of Churches became a presence.[15]

Recent decades, of course, have seen a wide expansion of liberal Protestant lobbying efforts.[16] The political agenda of liberal Protestant groups has lengthened, and all sorts of groups—the National Council of Churches, the General Board of Church and Society of the United Methodist Church, the Lutheran Council, assorted other mainstream denominational agencies, *Impact,* the interdenominational Protestant action organization, and others—are busy promoting it.[17] Many of these organizations, or similar ones, can also be found at the level of state government, though their existence and activity is often more episodic and ad hoc in the halls of state capitols than they are in Washington.[18]

However, while liberal Protestants are organized and participate vigorously in the group process that is American politics, their influence is distinctly limited, making their challenge even less potent in practice than it is in theory. They have a reputation in Congress for ineffectiveness, and it is difficult to suggest where they have had much impact, at least on domestic policy. Almost always aligned with forces seeking more

14. See Fowler, *Religion and Politics in America,* pp. 175-84; Reichley, *Religion in American Public Life,* pp. 267-81. Hertzke is more inclined to rate liberal Protestantism's effect at a greater level, especially in foreign affairs; see n. 17 below.

15. Reichley, *Religion in American Public Life,* p. 244.

16. *Ibid.,* pp. 244-81, 331-39.

17. The best feel for these groups and their leaders may be found in Hertzke, *Representing God in Washington.*

18. For a pioneering effort here, see William De Soto, "Religious Interest Groups in Madison," unpublished paper, 1985.

domestic spending, especially for the poor and disadvantaged, they have suffered defeat after defeat in this age of Ronald Reagan. Nor have they succeeded in their frequent endeavors to reduce the defense budget, much less eliminate nuclear arms. And on "lifestyle" issues, above all abortion, Congress has spurned their liberal stands.

Matters are much less clear in foreign affairs. Both opposition to U.S. involvement in Central America and intense support for détente and arms reductions with the Soviet Union have become almost crusades for liberal Protestant groups, some of whom appear to spend more and more time on these questions as their domestic agenda has stalled. It is a matter of some dispute how effective this liberal church lobby has been in the foreign affairs area. Hertzke is impressed with their successes in Congress: where they have not won, they have had a role in slowing others' options. He makes a good case.[19] On the other hand, most foreign policy is not made in Congress but in the White House; here the liberal Protestant lobby in the Reagan years got absolutely nowhere.

The modest success of mainstream Protestant social activism is surprising—perhaps one should say astounding. After all, mainstream Protestantism *was* America for a long time in religious terms. It dominated our culture, and it still claims to speak for a third or so of Americans in some loose sense. While the actual church members of mainstream Protestant denominations are a much smaller proportion of the population than that, they are more educated, more affluent, and more informed than most Americans. Each of these strengths constitutes an important potential political resource.[20] Moreover, Protestants from the liberal Protestant denominations are vastly overrepresented in elite circles in America—among business leaders, for instance. Indeed, a majority of Congress members and top government leaders are mainstream Protestants, now as in the past.[21] Finally, as we know, liberal Protestants have long been organized into interest groups; their organizational structures are established and their activists are often highly experienced.[22]

Yet their influence simply does not match all these advantages.

19. Hertzke, *Representing God in Washington,* ch. 5.

20. *Religion in America: 50 Years, 1935–1985* (Gallup Report No. 236, May 1985), pp. 35-37.

21. "Members of Congress Hold Ties to 21 Religious Groups," *Christianity Today,* 18 January 1984.

22. Allan Hertzke is superb on liberal Protestant organization, experience, and strategy, based on his interviews of organizational leaders and congressional staffers; see *Representing God in Washington,* chs. 2, 3.

Why? Obviously, something is wrong. There is no single explanation. Rather, there appears to be a set of factors working together to render politically organized mainstream Protestants relatively impotent, thus deflating their "challenge." Church organization among Protestants remains loose both within and among the denominations. Localism is still a powerful factor, even in nominally hierarchical denominations such as the Methodist church.[23] Protestants remain separated into distinct denominations largely on the basis of tradition and history rather than current beliefs. And although the movement toward ecumenism may be growing, as illustrated by the union of the two main Presbyterian churches and the two largest Lutheran bodies in recent years, there is no one voice for liberal Protestantism, including the multidenominational National Council of Churches.

Next is the question of *how* to be effective. Liberal Protestant organizations have made some efforts, notably those by *Impact*, to build lobbying organizations that can generate pressure from the local level. Some peace churches and some of the peace groups such as Bread for the World have done very well at maintaining local level contacts.[24] These make a difference; but on the whole, mainstream Protestant groups do not have much of a local constituency, that is, people organized into networks they can mobilize to apply pressure. Their strategy still concentrates heavily on lobbyists and visits by religious delegations, whose impact is doubtful.[25]

Moreover, unlike some other religious forces in American life, mainstream Protestants have not become much involved in electoral politics. Such a connection impresses politicians and bureaucrats alike, and activist Protestantism's well-known weakness here hurts it badly. Church-state barriers are still powerful constraints. So is the fact that, even if they wanted to, Protestant groups cannot really develop an explicit and wide-ranging electoral connection. The main reason for this serious constraint is straightforward: much of the political concern and the specific agenda of Protestant political activists is not shared by the laity. The activists are leaders who often lack followers.

23. One gets a sense of this by looking at the actual diversity. For the United Methodist Church, see, e.g., Robert L. Wilson and William H. Willimon, *The Seven Churches of Methodism* (Durham, NC: Duke University Press, 1985); Sue Plasterer, "A Study of the 11 United Methodist Churches of Madison, Wisconsin," unpublished paper, 1982.

24. Hertzke, *Representing God in Washington*, pp. 49-50; also his interview notes on *Impact*.

25. Fowler, *Religion and Politics in America*, pp. 179-80, 184; Reichley, *Religion in American Public Life*, pp. 268-69.

Beginning in the 1960s, growing evidence showed that clergy and laity within mainstream Protestant denominations diverged, often sharply, on political issues and political candidates.[26] This gap has definitely not diminished over time. In 1980, as liberal Protestant denominational leaders or social action councils mounted one challenge after another to policies of the American government, Protestant laity proved to be far more conservative, on the whole, than were their religious "leaders"—indeed, more conservative than the general population of the country. Surveys during the 1970s and 1980s of Presbyterians, Lutherans, and Methodists found many gaps between denominational elites and the laity on policy and political activism.[27] This was especially true on many economic and criminal justice policy issues; it was less true, though still existent, on such matters as abortion and foreign and military policy, exactly the areas where Protestant elites and activist groups have been most committed.[28]

Allan Hertzke insists that the evidence is mixed, that it varies by liberal Protestant denomination and by issue. He argues that the gap is clear and covers more issues in denominations such as the Episcopalians and the Presbyterians than it does in more liberal denominations such as the United Church of Christ. He also offers data suggesting that on some issues—particularly environmental spending, abortion, peace concerns, and Central American policy—elite and laity tend to be closer in a number of liberal Protestant denominations. But he confirms that on a number of other issues this is not the case.[29]

Hertzke suggests that foreign policy issues in particular make up the realm where the gap is smallest. On Central American policy he is correct to the extent that both elites and laity do not have much stomach for U.S. involvement.[30] Otherwise, once one grants that everybody can agree on such pleasant generalities as the wisdom of "peace" and "disar-

26. See such classic studies as Jeffrey K. Hadden, *The Gathering Storm in the Churches* (Garden City, NY: Doubleday, 1969); Lawrence K. Kersten, *The Lutheran Ethic: The Impact of Religion on Laymen and Clergy* (Detroit: Wayne State University Press, 1970); Harold E. Quinley, *The Prophetic Clergy: Social Activism among Protestant Ministers* (New York: John Wiley, 1974); Thomas C. Campbell and Yoshio Fukuyama, *The Fragmented Layman: An Empirical Study of Lay Attitudes* (Philadelphia: Pilgrim, 1970).

27. Reichley, *Religion in American Public Life*, pp. 270-71, summarizes well the current literature.

28. *Ibid.*, pp. 269-73.

29. Hertzke, *Representing God in Washington*, ch. 5.

30. *Ibid.*, ch. 5, pp. 14-20; for an example of elite attitudes regarding the contras, see "Church vs. *Contra* Aid," *Christian Century*, 9 April 1986.

mament," the evidence looks thin. Highly popular moves such as President Reagan's retaliatory bombing of Libya in 1986, popular across all major groups in the United States, expose the gap quite nakedly. Despite popular approval, the National Council of Churches denounced the raids in a strongly phrased statement; the president of the United Church of Christ attacked it; and leaders of the liberal American Baptist Church agreed. Examples of the gap go on and on.[31] Nor was there any evidence of broad support within the Methodist church for its bishops' bold statement in 1986 calling for unilateral disarmament and the rejection of deterrence theory, much less a popular movement within Protestant denominations for the radical Protestant-based "Pledge of Resistance," a fiery 1986 statement threatening militant resistance at home to any U.S. invasion of Nicaragua.[32]

On the whole, granting some qualifications—especially liberalism on abortion and environmentalism, vague support for peace, and specific lack of interest in Central America—the gap between liberal Protestant clergy, especially intellectuals, and their laity is large. That is reflected and to some degree summarized by the similar gap that exists in voting behavior between Protestant clergy and laity. While hardly radicals, mainstream Protestant clergy tend nowadays to be liberal Democrats and to vote that way. But majorities of the laity have voted differently: the majority of mainstream Protestant clergy rejected Ronald Reagan in 1980 and 1984; the laity voted otherwise.

Laity—Percent for Reagan	1980	1984[33]
Episcopalians	69	60
Lutherans	56	66
Methodists	53	65
Presbyterians	67	68
Percent of USA	51	59

The gap exists and generally grows greater the farther one is up in a denomination's hierarchy of decision making. The more elite one's position, the more liberal one's policy, which a study established, for ex-

31. About 80 percent of the American public supported the raids. For elite religious reactions, see "Responses to Libya Attack," *Christian Century,* 7 May 1986.

32. For the Methodist bishops' effort, see "In Defense of Creation: The Nuclear Crisis and a Just Peace," *Christian Century,* 14 May 1986.

33. Reichley, *Religion in American Public Life,* pp. 273-75; Fowler, *Religion and Politics in America,* pp. 63-67.

ample, regarding the United Methodist Church.[34] Even though churches such as the U.M.C. have substantial lay participation at all levels—in general governance and in various church agencies, boards, and commissions—this apparent paradox is resolved by the well-known process of selective (including self-selective) lay recruitment. Like select like, and lay representation often becomes merely a lay echoing of clerical elites.[35]

Complaints about this sort of failure to represent the laity abound, but they are based on the hardly self-evident proposition that this is what church leaders are called to do. Among liberal Protestant activists there is substantial conviction, encouraged by liberation theology, that Christians should speak prophetically. Speaking prophetically means proclaiming God's word as the "prophets" understand it, regardless of the consequences. For example, Protestant activists assume that they are called as Christians to speak for the poor and other social "victims" regardless of lay opinion—and at times somewhat in scorn of it. In fact, this attitude is common today.[36]

Other Protestants emphasize the legitimate place for the representation of church institutions quite apart from lay opinions. This position is often incorrectly associated only with the Catholic Church, but this ignores the fact that the Episcopal and Methodist churches, to cite two significant examples, are not at all structural democracies. Their bishops, while constrained in a number of ways, also have independent authority. Various leadership groups in many liberal Protestant denominations, in fact, feel quite comfortable in speaking for their church—or their church's theology—quite apart from the claims of the laity. Finally, a number of liberal Protestant churches have close international contacts with other branches of their denominations, the Lutherans and Episcopalians, for instance. As a result, some leadership elites portray themselves as internationalists, representing peoples very far from the United States—and their laity here.[37]

Representation, in short, is a complex business among liberal Protestants. For some leaders, representing lay opinion is, at best, only one factor that deserves to be taken into account. And yet lay opinion is im-

34. James Foyle Miller, *A Study of United Methodists and Social Issues* (New York: United Methodist Church, 1983), pp. 8-10.

35. But there are limits, as the "great" fight over the most recent Methodist hymnal demonstrated: Jean Caffrey Lyles, "'Military' Psalms Restored to Hymnals," *Washington Post,* 5 July 1986.

36. For a contemporary defense of the prophetic approach, see the essay on the Episcopal bishop of New York in Anderson, "Standing out There on the Issues: Bishop Paul Moore, Jr.," pp. 41-42, 45-48, 53-54, 73-95.

37. Hertzke, *Representing God in Washington,* ch. 4.

portant when one talks about influence, especially on major policy questions. If it is missing, all the theories of "proper" and multiple representation in the world won't convince a skeptical member of Congress that he or she must pay attention to any earnest mainstream Protestant pastor lobbying at the door.

Further complicating matters is the sometimes painful issue of whether clergy and the churches should be involved in politics in the first place. The American ideology of separation of church and state often means separation of church and politics for laity, which is predictable since we know that few of them go to church to get swept up into politics. Lay objections to such churchly involvement in politics have been repeatedly documented in liberal Protestant denominations over the past twenty years, and those objections continue strong.

For example, a recent study in the Presbyterian church showed clergy overwhelmingly in favor of church commitment to activism; yet only 30 percent of the laity were. A study of Episcopalians found that more than 75 percent of the laity wanted the church to concentrate on worship and spiritual matters and refused to view the church as an agent of political change.[38] The effect of this attitude on church figures in Washington or at denominational headquarters is obviously modest. It is likely to be much greater on the local minister because he or she must face the laity daily and can find out very quickly how they feel about political activity and the church. Protestant ministers who serve on campuses, in denominational agencies, or in Washington usually feel freer and are, consequently, more likely to be engaged in politics.[39]

No wonder mainstream Protestantism's alleged radical challenge has not amounted to much.[40] Its ideology so far is not very radical, and its political effectiveness is distinctly modest. Above all, the church's center, its laypeople, simply are not attracted to political reform, much less radicalism or the idea of political action by the church. Indeed, classic Protestantism is largely untouched by politics—radical or integrative—on a daily basis. It is, instead, a traditional religion, that is, concerned with spiritual truth, faith, prayer, and fellowship. Most laypeople belong for these things. Some mainstream Protestant elites may aspire to mount

38. William R. Wineke, "Social Issues Split Presbyterians," *Wisconsin State Journal*, 23 November 1985; Ostling, "Opting for the Browning Version"; Reichley, *Religion in American Public Life*, pp. 269-71; Fowler, *Religion and Politics in America*, pp. 181-82.

39. Wald, *Religion and Politics*, p. 246; Fowler, p. 182.

40. For a left-leaning critique, which agrees, see William Willimon, "A Crisis of Identity: The Struggle of Modern Mainline Protestantism," *Sojourners*, May 1986, pp. 24-28.

a challenge to our political order, but their church as a whole does not pose any such challenge, and at present it cannot.

This "cannot" is obviously crucial. It does not come solely from erroneous images of mainstream Protestantism's radicalism or its lack of political effectiveness; it also derives from its image, hardly grounded in fantasy, as a declining branch of American religion. The numbers are clear enough: the majority of Protestants no longer identify with theological "mainstream" Protestantism. The large denominations of liberal Protestantism show little growth these days. They are well below their 1950s proportionate strength of the total U.S. population *and* in absolute numbers. In the decade 1970–1980, for instance, the Episcopal Church declined 15 percent, the United Church of Christ 11 percent, the Lutheran Church in America 8 percent, the United Methodist Church 10 percent, the United Presbyterian Church (north) 21 percent.[41]

Some liberal Protestant observers believe that the situation is not so serious now. The declines have slowed, though they have hardly reversed. It is also quite possible to argue with the numbers (though not the trend) by pointing out that membership figures today remain far higher than in most other eras of American religious history, eras that also had their now-forgotten crises over future religious prospects. And it is frequently—and sometimes a bit too smugly—argued that smaller is better. The chaff is gone, the argument goes, and Protestant churches are better for it.[42]

However, the sharp numerical declines over the past several decades remain. So does the question "why?" The explanations are many, and the evidence is murky. Political opponents of liberal Protestant elites blame church activism, as do others for whom politics of any sort does not belong in church. According to another view, the increasing individualism of many college-educated, middle-class people has led them away from their traditional Protestant homes. And the trend in recent decades for middle- and upper-middle-class families to have fewer children is an important demographic factor.[43]

But as least as plausible as these reasons is the view that liberal Protestantism's decline in America to one religion among many derives from its loss of a special identity. It simply does not stand for theological absolutes in an age when religions that do are strong and growing. There

41. For decline data, see Reichley, *Religion in American Public Life,* p. 278.

42. William R. Hutchison, "Past Imperfect: History and the Prospect for Liberalism (I)," *Christian Century,* 1-8 January 1986.

43. The subject is a complex one. Perhaps the best single volume on the subject with regard to Protestants—even though it is weak on its cultural analysis—is Dean R. Hoge and David A. Roozen, eds., *Understanding Church Growth and Decline, 1950–1978* (New York: Pilgrim, 1979).

is no question that its religious style, which is open, pluralistic, accepting, and nonjudgmental, attracts some Americans. But it is equally certain that this style denies mainstream Protestantism a clear image and thus broader appeal in an age when certainties and standards are not out of fashion among laypeople. To be sure, many mainstream denominations are very clear in their political stands at the top; but people do not join churches for their political programs. Lacking elaborate ritual (in most cases) and strict theological beliefs, liberal Protestantism presents a blurred public image.[44]

We should not forget that millions of Americans continue to be members of liberal Protestant denominations, many of them members of vibrant, healthy congregations. But neither should we ignore the overall pattern of declining membership of the past twenty years, especially in light of the ironic hypothesis that, despite a great deal of challenging political rhetoric, liberal Protestantism's image is vague and certainly not perceived as an alternative to our culture, or even a retreat from it. Indeed, declarations from denominational headquarters aside, mainstream Protestantism is superbly integrated into American culture—no challenge at all. It remains the citadel of respectability in American religion, and its class basis reflects this fact.[45]

Recognition of this fact spurs on some leaders, such as the NCC's Arie R. Brouwer, to encourage more direct confrontation of society not only through politics but through evangelism, the message of Christ as Savior.[46] For some others, mainstream Protestantism's conformity (integration) elicits thinly disguised contempt: "What in American society would be left undone, what vacuum in private life unfilled, if liberal Protestantism were suddenly to disappear? Any unfinished business could be quickly polished off by a presidential commission or the community chest."[47]

44. For an interesting treatment, see Wade Clark Roof, "America's Voluntary Establishment: Mainline Religion in Transition," in *Religion and America: Spirituality in a Secular Age,* ed. Mary Douglas and Steven Tipton (Boston: Beacon, 1983), pp. 130-49; Paul Seabury, "Trendier than Thou: The Episcopal Church and the Secular World" (Washington, DC: Ethics and Public Policy Center, 1978), pp. 1-7.

45. The elite position of the Episcopalians and Presbyterians comes through in Gallup's surveys, but so does the entire "mainstream" group in comparison with other Protestants; see George Gallup, Jr., and Jim Castelli, *The American Catholic People* (Garden City, NY: Doubleday, 1987), ch. 1.

46. Ari L. Goldman, "Church Council Urged to Change," *New York Times,* 16 May 1985.

47. Edwin Scott Gaustad, "Did the Fundamentalists Win?" in *Religion and America: Spirituality in a Secular Age,* pp. 176-77.

Such a view is uncharitable and overlooks the many who find real needs fulfilled in their Episcopal or Methodist church. Frequently those needs are for temporary respite from the larger culture, something that in the typical "liberal" Protestant congregation often remains available. But such "retreat" comes through a very respectable vehicle in our culture, "mainstream" Protestantism. Tied to middle-class culture, it is almost an ideal *temporary* retreat, because it is so safe. This reality every bit as much as the image of decline which surrounds liberal Protestantism today undermines any challenge its leaders seek to lead.

The Roman Catholic Church

THE HYPOTHESIS that challenge to liberal culture is more and more the order of the day for American religion must include today's Roman Catholic Church. After all, it is in the headlines far more often than all liberal Protestant denominations combined, an inevitable result not only of its vast numbers (between 20 and 25 percent of all Americans claim to be Roman Catholics)[48] but also of its extensive participation in our national public policy debates. Moreover, unlike liberal Protestant churches, which have a long record of public involvement, the Roman Catholic Church's recent burst of activity represents a substantial departure from its past, at least in the United States.

When it was an ethnic church, Catholicism sought to exercise its political will, to be sure; but its efforts were usually local and in the service of protecting its detached world (above all, seeking government aid for its parochial schools). Its face turned outside to politics only to protect its inner world. Most white Catholics have long since left their grandparents' and great-grandparents' ghettos, a historic movement symbolized in the 1960s by the emergence of John F. Kennedy as a successful public figure. Coming from immigrant Catholic stock two generations before, Kennedy was the epitome of the integrated suburban Catholic in the 1950s and early 1960s.[49]

Every measure of contemporary Catholics in terms of education and economic status, as well as in attitudes toward politics and issues (except abortion), demonstrates how closely they parallel the larger American society. The life situations and the attitudes of Catholics are as diverse as are the population's as a whole, and the patterns of their diversity resemble

---

48. *Religion in America* (Gallup Report), p. 30.

49. For a good treatment of these matters, see Jay P. Dolan, *The American Catholic Experience: A History from Colonial Times to the Present* (Garden City, NY: Doubleday, 1985), chs. 5, 14, 15.

those of the entire country. They are no longer a people apart.[50] The internal changes in the American Roman Catholic Church since Vatican II (1962–1965) have also been a weighty factor in freeing the Catholic Church from its once isolated situation in the United States. While it is debatable whether the resulting church became largely "Protestant," what is not debatable is that the changes, especially the use of English and much greater lay participation in the mass and in local church affairs, brought the church more in accord with "normal" American religious practice. The old authoritarian, Romish, and remote Catholic Church is not dead, but in the United States it is greatly transformed.[51]

Today there is little doubt that non-Catholic Americans view the Roman Catholic Church and its millions of adherents as a legitimate and respectable part of American society. There is some lingering prejudice among secular intellectuals and religious fundamentalists; and Roman Catholics are seen in a more positive light by Protestants and Jews on the whole than either of them are by Catholics. But the general mood is one of tolerance and acceptance.[52] Thus the Catholics of today are perceived accurately: they are integrated into the United States. No doubt it was a recognition of this fact that allowed President Reagan to establish diplomatic relations with the Vatican in 1984—politics often being the last realm to acknowledge changed social realities—and explains why the opposition to this move was so weak and ineffective.[53]

Even the most pressing current problems of the Roman Catholic Church attest to its integration into American life. Its declining—if still huge—parochial school system simply can no longer count on either the once proportionately greater birthrate among Catholics (except for Hispanic Catholics, there is no Catholic/non-Catholic difference in birthrate today) or on Catholics' own sense of distance or alienation from the larger society to keep the system robust. People are happy with parochial schools, but there is no widespread urgent sense of their need among

50. Gallup and Castelli, *The American Catholic People,* ch. 1; Andrew M. Greeley, *American Catholics since the Council: An Unauthorized Report* (Chicago: Thomas More, 1985), chs. 2 and 3; *Religion in America* (Gallup Report), p. 30; Jay P. Dolan and David C. Leege, "A Profile of American Catholic Parishes and Parishioners: 1820s to the 1980s," in *Notre Dame Study of Catholic Parish Life,* Report No. 2 (February 1985), p. 8.

51. For two views, see Eugene Kennedy, *The Now and Future Church* (Garden City, NY: Doubleday, 1984); and James Hitchcock, *The Decline and Fall of Radical Catholicism* (New York: Herder and Herder, 1971).

52. Greeley, *American Catholics since the Council,* ch. 12.

53. Steven R. Weisman, "U.S. and Vatican Restore Full Ties," *New York Times,* 11 January 1984; Kenneth A. Briggs, "Church Groups Protest," *New York Times,* 11 January 1984.

either the laity or clergy to keep them as strong as they were even twenty-five years ago.[54] Similarly, the steep drop in vocations among both Catholic men and women reflects an unwillingness among even a small percentage of Catholic youth to undertake a life of celibate service in the church. That life is now perceived by almost all young Catholics as too remote from American cultural norms.[55]

By now the appropriate question is this: Why would anyone see Catholics, or the Catholic Church, as a challenge to the liberal culture? Indeed, the direction in which Catholics have been moving seems to lead them into an ever-closer embrace with their society, and in the 1980s this trend has steadily accelerated. While Catholics continue to be less conservative on most issues than are Protestants as a whole—though much less liberal than Jews—and identify themselves as and vote Democratic more than Protestants do, their political attitudes and voting behavior closely parallel those of the larger society. In the 1980s, predictably, there was a conservative direction: identification with the Democratic party eased, Republican identifiers were more common, and Ronald Reagan easily carried the majority of Catholic voters in 1980 and 1984. In 1984, 55 percent of Roman Catholic voters voted for Reagan, a modest 44 percent for Mondale. To be sure, Mondale did better, as always, with Catholics than with Protestants, but his support was still weak; and there were no other signs of a broad-based movement of lay liberalism, much less radicalism, among Catholic laity.[56]

Yet it remains true that the integration of Catholics into American culture—if not the current rather conservative tilt—has been essential to the burst of Catholic political activism during the last two decades. Catholic defensiveness is gone; fears that its activities will attract a backlash threatening the church are gone. Catholics are self-confident, and so is the church hierarchy. This self-confidence allows the church to reach out to the larger political and social world. The process has been absolutely essential for the modern, political Catholic Church.

The other side, though, is that the integrated, pluralistic laypeople hardly constitute an immediately available resource for a powerful challenge of the American liberal order. It may be that integration, or at least acceptance, of the Roman Catholic Church into the United States has

54. Greeley, *American Catholics since the Council,* ch. 8; his data (about which there is little disagreement) but my interpretation (not especially controversial either).

55. A good and diverse discussion of the problem is in "The Catholic Priesthood," *Overview* 19 (no. 10): 1-8; Greeley, *American Catholics since the Council,* ch. 7.

56. Reichley, *Religion in American Public Life,* pp. 299-302.

provided its bishops with enough confidence to edge toward a more prophetic role. But in an age in which Catholic laity are very much in tune with their country's culture (and in which the bishops' influence on the laity has declined) it is doubtful whether integration will incline a diverse laity to join them. It is not just the pope who lacks divisions; his American bishops do as well.

It may not be fair to say that the price of integration is the loss of distinctiveness and coherence and thus the potential political muscle of a large united church, but this seems to be the present situation. Andrew Greeley complains that Catholicism has become very much a part of American culture because Catholics blithely practice a selective (or individualistic and subjective) Catholicism, choosing those parts of the religion they like and ignoring or even denouncing those parts they don't like.[57] To be sure, one may argue that the pluralism that characterizes the Catholic church and its communicants today does not mean Catholics have no points of unity. Richard McBrien has suggested three—emphasis on sacrament, the church, and community.[58] Greeley agrees these are the significant elements, especially sacramentality and community. Leege's study of Catholic parishes establishes that a sense of community is, in fact, a central goal of active Catholics, as we would expect. After all, being integrated to American society today means in part seeing church in community terms (and being willing to seek there temporary refuge). But Leege does not report any evidence that Catholics see community and church as a statement of opposition toward the larger society and its values.[59] Greeley complains that neither church leaders nor laity take community very seriously beyond formal endorsement.[60]

Still, the impression remains, often inside as well as outside Catholicism, that American Roman Catholicism is challenging the very social order its people reflect and participate in so thoroughly. This impression's modest degree of truth derives from the actions of the National Conference of Catholic Bishops, the hierarchy. They are increasingly taking the official church from its timid American past toward a controversial political present. In many instances, they have garnered major support from

57. Andrew M. Greeley and Mary Greeley Durkin, *How to Save the Catholic Church* (New York: Viking, 1984), ch. 1.

58. Richard P. McBrien, "Roman Catholicism: E. Pluribus Unum," in *Religion and America: Spirituality in a Secular Age,* pp. 179-89. For a much fuller discussion by McBrien, see his *Caesar's Coin: Religion and Politics in America* (New York: Macmillan, 1987).

59. David C. Leege, "The Parish as Community," in *Notre Dame Study of Catholic Parish Life,* Report No. 10 (March 1987).

60. Greeley and Durkin, *How to Save the Catholic Church,* chs. 3, 6, and 7.

the priests and sisters of the church. The absence, on the whole, of corresponding support from the laity suggests that the Catholic Church may follow the pattern of liberal Protestant denominations before long: liberal, even radical, elites sharply separated from a diverse but much more nonpolitical and often conservative laity—with all the attendant problems of political effectiveness.[61]

There is some irony here, because on more strictly intrachurch questions the laypeople are often much more liberal than pastors are. On issues such as whether women should be priests, whether the church's stance on divorce should be eased, whether priests may marry, and the like, the laity is notably more change-oriented. But the irony fades when we realize that lay opinion is simply reflecting general American cultural attitudes on these issues. It is, if you will, merely more evidence of how acculturated or integrated Catholic laypeople are. The relative conservatism of pastors on these issues is, similarly, another signal of their detachment from the liberal culture's imperatives.[62]

The Catholic hierarchy has moved to the political forefront in recent times on three political issues: abortion, nuclear war, and the American economy. Unlike with the issue of abortion, the bishops, operating through the National Conference of Roman Catholic Bishops by tackling the subjects of nuclear war and disarmament and the American economic order, chose to enter the realm of political controversy on their own. In both instances their "letters" have hardly been essays in complacent conformity with current American norms, though they have also been less than full-scale challenges.[63]

In 1983 the bishops issued their pastoral letter, *Challenge of Peace*, after a lengthy period of public and private discussion within and without the church. It was a process that took the document through a refining process involving several drafts and innumerable controversies.[64] Mary

61. For a good, if brief, discussion of trends regarding laity and leadership in the U.S. Roman Catholic Church, see Reichley, *Religion in American Public Life*, pp. 285-302.

62. David C. Leege and Joseph Gremillion, "The People, Their Pastors, and the Church: Viewpoints on Church Policies and Positions," in *Notre Dame Study of Catholic Parish Life*, Report No. 7 (March 1986), p. 4.

63. See Kennedy, *The Now and Future Church*.

64. See "Challenge of Peace: God's Promise and Our Response," *Catholic Herald*, 7 April 1983; Jim Castelli, *The Bishops and the Bomb: Waging Peace in a Nuclear Age (with text of the Bishops' 1983 Pastoral)* (Garden City, NY: Doubleday-Anchor, 1983); Mary T. Hanna, "From Civil Religion to Prophetic Church: American Bishops and the Bomb," unpublished paper, pp. 1-18; John K. O'Connell, "The Catholic Church on Nuclear Arms and Warfare,"

Hanna's analysis is the best I have seen on the document's historic importance, which cannot be summed up by its actual contents.[65] Its attack on the possibility of nuclear war, its denunciation of the first use of nuclear weapons, its general "peace" orientation, and particularly its invocation of the central religious duty to protect human life were important. But though somewhat unusually dressed in theological garb, these themes were familiar as themes of current liberal and left-wing peace politics in American life. There was nothing very radical there. Significantly, the bishops did not renounce just war theory, urge unilateral nuclear disarmament, or support pacifism.

What was historic was the decision of the bishops to propel themselves and their more or less collective opinion into larger policy debates not traditional in the American church (unlike abortion policy). That is, the church leadership leaped into politics beyond its normal provinces, and it appears eager to stay right there. Also historic was the bishops' position on war in light of the Catholic Church's American past, a past marked by a sometimes hyperaggressive patriotism.

Both dimensions have significance for the future in that they may lead to a Catholic Church that is both ready to enter politics and ready to clash with conventional notions of patriotism. Such perspectives would be essential for any serious challenge to American liberal order. But the fact remains that the specifics of the bishops' letter on nuclear war, granting that it did not accord with the Reagan policy of the time, simply was not a radical challenge.

The same is true of their letter on the U.S. economy, *Economic Justice for All*, which followed in the mid-1980s. As with the nuclear war letter, the letter on the economy went through several drafts. The first draft, published in 1984, was the subject of considerable debate and discussion;[66]

unpublished paper, 2 December 1982, pp. 1-11; Roger Mahoney, "The Catholic Conscience and Nuclear War: Becoming a Church of Peace Advocacy," *Commonweal* 109 (23 March 1982): 137-43.

65. Hanna, "From Civil Religion to Prophetic Church"; on the issue overall, see Reichley, *Religion in American Public Life*, pp. 294-99.

66. "Excerpts from Draft of Bishops' Letter on the U.S. Economy," *New York Times*, 12 November 1984; see "The Bishops' Pastoral on the U.S. Economy: Reaction to the First Draft," *Overview*, February 1985, pp. 1-6; "Catholic Bishops and American Economics: A Survey of Comment, and Some of Our Own," *Religion and Society Report*, March 1985, pp. B1-B10; Eugene Kennedy, "America's Activist Bishops: Examining Capitalism," *New York Times Magazine*, 12 August 1984; Joseph Berger, "U.S. Bishops Laud Economic Letter," *New York Times*, 14 November 1985; Charles P. Alexander, "An Unwavering Voice for the Poor," *Time*, 14 October 1985.

the second draft opened in 1985.[67] The third and final draft of *Economic Justice for All*, issued in 1986, reflected the dialectic over previous drafts, but its form did not eliminate its controversy, to the probable relief of its authors.[68] Controversy has emerged at every stage. Some in the media have suggested that the letter is some kind of a basic attack on the U.S. economic arrangement.[69] Some leading conservative Catholics, especially Michael Novak and associates, agreed with the media and released a counter "lay letter" in anticipation of the third draft's publication, called *Toward the Future: Catholic Social Thought and the U.S. Economy*.[70] Others have faulted the document for numerous other reasons: its confidence about extremely complex issues, its lack of technical expertise, its taste for failed statist policies.[71]

The bishops' letter makes a serious effort to ground its teachings in Christianity, undertaking specifically to be biblical. It is careful to underscore the biblical basis for its economic outlook by emphasizing biblical injunctions on behalf of people as creations of God, the value of community, the call to discipleship, concern for the poor, and the duty to love one's neighbor. For the bishops, indeed, every economy is properly understood as "men and women working together to develop and care for the whole of God's creation."[72]

When the letter gets down to the U.S. economy, the mood becomes negative. Its economic picture of America includes "massive and ugly" failures at home and considerable U.S. responsibility for world poverty and starvation. Unemployment is the worst evil, one that the bishops link directly with America's "harsh poverty." Moreover, poor people too often struggle to cope, alienated, powerless, and without much community. The bishops give considerable attention to what should be done, granting that their policy proposals cannot carry the moral authority of

67. Philip F. Lawler, *How Bishops Decide: An American Catholic Case Study* (Washington, DC: Ethics and Public Policy Center, 1986).

68. National Conference of Catholic Bishops, *Economic Justice for All: Catholic Social Teaching and the U.S. Economy* (Washington, DC: National Conference of Catholic Bishops, 1986).

69. E.g., Alexander, "An Unwavering Voice for the Poor."

70. See *Toward the Future: Catholic Social Thought and the U.S. Economy: A Lay Letter* (New York: Lay Commission on Catholic Social Teaching and the U.S. Economy, 1984).

71. For a good range, see Robert Royal, ed., *Challenge and Response: Critiques of the Catholic Bishops' Draft Letter on the U.S. Economy* (Washington, DC: Ethics and Public Policy Center, 1985).

72. National Conference of Catholic Bishops, *Economic Justice for All*, p. 1, ch. 2.

their biblically based analysis. The result is a cornucopia of proposals on virtually every imaginable subject possibly related to economic life, which may be summed up as an enthusiastic endorsement of a vastly expanded welfare state.[73]

This is not exactly radicalism. The letter explicitly defends private property; and it specifically opposes statism: "The Church opposes all statist . . . approaches to socio-economic questions. Social life is richer than governmental power can encompass."[74] Otherwise, the letter's ideas are no more radical than those of conventional left-liberals in the Democratic party, as others have pointedly observed. Andrew Greeley remarks: "The bishops . . . have produced a document that is little more than a rehash of the party-line liberal conventional wisdom of five to fifteen years ago. . . . They have . . . provided religious underpinning for the latter-day New Deal of the . . . Democratic party platform."[75] Charles Krauthammer agrees: "The bishops' . . . remedies . . . amount to more Great Society programs. . . . Where have they been for twenty-five years?"[76] No doubt the bishops' approach is unpopular in the United States today, even in the Democratic party. But this is not the same as viewing the letter as evidence that the church (or its bishops) is taking up the role of radical prophecy.

Coming on the heels of the nuclear war pastoral, however, the pastoral on the U.S. economy strengthens the idea that the ground is being laid for such a role, if the American bishops elect to pursue it in the future on some issues. Whether they will go that route is uncertain; but even more uncertain is whether "the church" will find many people prepared to follow along, judging from lay reaction to those first two pastorals. One might say that it is perhaps too early to tell from the letter on the U.S. economy. The evidence regarding the less controversial nuclear war pastoral seems at best ambiguous. Kenneth Wald interprets Roman Catholic lay opinion studies to suggest that the nuclear letter made an impact. Catholic opinion regarding defense spending and related issues has grown more liberal.[77] Perhaps this is true, but no mobilization for change in our nuclear policies has taken place from the pews.

73. *Ibid.*, pp. 1, 4, 5, 18-32, ch. 3.

74. *Ibid.*, pp. 31, 33-34.

75. Andrew M. Greeley, "A 'Radical' Dissent," in *Challenge and Response*, p. 33.

76. Charles Krauthammer, "Perils of the Prophet Motive," in *Challenge and Response*, p. 52.

77. Kenneth D. Wald, *Religion and Politics in the United States* (New York: St. Martin's, 1986), pp. 228-29.

Thus it remains true that while the bishops may make pronouncements just as the National Council of Churches does, that is something far different from a united church, organized and committed to change. We can characterize those pronouncements merely as a church representing potential challenge.

A third issue, opposition to abortion, obviously has also attracted strong support from the Catholic hierarchy.[78] But the first activists from Catholicism on this issue after the 1973 *Roe v. Wade* decision were laypeople. On this issue more than any other, the leadership and the laity of the Catholic church are relatively united.[79] Catholics of all sorts are involved in a variety of groups fighting abortion and seeking changes to deny abortions (though a few Catholics are also prominent in the "pro-choice" movement). However, despite impressions to the contrary, the organizations opposing abortion on demand are not merely arms of the Roman Catholic Church, nor do Catholics constitute almost all the opponents of abortion.[80] The truth is much more complicated. Some organizations are closely affiliated with the Catholic hierarchy, others are definitely not; most today are coalitions of many people, certainly including a great many evangelical and fundamentalist Protestants, for whom opposition to abortion has become more and more important in recent years.[81]

The antiabortion struggle demonstrates that when many laypeople within the Catholic Church join with influential and committed elements of the hierarchy, things happen politically. Abortion foes have not succeeded in reversing *Roe v. Wade;* but if they have not scaled the heights on which the Supreme Court sits or found two-thirds of Congress ready to pass a constitutional amendment to their liking (in part because of dis-

78. A good summary is in Reichley, *Religion in American Public Life,* pp. 291-94.

79. Data on abortion and Roman Catholic views of various sorts is abundant; see, e.g., "The Views of American Catholics," *New York Times,* 25 November 1985; Fowler, *Religion and Politics in America,* pp. 187-88; Greeley, *American Catholics since the Council,* pp. 82-83; probably the best and most wide-ranging discussion of assorted Catholics and abortion may be found in Mary T. Hanna, *Catholics and American Politics* (Cambridge: Harvard University Press, 1979); see also Hertzke, *Representing God in Washington,* ch. 5.

80. For a good illustration of such an error, see Frederick S. Jaffe et al., *Abortion Politics: Private Morality and Public Policy* (New York: McGraw-Hill, 1981); for an informed response, see Peter Skerry, "The Class Conflict over Abortion," *Public Interest* 52 (Summer 1978): 69-84.

81. Franky Schaeffer, *A Time for Anger* (Westchester, IL: Crossway Books, 1982). This is the classic anti-abortion, pro-action evangelical book.

agreements over what exactly it should say), they have been extremely successful in Congress in stripping away all national funding support for abortions.[82] And this success has come despite the fact that while the nation's majority shares their dislike for abortion on demand, it also supports a woman's right to choose whether or not to have an abortion.[83]

On this issue Catholic political involvement is obvious, and so is its noticeable record of success. But does the Roman Catholic Church's (and its allies') antiabortion struggle constitute dramatic evidence of organized religion as a challenge to contemporary American liberalism? A case can be made for it and, in fact, has been made, especially through books by such evangelicals as Franky Schaeffer and John Whitehead.[84] They insist that abortion foes represent "the people" and the traditions of Americans in a contest with liberal elites now in control of the soul of America. These critics maintain that they are radicals of a special sort, radical in opposition to the un-American, secular usurpers who have seized American culture. This posture represents challenge, but I think we can best term it a conservative or reactionary challenge.

Among Catholic activists, however, a new radicalism is less often their conception of what is going on; they rarely operate at so theoretical a plane. Their main argument is concrete: the straightforward and familiar "right-to-life" position, one that they do not see as radical at all. And indeed, who *could* see it as radical in philosophical terms? After all, ours is a "liberal" culture with a great emphasis on rights and the individual.[85] In practical terms, though, Catholic forces are in substantial conflict with the culture on abortion; and the potential is there for similar clashes on nuclear policy, economic policy, and more. At present, though, neither the Catholic Church leadership nor its laity is committed to such confrontations. The pastorals on war and economics have been somewhat timid, and lay support usually has been mild, guaranteeing that a disciplined, effective organization for political change is absent.

One crucial factor in assessing the future is the role of the papacy. How much will it encourage a more prophetic role for the church? How much will it advise a more political application of prophecy? It will also be important how much liberation theology pervades the American

82. Fowler, *Religion and Politics in America,* pp. 186-89 and 191-92; Reichley, *Religion in American Public Life,* pp. 291-94.

83. Victoria A. Sackett, "Between Pro-Life and Pro-Choice," *Public Opinion,* April-May 1985, pp. 53-55.

84. See Schaeffer, *A Time for Anger;* John W. Whitehead, *The Second American Revolution* (Elgin, IL: David C. Cook, 1982).

85. A lot of other things are also at stake. See Kristin Luker, *Abortion and the Politics of Motherhood* (Berkeley: University of California Press, 1984).

Catholic Church—as well as Vatican reaction to it. Up to this point, liberation theology has received a mixed reception at the Vatican. The unmistakable connection with Marxism, including the latter's emphasis on class and conflict (sometimes including approval of violent conflict), has not gone over well in Rome. Neither have attacks on hierarchical church principles. On the other hand, Rome has applauded liberation theology's concern for the poor and for developing institutions exemplifying an egalitarian and communal order.[86] Liberation theology has not as yet penetrated the great body of the American Catholic Church. Some clergy and bishops are obvious enthusiasts, and so are orders such as the Maryknolls, especially some orders of nuns. But despite the enthusiasm of such publications as the leftish *National Catholic Reporter,* lay knowledge—not to mention support—appears scanty.[87]

In another day or another era the story may be different. But even then liberation theology will face what the National Council of Catholic Bishops faces: a diverse Catholic laity who will not easily agree on, much less mobilize for, *any* agenda for the public arena. It will also face a laity that does not look to the church for a political agenda, certainly not for radical politics. And it would have to grapple with a laity that may, if anything, be growing more conservative over time.[88] The laity simply does not appear to be available for a change-oriented Catholic politics. There is little sign—except regarding abortion—that the hierarchy's official ethical-political teachings penetrate the laity and generate a consensus. It may be that religion plays some role in many Catholics' political attitudes; but if so, the existing evidence suggests that *varying* images of God are much more important than pastors' homilies or bishops' letters.[89]

The continued opposition of Rome and the American bishops to overt electoral participation by the church, strongly reinforced by lay approval of at least this aspect of separation of church and state, is another

86. Kenneth Woodward, "The Holy Seesaw: Up and Down on Liberation Theology," *Newsweek,* 14 April 1986.

87. Reichley, *Religion in American Public Life,* pp. 301-2.

88. *Ibid.,* 299-302; for another view on the political drift of Roman Catholicism, see Greeley, *American Catholics since the Council,* ch. 3.

89. An interesting approach here is in Thomas John Hoffman, "Religion and Politics: An Empirical Inquiry," Ph.D. diss., University of Arizona, 1982. Much more work is needed in this, and it will very definitely have to start from a position of great awareness regarding the degrees and kinds of church involvement of lay Catholics. A place to start is David C. Leege and Thomas A. Trozzolo, "Participation in Catholic Parish Life: Religious Rites and Parish Activities in the 1980s," in *Notre Dame Study of Catholic Parish Life,* Report No. 3 (April 1983), pp. 1-8.

significant impediment to the metamorphosis of the Roman Catholic Church into an institution concerned with effective radicalism. The old Catholic strategy of politics through the back door, even when it is "modernized" by public declarations and lobbying, still leaves out an electoral connection. Only on abortion, and there only through allied organizations, have church leaders countenanced direct electoral interventions. One suspects that this policy will have to change dramatically before prophecy can become serious politics, and the prospects for that are nonexistent at present. For all its bishops' tentative gropings toward prophecy, the Catholic Church is far too integrated into liberal America to risk such strategic radicalism.[90]

An Afterword on the Sanctuary Movement

DURING THE MID-1980s, involvement in what became known as the "sanctuary movement" was for a time *the* issue among politically liberal Protestants and some similarly inclined Catholics. The movement sought to offer asylum to refugees from Central American countries (though not from Nicaragua) who, they believed, were fleeing a political persecution the U.S. government would not acknowledge—and was often the cause of. The refugees they protected were illegal refugees in the United States, and conflict with the U.S. government in the courts and elsewhere was integral to the history and the symbolism of this issue. The sanctuary struggle has had its ironies, notably that liberal Protestant churches have been engaged in assisting mostly Catholic Central Americans who are fleeing to a country many feel is the cause of their political persecution.

Why this movement took on such intense overtones among its liberal Protestant supporters is not immediately obvious. Part of the answer lies in the concreteness of the issue: single churches can "do something" to reduce the suffering in God's world by offering sanctuary to actual individuals or families. Perhaps another part of the explanation lies in this chapter's analysis: the popularity of the sanctuary movement may rest in part on its rather fascinating combination of political and private religion. Its political side, with its entry into public space, its challenge to government law and practice, and its insistence on religion's command to undertake such prophetic action is perfectly obvious. In this sense it seems to be standard fare for the political parts of politically liberal or

90. More and more the degree and kind of appropriate political action for the church is contested. Contrast Kenneth A. Briggs, "Leader of Catholic Bishops Drafts Statement Opposing Partisanship," *New York Times*, 9 August 1984; and "Catholics Urged to Press Views," *New York Times*, 10 August 1984.

leftist Protestantism and Roman Catholicism. On the other hand, it reaches deep into the traditional, nonpolitical well of American religion. For the sanctuary movement in name and practice is about an escape from politics—the politics of a foreign government as well as the politics of our government. It is about retreat, escape, sanctuary, and in this sense it evolves an image of church and religion that is close to what most Americans both understand and treasure. It is thus almost an appropriately ambivalent political-nonpolitical issue for religious activists. Moreover, in its concentration on the adoption of refugees by a local church, the sanctuary movement routinely emphasizes its view of the church and religion as community-oriented. It affirms community both in the sense that church and religion can serve as a refuge from a warring world and in the sense of concretely realizing God's teaching of the truth that we are all one human family. From this analysis, then, the sanctuary movement was and is no fluke. It reflects (for those who share its political assumptions) both the inward and outward inclinations of American religion. It is about prophetic politics, refuge from politics, and the affirmation of our common membership in God's community.[91]

91. On the sanctuary movement see: Richard Ostling, "A Defeat for Sanctuary," *Time*, 12 May 1986; sanctuary issue of *Sojourners*, March 1985; Art Laffin, "The Final Verdict," *Sojourners*, March 1986, p. 35; Christina Medvescek, "Sanctuary Convictions; Law over Justice," *Christian Century*, pp. 4-11 June 1986; Vicki Kemper, "'Guilty of the Gospel': Convicted Sanctuary Workers Vowed to Continue Work," *Sojourners*, June 1986, pp. 8-9; William C. Ryan, "The Historical Case for the Right of Sanctuary," *Journal of Church and State* 29 (1987): 209-32.

CHAPTER SEVEN

Conservative Protestants: The Challenge That Is Not

THE CHANGE THAT HAS DRAMATICALLY ALTERED THE LANDSCAPE of religion and politics in the United States in the last ten to fifteen years has been the sharp opening to politics by many Protestant fundamentalists and evangelicals. Fully one-quarter of the nations' population identify themselves in this religious tradition. Moreover, while mainline Protestant denominations continue their relative and often absolute decline in numbers, conservative Protestantism continues its steady growth.[1] It could well claim to be the "mainline" form of Protestantism in the United States today.

The partial—and often self-consciously ambivalent—embrace of politics by many in the theologically conservative Protestant movement (evangelicals and fundamentalists) in recent years is historic. While there have been highly political moments in Protestant religious history, such as the crusade for Prohibition, the dominant motif among theologically conservative Protestants since the 1930s has been nonpolitical, often antipolitical. Politics and salvation were realms that had little or no connection.

This very shift from quiet avoidance of politics to a not unmixed engagement with politics by conservative Protestants may be the most important evidence of challenge in American religion today. On the surface, at least, the shift hardly reflects a politics of accommodation with the basic "modernist" values of contemporary culture.[2] Conservative Christians are

1. A. James Reichley, *Religion in American Public Life* (Washington, DC: Brookings, 1985), p. 324; *Religion in America: 50 Years, 1935-1985* (Gallup Report No. 236, May 1985), p. 11; Phillip Barron Jones, "An Examination of the Statistical Growth of the Southern Baptist Convention," in *Understanding Church Growth and Decline, 1950-1978,* ed. Dean R. Hoge and David A. Roozen (New York: Pilgrim, 1979), pp. 160-78.

2. For a rich source of data on future evangelical elites—which unconvincingly suggests the future might be quite "modernist"—see James Davison Hunter, *Evangelicalism: The Coming Generation* (Chicago: University of Chicago Press, 1987).

in politics to change our culture. They want to abolish much of modern America, and recover the past. Pat Robertson, for example, stresses over and over the theme of "loss." So much has been lost to Americans. The majority have lost their rights; our nation's spiritual basis is lost; our government has lost a sense of "fiscal responsibility"; and so on. The answer is for Christians to get into politics and change things.[3]

The theme that conservative Christians who have turned to politics represent a radical challenge from a new source obviously poses a major problem for my theory of the relationship between religion and culture today. If religion indirectly supports the established culture in America, how can one explain the emergence of the religious right? And how can one come to terms with its apparent challenge in principle and in practice?

The burst of political energy from conservative Protestant circles over the past ten years has, of course, drawn a great deal of attention. Some commentators calmly stress that this activity does not mean much of anything of significance in the impact of particular religious values on the society as a whole. Some suggest that the United States is too stable and integrated a nation for extremists to mount a successful cultural challenge.[4] Others have argued that much of the renewed interest in public affairs largely reflects conservative Protestantism's desire to be heard, motivated by its leaders' acute sense that their influence on society's elites and culture in general is steadily diminishing. In this view, the resurgence of interest in politics by conservative Christians constitutes no particularly startling statement about the relationship between religion and American culture.[5]

Perhaps surprisingly, a number of other analysts see evidence that the emergence of Christian conservatives does nothing to undermine the idea that religion in America is continuing in its longtime integrative role. One version argues that the very interest in politics among these Christians is a major step toward integration, especially among fundamentalists, most of whom have traditionally adopted an ethic of radical separatism.[6] Another view proposes that we examine the moral program at the center of conservative Christian demands: its emphasis on

3. Pat Robertson, *America's Date with Destiny* (Nashville: Nelson, 1986), pp. 84-85, 185, 193-94, 300-304, ch. 14.

4. As argued in John H. Simpson, "Moral Issues and Status Politics," in *The New Christian Right: Mobilization and Legitimization,* ed. Robert C. Liebman and Robert Wuthnow (New York: Aldine de Gruyter, 1983), ch. 10.

5. Richard John Neuhaus, *What the Fundamentalists Want* (Washington, DC: Ethics and Public Policy Center, 1985).

6. James A. Speer, "The New Christian Right and Its Parent Company: A Study in Political Contrasts," in *New Christian Politics,* ed. David G. Bromley and Anson Shupe (Macon, GA: Mercer University Press, 1984), pp. 19-40.

conventional sexual behavior and sexual models, its support for prayer in schools, its opposition to drugs, its criticism of pornography, and other programs align it closely with established—and popular—moral beliefs in society. This is hardly radical.[7] A third view underscores status tensions as the cause of the upheaval produced by conservative Christians' entrance into politics. By this analysis, they are angry people who feel dispossessed and left out of American life. There is, these theorists suggest, nothing radical or revolutionary here, just another ugly fight over status and position in America.[8] There is an even more conspiracy-oriented interpretation, which points to the new religious right as a tool of capitalist economic interests and sees it as a fundamentally conservative, or integrative, force. In this view, the activist religious conservatives seek to prop up very established economic elites and institutions.[9]

I think it is clear, however, that the sometimes furious assault on the political activism of evangelicals and fundamentalists has proceeded from a suspicion that the challenge rather than the integration hypothesis is correct. While the sense that conservative religious forces are an immediate threat has lessened, an attitude of deepfelt antagonism remains among many liberals, and that antagonism is rooted in the sense that these opponents seek to change the basic contours of liberal, modernist America. No wonder the national Democratic party, *Time, Newsweek, The New York Times, The Washington Post,* the American Civil Liberties Union, Norman Lear's People for the American Way, and so many others have taken up the cudgels of assault.[10] Denunciations from within American religion have joined these secular assaults, with voices being raised in the American Jewish Committee, the National Council of Churches, the Lutheran Council, the United Methodist Church, and the United

7. John H. Simpson, "Support for the Moral Majority and Its Sociomoral Platform," in *New Christian Politics,* pp. 65-68.

8. Simpson, "Moral Issues and Status Politics."

9. Charles L. Harper and Kevin Leicht, "Explaining the New Religious Right: Status Politics and Beyond," in *New Christian Politics,* pp. 101-10.

10. Several recent examples of elite media treatments are Richard N. Ostling, "Power, Glory—and Politics: Right-Wing Preachers Dominate the Dial," *Time,* 17 February 1986; Harold Kurtz, "Lobbying—the Opposite of Crusade: How Norman Lear's Group Battles to Keep Religion out of Public Affairs," *Washington Post National Weekly Edition,* 17 February 1986; Tina Rosenberg offers some skepticism about the sense of the media assault in "How the Media Made the Moral Majority," *Washington Monthly,* May 1982, pp. 26-29, 32-34; on the general leanings of media elite, see S. Robert Lichter, Stanley Rothman, and Linda S. Lichter, *The Media Elite* (Bethesda, MD: Adler and Adler, 1986); for an able and nonmedia version, see James Guth, "The Politics of the 'Evangelical Right': An Interpretive Essay," paper read at the American Political Science Association, 1981.

Church of Christ, among others.[11] Together they have forged an alliance of politically liberal religious and secular forces determined to repulse the drive of the religious right. Their intensity has easily matched their opponents; and, ironically, may well have assisted in the formation (if not the goals) of the religious right.[12]

Much of the argumentation between these two sides has been less than ennobling. The air has been poisoned with wild charges, absolutist declarations, and intentional scare tactics. Each side's charges have mirrored the other side's.[13] Some criticisms of the religious right have been embarrassing, particularly religious and secular liberals' charges that conservative Christians are violating sacred boundaries of church and state. Such claims imply that these boundaries are or have been fixed for all time in the form in which the Warren Supreme Court cast them, an error either of ignorance or cunning that begs the real question of what are the proper boundaries of church and state, religion and politics. Moreover, such alarms display an irritating hypocritical side that has been frequently noted.[14] Somehow conservative Christian activity in politics threatens the First Amendment, but there were no such anxieties in the 1960s when liberal churches rushed to back the civil rights movement. Nor do we hear many expressed today when the National Council of Churches pronounces on this or that public question.[15] On the other hand, some criticisms have concentrated on the substantive proposals of conservative Christian groups, a growing part. Critics object to these groups' persistent challenging of existing policies on welfare, abortion, and ecology. And at a deeper level critics insist that conservative religious activists threaten the basic American compact encouraging diversity and tolerance of opinions as well as lifestyles.[16] The tone is usually urgent and intense, moreover, because they perceive these challenges to be real. To its liberal critics, the religious right is no paper tiger.

Because of the rather charged atmosphere surrounding the Chris-

11. Robert Booth Fowler, *Religion and Politics in America* (Metuchen, NJ: Scarecrow Press, 1985), pp. 183-84; for more detail see Allan Hertzke, *Representing God in Washington: The Role of Religious Lobbies in the American Polity* (Knoxville: University of Tennessee Press, 1988).

12. Rosenberg, "How the Media Made the Moral Majority."

13. See, for example, James Davison Hunter, "The Liberal Reaction," in *The New Christian Right,* ch. 8.

14. Robert W. Lee, "The Hypocrisy about Religion and Politics," *Conservative Digest,* December 1986, pp. 85-94.

15. As pointed out in Neuhaus, *The Naked Public Square: Religion and Democracy in America* (Grand Rapids: Eerdman, 1984), p. 10.

16. See, e.g., "Oh So Sure They're Right," Editorial, *New York Times,* 9 September 1984, p. 24E.

tian conservative movement, it remains appropriate to step back and dispassionately analyze its implications. Its vocabulary often resonates with challenge, but challenge to what? And what lies behind the vocabulary? How much serious alienation from the American liberal order really exists among conservative Protestants today?

I suspect the mood of challenge from conservative Christians is probably more rhetorical than fundamental. But the rhetorical dimension cannot be ignored; to do so would be to brush aside the self-image of conservative Christian leaders. After all, they insist that they are Christians who are confronting American culture, posing challenges that no committed Christian dare avoid. They believe that they must do so despite the criticism that liberal culture inflicts on them. This is a price, they proclaim, that must be paid, since "as Christians we have a higher calling than being 'open-minded' or even of being 'good Americans' or 'pluralistic.'"[17] The task is formidable, they say, because the "secularist alternative to the Judeo-Christian vision is no longer an 'alternative' or even 'radical' but has, in fact, become the *establishment*." Meanwhile, "we who are Christians . . . are the *new radicals and the true alternative minority*."[18]

Obviously, the alarms sounded by Rev. Jerry Falwell on the airwaves and in his books are the best-known expression of this mood within both fundamentalism and the general public.[19] Franky Schaeffer and John Whitehead have been at the forefront of those sounding the alarms within evangelicalism. These voices and others repeatedly insist that American society is all but abandoned to a soul-destroying "secular humanism" (liberalism), disloyal to God, worshipful of "relativism, Mammon, and libertinism." It is for them a time of the greatest possible crisis for American Christians, almost the last days for their influence in this civilization. No wonder they spend much of their time urging major changes by increasingly radical means.[20]

But this is not the whole story. The Christian right's challenge exists, but it is very selective: its essence is an attack on the *secular* nature of modern liberal America. They mount this attack in fear—almost desperation—at times, but it is not a challenge to the liberalism of Amer-

17. Franky Schaeffer, *Bad News for Modern Man: An Agenda for Christian Activism* (Westchester, IL: Crossway Books, 1984), p. 78.

18. *Ibid.*, p. 71.

19. The best way to follow the Jerry Falwell view of the past decade—even better than TV—is to read *The Moral Majority Report;* also his books, such as *Listen America* (Garden City, NY: Doubleday, 1980).

20. See Schaeffer, *Bad News for Modern Man;* John Whitehead, *The Second American Revolution* (Elgin, IL: David C. Cook, 1982); William A. Stanmeyer, *Clear and Present Danger: Church and State in Post-Christian America* (Ann Arbor: Servant Books, 1983).

ican culture, historically understood. Far from it. Indeed, it is a staple of this conservative challenge to object to contemporary liberalism in the name of the American liberalism of the past, a liberalism that included a broad role for religion in general and Protestant Christianity in particular.[21] It is standard fare for the religious right to affirm the legitimacy of considerable personal liberty and to contrast that with the liberty-denying policies of current secular elites. Their praise for the consent of the governed and republican government is frequent, and they contrast it with rule by media and Washington elites. And despite charges by their critics, they celebrate selective tolerance, a tolerance especially for the properly religious. Nor does the conservative Christian movement fault most of the traditional liberal institutions. On the contrary, its spokesmen usually laud government institutions; and the same is true, predictably, of the American economic system. They even criticize the public school more in sadness than anger: if only it were the school of old, devoted to basics, including instruction in "fundamental" religious and ethical values, it would be excellent.[22]

In conservative Christian jeremiads, a clearly demarcated other creature is at fault: *contemporary liberalism*. It has shamelessly tried to drive religion out of public life and all of American culture; it has turned to elitism and state-worship; it has threatened capitalism, constitutional government, and our very nationhood (by its softness on communism); it has allowed neighborhoods to be polluted by pornography, abortion on demand, dirty movies, and vulgar rock music. The list is endless.[23] This same thesis, that the unease among conservative Protestants has its roots in a distaste for contemporary liberalism rather than for our fundamental liberal order, finds confirmation in data on lay attitudes. Lay opinions reveal marked discontent with the present operation of a wide range of American institutions; but there are no such complaints about the institutions themselves. These they applaud. It is their policies and practices that they single out. This distinction may be more imagined

21. Whitehead perfectly articulates this view in *The Second American Revolution*, chs. 3-6.

22. Typical "conservative" Christian views are found in Colonel V. Doner, ed., *The Christian Voice Guide: Strategies for Reclaiming America* (Pacific Grove, CA: Renod, 1984); Schaeffer, *A Time for Anger* (Westchester, IL: Crossway Books, 1982); Whitehead, *The Second American Revolution;* Falwell, *Listen America*.

23. Examples of attacks on contemporary liberal values and their social consequences are: (1) pro-abortion policy: Schaeffer, *A Time for Anger;* (2) loose construction of the Constitution: Whitehead, *The Second American Revolution;* (3) everything: Falwell, *Listen America*.

than real, in fact, but its presence demonstrates discernible limits of lay discontent.[24]

One must conclude that the religious right, and conservative Christians in general, cannot be easily labeled as radicals in any sweeping sense. They *are* change-oriented, and they have already made a change of undeniable importance by activating a portion of conservative Protestantism and directing it into American politics. Their leaders do intend to make a difference in the way liberalism is interpreted and in the way our institutions operate. But again, though some of their leaders say that they are radicals, echoing their opponents—the ACLU, Norman Lear and the People for the American Way—the evidence is not there.[25] They are really neither radicals in a reactionary sense nor status quo conservatives. *Traditionalist*— if one grants for a moment their understanding of traditional American institutions and traditional liberalism—is the better term. As traditionalists they do represent opposition to many elites and current practices in our culture, but not to the culture itself in any fundamental fashion.

In any case, there is good reason to deprecate the challenge of the religious right from a purely practical point of view. Granted, new religious right groups such as the Moral Majority, Religious Roundtable, and Concerned Women of America, even as young as they are, have made an impact on the American political scene. Yet the distance they need to travel for long-term, sustained influence looks longer.[26] This judgment is roundly underscored by the failed 1988 Pat Robertson campaign for the Republican presidential nomination. The Moral Majority (now absorbed into the Liberty Federation) illustrates well the once underestimated practical limitations facing mobilized Christian conservatives. Especially during the early 1980s, the Moral Majority radiated confidence and a sense of power. Their opponents in the secular media and elsewhere expressed fear, but sustained influence was harder to achieve than it seemed.[27] Indeed, it looks much harder from a current perspective. The scare stories have stopped now, and sober, practical assessments of these groups have come to the fore.[28]

24. Reichley, *Religion in American Public Life,* pp. 314-31, sums up the data here nicely.

25. *Ibid.,* p. 331.

26. For a reflective discussion of the main groups, their strengths, their weaknesses, and their future, see James L. Guth, "The New Christian Right," in *The New Christian Right,* ch. 2; see also Fowler, *Religion and Politics in America,* pp. 203-27.

27. Larry Martz, "Trouble on the Far Right: Has Success Spoiled Political Fundamentalism?" *Newsweek,* 14 April 1986.

28. *Moral Majority Report,* 17 November 1980; Lisa Meyers, *Washing-

In retrospect, the frantic alarms seem puzzling; the actual impact of the Moral Majority on policy (as opposed to popular rhetoric) appears very modest at best. Even claims about the Moral Majority's clout in the 1980 and 1984 elections are in inverse proportion to the slim social science data to sustain them.[29] Once again the American political system has proven more complex and intricate and far harder to overturn than it might appear.

This lack of evidence that the Moral Majority has taken the country by storm is now no surprise. We know that popular support for the Moral Majority has consistently been extremely limited. In 1980, for example, only 5 percent of the electorate judged themselves strong supporters of the organization and its aims; perhaps another 7 percent were sympathetic to some degree; while an overwhelming 68 percent were hostile. And subsequent surveys show no particular increase in support. It is far from a popular group.[30]

It may see more controversial to argue that the Moral Majority has struggled with equally limited success to obtain power within the presidency. Yet that is what the record shows. One can easily point out that Ronald Reagan, following Jimmy Carter, openly and eagerly courted conservative Christians; but what this meant concretely for the Moral Majority is something else again. The Moral Majority got nowhere in-

ton Star, 30 June 1980; "A Tide," *Newsweek*, 15 September 1980; "Falwellians' Force Is Hard to Resist," *Milwaukee Journal*, 25 October 1983; Ben Stein, "The War over What We'll See on TV," *Chicago Tribune*, 22 February 1981; Stein, "Norman Lear vs. the Moral Majority," *Saturday Review*, February 1981, pp. 23-27; John Scanzoni, "Resurgent Fundamentalism," *Christian Century* 97 (10-17 September 1980): 847-49.

29. Reichley, *Religion in American Public Life*, pp. 319-27; E. C. Ladd, *Where Have All the Voters Gone?* (New York: Norton, 1982), pp. 99-100; Seymour Martin Lipset and E. Raab, "The Election and the Evangelicals," *Commentary* 71 (March 1981): 25-31; E. H. Buell, Jr., "An Army That Meets Every Sunday? Popular Support for the Moral Majority in 1980," paper presented at the Midwest Political Science Association, 1983; Robert Zwier, *Born-Again Politics: The New Christian Right in America* (Downers Grove, IL: InterVarsity, 1982), ch. 5; Corwin Smidt, "Evangelicals vs. Fundamentalists: An Analysis of the Political Characteristics and Importance of Two Major Religious Movements within American Politics," paper presented at the Midwest Political Science Association, 1983; Ronald Stockton, "The Falwell Core," paper presented at the American Political Science Association, 1985.

30. Buell, "An Army That Meets Every Sunday?"; Anson Shupe and William Stacey, "The Moral Majority Constituency," in *The New Christian Right*, p. 105; Simpson, "Support for the Moral Majority and Its Sociomoral Platform," pp. 65-68; Stockton, "The Falwell Core."

side the Carter presidency, as it knows so very well. This explains in a good part why its leadership turned against Carter with such intense—and thinly disguised—animosity. The Reagan record is more complex. President Reagan praised leaders and allies on the religious right time and again. He supported their central concerns, such as banning abortions, reintroducing prayer in the public schools, fighting communism, and reinforcing our national defense. Moreover, President Reagan appointed officials who—at one time at least—met with the Moral Majority's highest approval, men such as Surgeon General C. Everett Koop and Bob Billings, former executive director of the Moral Majority.[31]

But the Reagan administration offered little but symbolic support. Talk has flowed, but President Reagan appointed no Christian conservative activist to any central policy-making position in his Cabinet. Nor did he show any real muscle in pushing the religious right's program, except for issues that command far broader support than their appeal to some religious conservatives (e.g., national defense). On the social issues in particular, the Reagan effort was modest indeed. He used none of his power to push for the wishes of groups like the Moral Majority on abortion or school prayer. As a result, the Moral Majority found itself in the embarrassing position of accepting Reagan's words as enough in order to maintain access.

The influence of the Moral Majority in Congress is harder to trace, but the indications we do have suggest that there is very little. The stimulating, pioneer study by Benson and Williams, *Religion on Capitol Hill*, does not address the specific impact of the Moral Majority; but it does report in detail on the Christian right in Congress, establishing that its congressional adherents are small in number and don't even count among their numbers much more than a majority of the evangelicals and fundamentalists in Congress.[32] What successes the Moral Majority has had in Congress—and that means those limited to the abortion issue—have come from cooperation with the members of Congress not otherwise sympathetic to the Moral Majority, especially Roman Catholics.

Allan Hertzke's more recent work with religious interest groups in Washington superbly documents the complexity and nuances of the pressure group situation for the wide variety of religious lobby organizations. He acknowledges that groups such as the Moral Majority can be effective actors in Washington and can represent quite a new factor in the balance of religious interest groups there. But he also found no sense that

31. D. Edwards, "Key Posts Please Conservatives," *Moral Majority Report,* 16 March 1981.

32. Peter L. Benson and Dorothy L. Williams, *Religion on Capitol Hill: Myths and Realities* (New York: Harper and Row, 1982), esp. ch. 10.

the Moral Majority or other Christian conservative organizations were anywhere near dominance in any policy area.[33] Kenneth Wald goes further and describes their overall public policy efforts as a "failure."[34]

The Moral Majority has not exercised discernible influence on the court system of the United States, as Moral Majority leaders and publications are all too aware. No arena appears to be more frustratingly inaccessible to new religious right efforts, though this lack of influence on the judicial system was the single most important causal factor in the creation of the new religious right. While the Moral Majority has hopes that time will give their persuasion dominance on the Supreme Court, that is at the moment only a hope. For now the federal courts are simply not on their side.[35]

The Moral Majority and a long list of other conservative Christian political groups are equally angry about their lack of influence in the media. This includes, of course, the cultural media, television, and the movies, where, apart from the Christian Broadcasting Network, assorted TV evangelists, and Christian "movies," their influence is low. Movies and TV programming are usually produced and directed by people who are frankly secular, and the rare Christian is not an evangelical or fundamentalist Protestant. Moreover, it is obvious to conservative Protestants, as to everyone else, that modern television programming and the movies usually ignore the subject of religion, as if it simply did not exist. Those references that do make it are not ordinarily flattering. To Christian conservatives, this looks very much like censorship of their world.[36] Even less palatable, however, is the news provided by the leading print media and the major TV news organizations. The issue is not whether there is coverage of the religious right; there has been a great deal of it since 1980. But conservative observers insist that the elite media have treated its ideals, leaders, and organizations with bias and even con-

33. Hertzke, *Representing God in Washington.*

34. Wald, *Religion and Politics in the United States* (New York: St. Martin's, 1986), p. 205.

35. The elevation of William Rehnquist to Chief Justice and Anton Scalia to Associate Justice, while warmly supported by the Christian Right, was symbolic of the half (or maybe better) "program" during the Reagan administration's remaking of the federal judiciary. Both appear to support the Christian right's social agenda. However, neither is a representative of that world; neither is a true son. The newest justice, Anthony Kennedy, appears even less so.

36. See Ben Stein, *The View From Sunset Blvd.* (New York: Basic Books, 1979); "TV: Where the Girls Are Good Looking and the Good Guys Win: But Whose World View Is This?" *Christianity Today,* 4 October 1984.

tempt.[37] In point of fact, some coverage of the Moral Majority (and conservative Christians, in general) has hardly been a model of objectivity.[38]

It would be surprising if it were, given the systematic profile data on Washington correspondents of major newspapers, TV news, and other newsgathering organizations, which show that as a group these individuals are overwhelmingly secular and notably liberal on social issues in particular. There is no evidence whatsoever of any sympathy for the Moral Majority in that world, nor that the Moral Majority has made the slightest dent in modifying newsgatherers' perspectives in directions it would like.[39]

Thus the idea that conservative religious groups were an unstoppable force in U.S. political life was wrong at the start and has stayed wrong. The Moral Majority, for example, has always been an improbable juggernaut for very practical reasons. It has encountered organizational and strategic dilemmas within the organization itself, and these have grown worse over time. Money proved to be harder to raise than it had seemed at first. Maintaining other support and participation also turned out to be difficult once the first glow was over.[40]

Then there were religious and political constraints imposed by the world outside the Moral Majority's conservative Protestant home. Consider the unexpectedly limited religious audience open to the Moral Majority's appeals. Its denials aside, the Moral Majority is not merely a political organization; its center is located in part of the Protestant fundamentalist community, and it seeks to rally religious people to build a movement for change. This might seem to be an advantage. After all, most Americans claim to be religious; most belong to a church, synagogue, or other religious institution; in any week about 40 percent of the population attends church. On the other hand, however, claims of religious interest or membership are not backed up by the majority, who do not even bother to attend church weekly. And once one delves below the fairly perfunctory measure of attendance and begins to talk about serious involvement in religion, organized or otherwise, the available numbers of the deeply "religious" appear to be a decided minority by any measure.[41]

37. E.g., Cliff Kincaid, "The Anti-Christian Bias of Man Media," *Conservative Digest*, December 1986, pp. 13-16.

38. See a rather negative example in note 27 above. But there are degrees; for a range, consider Frances Fitzgerald, "A Disciplined Charging Army," *New Yorker*, 18 May 1981; Ostling, "Power, Glory—and Politics"; Jeffrey K. Hadden, "Televangelism and the Future of American Politics," in *New Christian Politics*, pp. 151-64.

39. See the data reported in Schaeffer, *A Time for Anger*, pp. 26-29.

40. Martz, "Trouble on the Far Right," pp. 24-25.

41. *Religion in America* (Gallup Report), pp. 40-44.

Equally important, a large portion of America's religions are not in sync with the Moral Majority and similar groups, which is no surprise given the incredible diversity that characterizes America's religions. The Moral Majority has been extremely sensitive to this fact, describing itself as a wide-open, nonreligious organization. Yet there has been little response among either Catholics or Jews; and even within the nominally more congenial world of Protestantism, the Moral Majority has come up against pluralism. While polls show that as many as one-quarter of all Americans are born-again Christians, and a majority of Protestants adhere to one or another conservative religious tradition, tens of millions of Protestants do not. The conservative theology and politics of the Moral Majority has simply not penetrated more liberal and mainstream Protestants or the black church.[42]

A third boulder in the path is the political pluralism of the United States. After all, the Moral Majority did not enter virgin territory when it suddenly appeared in 1979; it entered an already filled "neighborhood" where it was the distinctly unwelcomed new kid on the block. And it found out immediately just how unwelcome it was. Established liberal interest groups turned on it, and new groups such as the People for the American Way mobilized against it, only to be attacked in turn by the right.[43] This was only to be expected. When a new group tries to break into American politics, particularly one that prepares to alter the public agenda, it can count on often fierce opposition. The result was that, rather than a monolith rolling to take over America, the Moral Majority proved to be just another entrant into the pluralist struggle.[44]

Another external constraint has been the American tradition (or myth) of the separation of church and state. Every survey demonstrates that almost all sectors of the public disapprove of a political religion and of churches and their clergy entering politics.[45] While the mood has

42. For the range and limits of Moral Majority appeal, see the data cited in note 30 above.

43. William P. Hoar, "Bashing Christians for Fun and Profit," *Conservative Digest,* December 1986, pp. 41-50.

44. For an analysis of the strategic situation that places the Moral Majority's situation with the rest of the so-called Christian right and similarly stresses obstacles (and thus prepares one for the Moral Majority's own concession of its challenges implied by its 1986 name change to Liberty Foundation), see Fowler, *Religion and Politics in America,* pp. 223-27.

45. Reichley, *Religion in American Public Life,* pp. 270-71; Kelley, *Why Conservative Churches Are Growing* (New York: Harper and Row, 1972); Jeffrey K. Hadden, *The Gathering Storm in the Churches* (Garden City, NY: Doubleday, 1969); Thomas C. Campbell and Yoshio Fukuyama, *The Fragmented Layman: An Empirical Study of Lay Attitudes* (Philadelphia: Pilgrim, 1970); Charles Glock,

shifted rapidly among some fundamentalists and evangelicals, resistance to the intertwining of religion and politics remains very much alive among theologically conservative Protestants. Their tradition has been one of strong support for a fairly thoroughgoing separation of church and state, which usually included staying away from politics, and efforts to sweep away that tradition have not been trouble-free.[46] At a conference of conservative Protestant clergy outside Chicago, the power of this belief was brought home to me during an address by a Moral Majority representative. Again and again his audience greeted his complaints about American society and politics with shouted approval. However, when he turned to calls for political *action* to remedy evils in America, approval cooled. Suddenly he was out of bounds.

Overall, conservative Christians have a distinct distaste for politics. Conservative Protestants go to church for politics even less than do most people in the United States; moreover, a large proportion of Moral Majority members themselves disapprove of religion entering politics.[47] This may change as groups like the Moral Majority have their impact and as a new generation of different-minded pastors comes to the fore in such worlds as the Southern Baptist Convention. For now, though, this reluctance to mix religion and politics is a major constraint on the Christian right.[48]

In addition, given the measurable resistance to religion in politics among the public at large, church-state complaints directed at the Christian right—and the Moral Majority in particular—get wide publicity and are often highlighted in the national media. The most common public fear is that such groups want to enact a despotism of their

---

et al., *To Comfort and to Challenge: A Dilemma of the Contemporary Church* (Berkeley: University of California, 1967); Mary Hanna, *Catholics and American Politics* (Cambridge: Harvard University Press, 1979); Lawrence K. Kersten, *The Lutheran Ethic: The Impact of Religion on Laymen and Clergy* (Detroit: Wayne State University Press, 1970); Harold E. Quinley, *The Prophetic Clergy: Social Activism among Protestant Ministers* (New York: John Wiley, 1974).

46. See Fowler, *Religion and Politics in America*, pp. 93-97; Carl F. H. Henry, "Church and State: Why the Marriage Must Be Saved," in *The Christian as Citizen* (Carol Stream, IL: Christianity Today Institute, 1985), pp. 9-13; Stephen V. Monsma, "Windows and Doors in the Wall of Separation," *The Christian as Citizen*, pp. 14-18; David L. McKenna, "A Political Strategy for the Local Church," in *The Christian as Citizen*, pp. 19-23; James Guth, "The Politics of Preachers: Southern Baptist Ministers and Christian Right Activism," in *New Christian Politics*.

47. Shupe and Stacey, "The Moral Majority Constituency," p. 109.

48. Hadden, *The Gathering Storm in the Churches* is the standard work here; James Guth, "The Politics of Preachers."

own dogmas.[49] No wonder the Moral Majority has spent so much time insisting that religious involvement in our political life is traditional, despite the American rhetoric of separatism. And no wonder the Moral Majority has done best when it is able to work with local party organizations and churches, outside the general blanket of criticism in which the media has wrapped the organization.[50]

A related problem for groups like the Moral Majority is the elite opposition they have faced. While the Moral Majority has symbolic support from the Reagan administration, one cannot possibly ignore the hostility among political, intellectual, media, and business elites that has certainly damaged it. This problem is one the organization believes to be very real, and *The Moral Majority Report* has often underscored it. The way the Moral Majority copes is to welcome such opponents and portray itself self-consciously as a populist group combating the rule of "secular humanist" elites.[51] In fact, this analysis is now very popular in conservative Christian circles, dramatically argued by Franky Schaeffer in *A Time for Anger.*[52]

Internal constraints also undercut the challenge of the new right. Analyses of the Moral Majority invariably note the enormous number of conservative Christians in the United States and their alleged rapid expansion. The implication is that this vast population is on the march religiously and could become united in the ranks of the Moral Majority— if they are not so already. But such an image displays little actual knowledge of the culture of conservative Christians, of the rich differences in history, religious beliefs, and politics that lie just below the surface of "conservative Christianity." The practice of referring to conservative Christians as fundamentalists continues to be extremely popular in the outside media and by those who are irritated by the existence of the Moral Majority. This practice is misleading because, in fact, most conservative Christians carefully distinguish themselves as either fundamentalists or evangelicals. This distinction is meaningful not because its lines are correct and impermeable but because it is made—it has a phenomenological significance that we cannot ignore—and because it has a discernible substance.

49. Simpson, "Support for the Moral Majority and Its Sociomoral Platform," pp. 65-68.

50. Robert C. Liebman, "Mobilizing the Moral Majority," in *The New Christian Right,* ch. 3.

51. A couple of examples are Lori Davis, "Elites Don't Understand," *Moral Majority Report,* 22 February 1982; Mark Edwards, "Liberals Using PAW to Pave the Way for Kennedy to Run for President," *Moral Majority Report,* 19 October 1981.

52. Schaeffer, *A Time for Anger,* chs. 9 and 2.

Fundamentalists have always had a sharper sense of the world's overwhelming sinfulness, a greater belief in the necessity of separation from the world, and a deeper suspicion of other Christians—including other supposed conservative Christians. They also suspect most institutions of society, educational and political institutions in particular. Much more than most evangelicals, they have seen themselves in conflict with, often in utter opposition to, the world; and they seek to build their own counterworlds. On the other hand, many evangelicals view fundamentalists as excessively separatist, often anti-intellectual, and unworldly in an unattractive, even ungodly, sense.[53]

Rev. Falwell and much of the Moral Majority come from a fundamentalist background, which explains a good deal of their problem with many conservative Christians.[54] On the one hand, many evangelical spokespeople and laity do *not* see the Moral Majority as one of their own; only outsiders lumping all conservative Christians together would make that mistake. This explains in large measure many evangelical leaders' dismissal of Falwell and his allies, as well as the celebrated spat between Billy Graham and the Moral Majority (which has since been papered over).[55] On the other hand, many fundamentalists still care deeply about maintaining a separation from the world, including from the state. They are often reluctant to rally to a movement, an action that would hardly affirm the wisdom of withdrawal from the sinful institutions in the larger world. This sense is reflected in the studied lack of interest in Falwell's efforts by many pentecostals and in the explicit attacks on him by fundamentalists such as Bob Jones III, who called Jerry Falwell "the most dangerous man in America."[56]

Fundamentalist-evangelical tension is just the beginning of the

---

53. Corwin Smidt, "Evangelicals vs. Fundamentalists"; Robert Booth Fowler, *A New Engagement: Evangelical Political Thought, 1966–1976* (Grand Rapids: Eerdmans, 1982), ch. 1; George Marsden, "Preachers of Paradox: The Religious New Right in Historical Perspective," in *Religion and America: Spirituality in a Secular Age,* ed. Mary Douglas and Steven Tipton (Boston: Beacon, 1983), pp. 150-68.

54. Sympathy with the Moral Majority highly correlates with fundamentalism: Shupe and Stacey, "The Moral Majority Constituency," p. 114.

55. E.g., the Moral Majority has not proven especially attractive to the evangelical portions of the Southern Baptist Convention: Guth, "Southern Baptist Clergy: Vanguard of the Christian Right?" in *The New Christian Right,* ch. 6; "Graham Lauds Moral Majority," *Moral Majority Report,* 16 February 1981; Reichley, *Religion in American Public Life,* pp. 328-29.

56. Fowler, *Religion and Politics in America,* p. 224; Reichley, *Religion in American Public Life,* p. 328.

complications that religious diversity within the world of conservative Christians presents to the Moral Majority. It is a realm of almost bewildering numbers of independent churches, denominations, and traditions, where cooperation is often slight and frequently nonexistent. There are, for instance, the Southern Baptist Convention (widely diverse in itself), numerous independent white Baptist traditions and churches, and several black Baptist conventions. Contrast the evangelical Reformed churches and their impressive intellectual credentials with the frequently anti-intellectual pentecostal churches. Contrast conservative Lutheran groups such as the Missouri and Wisconsin synods with the evangelical peace churches such as the Moravians, Brethren, and conservative Quakers. The diversity goes on and on.[57]

We also need to remember that the norm among conservative Christians has always been local sovereignty for each individual church. Not only are there an endless number of strictly independent conservative Christian churches, but most of the large denominations—very much including the Southern Baptist Convention (the largest)—have no authority over their "member" churches. Each is, so to speak, a single American individual, and nowhere in America is there a more prickly sensitivity to "individual rights" than here.

Even within the presumably congenial political realms of those who identify with the Christian right, each group like the Moral Majority has proven to be a voice in less than full chorus. For example, Falwell attempted to direct conservative Christian sentiment toward the 1988 presidential election by his early support of Vice President George Bush. Pat Robertson's later campaign for the presidency led to divisions in conservative Christian ranks when his cause won the support of many of the faithful, including such ordinarily nonpolitical figures as Oral Roberts and the now embarrassing Jimmy Swaggart. This division was very public, and it was a part of an old pattern of political conflicts.[58]

No doubt, at certain times there has been considerable consensus among theologically conservative Protestants. The 1984 presidential election was one such moment: evangelicals and fundamentalists did unite and back Reagan (75 percent to 25 percent). He almost perfectly mirrored the widespread unease among these Protestants over the *opera-*

57. A good introduction to diversity within Protestants as a whole and over time is Martin E. Marty, *Righteous Empire: The Protestant Experience in America* (New York: Dial Press, 1970); for diversity within evangelicalism itself, see Fowler, *A New Engagement.*

58. Thomas B. Edsall, "Bush Isn't Just Pandering to Conservatives, He's Splitting Them," *Washington Post National Weekly Edition,* 10 March 1986.

tion of the American liberal order, while at the same time he enthusiastically supported it—indeed, headed it.[59]

Nonetheless, religiously conservative Christians are not monolithic in political terms. Beatty and Walter have demonstrated that great diversity in political beliefs exists within religiously conservative denominations.[60] Wilcox found somewhat more cohesion among those he identified as "born-again fundamentalists" (BAF) on a number of political variables, but he found that they often *differed* from another religious grouping, the base of groups like the Moral Majority, which he called the "new Christian right" (NCR). Specifically, BAF opinion was not especially alienated from the American political order, while NCR views were; BAF were likely to be Democrats, NCR Republicans; BAF were not particularly conservative in economic ideas, NCR decidedly were. While both groups were conservative on social issues, disagreements abounded on many other political issues. Thus he wondered how much potential there was for the new Christian right, including the Moral Majority, to expand in the terrain of "born-again fundamentalists."[61] Wilcox also found major differences among fundamentalists defined by denomination or defined by belief.[62] Smidt found pronounced differences between fundamentalists and evangelicals both on party affiliation (with fundamentalists much more likely to be Democrats), and at least in the 1980 presidential election in voting behavior (with fundamentalists much more devoted to Jimmy Carter).[63]

Smidt has noted, as has Wilcox, considerable congruence between the two groups on social issues.[64] This congruence, of course, has been the basis for what popular support the new Christian right has generated; and there is some evidence that on such issues as pornography, abortion, and the like, support for the Moral Majority's positions

59. Corwin Smidt, "Evangelicals and the 1984 Election: Continuity or Change?" paper presented at the Society for the Scientific Study of Religion, 1985; Reichley, *Religion in American Public Life,* pp. 326-27.

60. Kathleen Murphy Beatty and Oliver Walter, "Religious Beliefs and Practice: New Forces in American Politics?" paper presented at the annual meeting of the American Political Science Association, 1982.

61. Clyde Wilcox, "The New Christian Right: Patterns of Political Beliefs," paper presented at the Midwest Political Science Association, 1983.

62. Clyde Wilcox, "Fundamentalists and Politics: An Analysis of the Effects of Differing Operational Definition," *Journal of Politics* 41 (1986): 1041-51.

63. Smidt, "Evangelicals vs. Fundamentalists."

64. Smidt, "Evangelicals vs. Fundamentalists," Table 4; Wilcox, "The New Christian Right," pp. 18-22.

far outruns support for the organizations that have made them important issues in the public realm.[65] Nevertheless, even within the ranks of Moral Majority supporters there is wide diversity of opinion once one gets away from the family-lifestyle issues.[66]

The issue with the religious right is whether their substantive aims represent a real threat to the liberal order of America and whether their political situation makes possible a challenge. I have made the point that on both there is ample reason for skepticism.

65. Stuart Rothenberg and Frank Newport, *The Evangelical Voter: Religion and Politics in America* (Washington, DC: Institute for Government and Politics, 1984), ch. 5; Reichley, *Religion in American Public Life*, p. 330.
66. Shupe and Stacey, "The Moral Majority Constituency," p. 114.

CHAPTER EIGHT

Other Challenges

So FAR MY ARGUMENT HAS CAST A GOOD DEAL OF DOUBT on the idea that religion in the United States has shifted from integration to confrontation with our liberal society. One could get such a misimpression from headlines but not from people in the pews, nor from religious activists. It is an outsider's impression, attractive to some and frightening to others, but in any case not true. Yet it is not wholly implausible by any means, especially if one looks at American religion today from the perspective of one of its most quiescent eras, such as the 1950s, or that of the Roman Catholic Church and the conservative Protestant denominations in most of their history in the United States.

But, as I have argued, the matter at hand is not mere activity; perhaps it is as much a matter of the *depth* of the challenge—depth in terms of theological position and of support among the more-or-less religious majority of America. From this angle, confrontation is hardly the right term for what is taking place.

Perhaps, however, I have looked in the wrong places. Perhaps there are more radical and serious challenges that I have not considered. My eye has focused on the several mainstreams of American religion; the advantage has been that I have had a chance to raise questions about the "radicalness" of these mainstreams. But in doing so, perhaps, the eye has not spied turbulent dissenting currents. Three possibilities come to mind. One is the host of self-conserving radical communities of "biblical" Christians seeking to transform themselves and our society toward the model of New Testament Christianity; a second is the large black church, which, diverse as it is, continues to be the center of the hopes of some black activists; the third is the world of the "cults," separatist on the whole and, it would seem, very much radical.

Radical Christian Communities

No SELF-CONSCIOUSLY RADICAL CHRISTIAN COMMUNITY of the present day has been more discussed than the Sojourners Fellowship, located in a poor black neighborhood of Washington, D.C. Its influence as a model is extensive. Its publication, *Sojourners* ("an independent Christian monthly"), is the modern-day bible for the radical Christian community movement in America. *Sojourners* discusses religious-political issues in broad perspective, though its link to the Sojourners community is reaffirmed monthly through the regular *Sojourners* feature "Euclid Street," which recounts events in the Sojourners Fellowship. The magazine pursues its broader concerns by drawing on a wide variety of writers from many different religious denominations and traditions; they are united, however, in sharing *Sojourners'* biblical focus and biblical interpretations regarding political, social, and economic life. Moreover, its feature column "Connections" serves as a bulletin board for similar communities or related causes from all over the country. *Sojourners'* aim is to encourage the forming of contacts with others in the movement.[1]

The Sojourners community was born out of the civil rights movement and the Vietnam War, especially the latter. As the most influential prophet of the movement, Jim Wallis, puts it, that was "the historical occasion for a revival of biblical faith."[2] In 1971, *The Post-American* (later renamed *Sojourners*) appeared as the voice of evangelical radicalism, declaring: "We require radical transformation, a new understanding of society and ourselves. As the analysis of our dilemma must be radical, so must our solutions."[3]

The continuing mood has involved extensive denunciations of war and racism, imperialism and capitalism, always with a firm finger pointed at the liberal society in the United States. *Sojourners* regularly expresses a deep belief that liberal America is evil, an example of the fallen world. William Stringfellow has proclaimed: "The nation *is* fallen. . . . America is a demonic principality."[4] Jim Wallis adds that America needs "a disloyal opposition."[5] Today this pessimism is extended to the world. In his influential book *The Call to Conversion*, Wallis insists that "the world ap-

1. On Sojourners Fellowship, its history, theology, etc., see *Sojourners* magazine; Jim Wallis, *Agenda for a Biblical People* (New York: Harper and Row, 1976); Wallis, *The Call to Conversion* (New York: Harper and Row, 1981); Robert Booth Fowler, *A New Engagement: Evangelical Political Thought, 1966–1976* (Grand Rapids: Eerdmans, 1982), ch. 7; Fowler, *Religion and Politics in America* (Metuchen, NJ: Scarecrow Press, 1985), pp. 90-93, from which part of this discussion is adopted.

2. Jim Wallis, *Agenda for a Biblical People,* pp. 6, 10, 12.

3. Wallis, "Post-American Christianity," *Post-American* 1, no. 1 (1971).

4. William Stringfellow, *An Ethic for Christians and Other Aliens in a Strange Land* (Waco, TX: Word, 1976), pp. 154-55.

5. Wallis, *Agenda for a Biblical People,* p. 108.

pears to be falling apart" and "the value of human life seems to be steadily diminishing."[6]

These Christian radicals come back time and again to the point that true commitment to serving God requires "incarnation": they mean that real belief requires direct and tangible evidence in one's life. It is not enough to say words, endorse creeds, or claim to be born again; there must be a genuine "conversion." In the process, disputes over biblical literalism or the meaning of inerrancy must take second place to translating the Bible for contemporary human lives. John F. Alexander puts it this way: "The central issue about the Bible is whether we live it."[7] And Jim Wallis says, "One's life rather than one's doctrine is the best test of faithfulness to Scripture."[8]

Achieving this requires, they believe, revolution. The revolution they seek has nothing to do with violence or destruction in a blast of fire or steel; but it does concern drastic, life-transforming change. The means of change, they contend, must vary from time to time and situation to situation; except for the fact that it must be peaceful, there are few limits on it. It can be radical, nonviolent action, if necessary, and it must proceed with a healthy and guilt-free recognition of "the inadequacy of moderation." Reconciliation is important, and so is the preservation of every human life. But it is also necessary to recognize that "to be a Christian is to be an extremist," and only those who are in conflict with the established order may present themselves as true Christians.[9]

At the heart of the "revolution" in liberal America that the Sojourners and other religious radicals seek is a shift to community and away from liberal individualism. For them, community is simply God's way, God's great commandment about how to live life: "Community is the great assumption of the New Testament." When people build community, real change takes place, they insist: "The creation of living, breathing, loving communities of faith at the local church level is the foundation of all the answers. That change is the creation of reborn, loving Christian persons."[10] Moreover, community is the proper center for all Christians, the place where they can participate, give and receive

6. Wallis, *The Call to Conversion,* pp. xi and xii.

7. John Alexander, "Editorial," *The Other Side,* July-August 1975, 63; obviously, the burden of Wallis's *Call to Conversion* is, similarly, concrete individual change.

8. Wallis, *Agenda for a Biblical People,* p. 4.

9. *Ibid.,* pp. 133, 153; John F. Alexander, "Politics, Repentance and Vision," *The Other Side,* March-April 1974, pp. 2-4, 52-54; Wallis, "The New Regime," *Post-American* 3, no. 7 (1974): 30.

10. Wallis, *The Call to Conversion,* pp. 113, 109.

love, experience intimacy—human solidarity under God's eye. It is also
the base from which efforts to promote a broader, more global community can arise.[11]

The kind of Christian community these radicals have in mind is
fairly clear. It is to be like a "household," in Dave and Neta Jackson's
term, disciplined in its service of God and loving in its devotion to God
and to each member as a child of God.[12] But this is not easy to achieve
or maintain. Graham Pulkingham, for instance, argues what all honest
people know: it is not easy to live together over time, and only fools and
romantics believe it is. All the more so in an enduring community. Structures will not save a failed community, just as marriage contracts cannot
save dead marriages. For Pulkingham the answer is discipline, love, determination, and a great deal of luck.[13] It is no surprise that the examples
of communities radicals often cite—the Sojourners Fellowship in Washington, D.C. or Koinonia in Georgia, to name two—do not report an
easy time. The challenge is obviously great.[14]

Concern for making this revolution work obviously calls the Sojourners, Wallis, and others of similar disposition to confront directly the
American liberal order. This disposition is obvious at the most superficial policy level. *Sojourners* can be counted on to oppose whatever policies and/or leaders hold sway in Washington. In this, of course, the Sojourners community behaves little differently from the religious left in
general. This reflexive opposition, in fact, suggests that the Sojourners,
like the religious left as a whole, are locked in an embrace (albeit not one
of love) with the culture, despite their protestations.[15]

In recent years *Sojourners* has gone beyond campaigning for nuclear
freeze and arms reductions to a position attacking the militarized state
altogether—while urging unilateral disarmament, pacifism, and nonvi-

11. For a recent statement by a major figure of influence, see Henri J. M.
Nouwen, "Creating True Intimacy: Solidarity among the People of God," *Sojourners,* June 1985, pp. 14-18.

12. Dave and Neta Jackson, "Living in Community, Being the Church,"
The Other Side, May-June 1973, pp. 8-13.

13. Graham Pulkingham, "The Shape of the Church to Come," *Sojourners,* November 1976, pp. 11, 13; Pulkingham, "Interview," *Sojourners,*
January 1977, pp. 21-23.

14. For a quite recent discussion, see "A Sign and a Choice: The Spirituality of Community—An Interview with Joan Chittister," *Sojourners,* June
1987, pp. 14-19.

15. There seems to be a constant push-pull in *Sojourners* between a desire
to get "beyond" a policy focus to larger issues and larger conceptions and a
deep desire to meet urgent policy issues.

olent resistance. It has gone beyond attacking the Reagan "opportunity" economy and reduced welfare state to a support of "socialism" (though this word is not theirs). It has gone beyond severely criticizing the administration's foreign policy in selected instances to condemning it wholesale and to eagerly supporting its opponents in many locations (e.g., Central America). It has gone beyond ardent sympathy for liberal Democrats and the electoral process to opposition to the entire liberal political process and all candidates for president. In 1976, for instance, *Sojourners* had no good words for Jimmy Carter, then a hero to political liberals in the American Christian community. In 1984 it spared no effort in its relentless attacks on President Reagan but mounted no campaign for Walter Mondale.[16]

In terms of focused policy efforts, *Sojourners* has concentrated on the two areas where Christian radicals agree that liberalism fails most concretely and most painfully, where the absence of community is unmistakable: poverty and war. Religious radicals contend that the goals of eradicating poverty and achieving world peace were central to Christ, yet are almost strangers to modern liberalism. They insist that the answers are not rapid economic development, expansionist economics, and materialism—the false goals of both liberal capitalism and Marxism. For them there would be plenty to go around if people in the United States lived simply and in that simplicity achieved liberation.[17] This does not mean a celebration of the life of the poor in the world. Simplicity and desperate poverty are not the same. The Sojourners contend that most people on our planet endure conditions that are shockingly below what Christ would approve, while the rich (and not only those in the USA) live a life of affluent sinfulness, oblivious to Christ's warning "But woe to you who are rich."[18]

During the late 1970s and the 1980s the struggle for peace became vital for these radicals. They urged governments, churches, and individuals to do all they could to increase the possibilities for peace. This meant a longstanding campaign against nuclear war and nuclear weapons, especially in *Sojourners*. In the 1980s, in particular, the publication stepped

16. The politics and policies of Sojourners are discussed at greater length in Fowler, *A New Engagement*, ch. 7; Fowler, *Religion and Politics in America*, pp. 90-93.

17. For example, Art Gish, "Simplicity," *The Other Side*, May-June 1973, pp. 14-16.

18. Ronald J. Sider has made the classic argument: *Rich Christians in an Age of Hunger: A Biblical Study* (Downers Grove, IL: InterVarsity, 1977); for a more recent example, see Jim Wallis, "Poverty Is a Scandal," *Sojourners*, November 1985, pp. 4-5.

up its antinuclear efforts. *Sojourners* had in the past given space to those proposing tax resistance and other nonviolent protests against war preparations; but by the 1980s it was clearly committed to complete abandonment of the nuclear arms race and virtual pacifism. Nowhere was its conviction stronger.[19]

At least as important, the Sojourners Fellowship and some of those associated with it have supported and sometimes participated in a series of actions in recent years, attempts to match words with deeds. This has been particularly true on the issues of disarmament, defense spending, and sanctuary for refugees from Central American conflicts in which the United States is involved. Pickets, sit-ins, tax withholding, and "symbolic" assaults on defense institutions and facilities have become almost common, all with the enthusiastic support of the Sojourners world.[20]

That this is radical stuff, just as it is meant to be, is not in dispute. There is little parlor radicalism here, nor secular left-wing Democratic party politics dressed up as religious radicalism, nor a confused belief that opposition to Reagan was serious radicalism. This does not mean, however, that Sojourners Fellowship and those who share its faith are a significant, religiously based challenge to our liberal society in any practical sense. Jim Wallis argues that they are and that the movement is very much on the way

19. For the 1970s, see as sample articles Deltun Franz, "Channeling War Taxes to Peace," *Sojourners,* March 1977, pp. 21-23; John Howard Yoder, "Why I Didn't Pay All My Income Tax," *Sojourners,* March 1977, pp. 11-12. In the 1980s virtually every issue pounds home the *Sojourners* version of "peacemaking" with its intense antinuclear and neopacifist themes. For examples, see the August-September 1985 issue entitled "The Hiroshima Decision," whose thrusts are the above with a heavy emphasis on the United States as the really guilty party from 1945 on; or see the recommended books on "peacemaking" in the same issue, pp. 38-39, a selection with a similar definition; or see the effort for "Peace and Pentecost 1985" in the May 1985 issue, pp. 22-23. These reveal a concern and focus that is emphatically antinuclear and sympathetic to pacifism. Also relevant here are such books as Ronald J. Sider's and Richard K. Taylor's *Nuclear Holocaust and Christian Hope* (New York: Paulist, 1982).

20. By way of illustration, see, in recent issues, Danny Collum, "Trident Resistance Actions North and South," *Sojourners,* March 1986, p. 12; Art Laffin, "The Final Verdict," *Sojourners,* March 1986, p. 35; Steven Hall-Williams, "Pledge Says 'No' to *Contra* Aid," *Sojourners,* June 1986, p. 10; Bob Campagna and Susan K. Delbner, "Faith and Resistance in Missouri," *Sojourners,* June 1986, p. 11; the celebration of Martin Luther King, Jr., issue: "Getting Ready for the Hero," *Sojourners,* January 1986; Sojourners Peace Ministry, "The Gospel Compels," *Sojourners,* March 1986, p. 6; Vincent Harding, "In the Company of the Faithful," *Sojourners,* May 1985, pp. 14-21.

up.[21] But his claim is simply not convincing. More people may agree with him than ever, but together they do not represent significant numbers of religious Americans. Few agree with their tactics of assertive nonviolent action, with their policy goals—except in the vaguest terms (who, after all, is against peace?)—or with their implicit collapse of any distinctions between religion, politics, and society. Popular support is simply not there by any objective standard of measurement we have.[22]

Nor can we be sure how radical in practice such groups as the Sojourners could be even if general public opinion were very different. These religious radicals are deeply ambivalent about all institutions, but especially government.[23] It is just not clear how well they could *act* in a societal sense, as opposed to isolated incidents of nonviolent protest or grand abstract affirmations of principle. The Sojourners community, then, and those in American religion who are sympathetic to its goals, policies, and means of change, are radical. But they do not pose any serious threat to the liberal culture they so detest. Someday they may, but for now they are an opposition without teeth.

Black Religion

A DECADE OR TWO AGO those attracted to the challenge hypothesis might have ignored both radical groups such as Sojourners and religious cults and looked instead to the realm of black religion as the place where challenge to liberal America was a reality both in theory and in fact. It is undeniable that in the last several decades the black church has become a potent political force. The Reverend Jesse Jackson is only the most famous current example. Black religious leaders are often (though far from always) willing to enter politics, even party politics. Some become famous at the national level, but more often they participate at local levels. Black clergy often endorse candidates and seek considerable sway with the laity at the voting booth, the typical black voter being an active church member. Black clergymen often run for political office, and many of them hold office. Even compared with that of the new evangelical right, the frequency of political endorsements and campaign involve-

21. Jim Wallis, "The Rise of Christian Conscience," *Sojourners,* January 1985, pp. 12-16.

22. A. James Reichley, *Religion in American Public Life* (Washington, DC: Brookings, 1985), pp. 269-81, 299-302, 319-31, nicely summarizes the data.

23. The classic statement of Sojourner's position was in Jim Wallis, "What Does Washington Have to Say to Grand Rapids?" *Sojourners,* July 1977, pp. 3-4. Nothing much has changed since.

ment from many black churches is extensive. They are at the frontier of the political church today.[24]

Whether this is evidence now, or in the past, for the view that black religion is the true center of challenge to liberalism within American religion is, however, something else. Indeed, from the perspective of today, the experience of the black church may provide a fitting cautionary note in the discussion of religious challenge in America today. For the much-heralded "challenge" posed by black religion in the 1960s was not only much less popular among religious blacks than the secular media thought; it also turned out to be much less of a fundamental challenge than many believed it would be fifteen or twenty years ago. Black religion today simply is not radical in any deep sense.

Blacks are more likely to belong to a church than are whites, and they attend church more frequently. Altogether the church is a much more important institution in the black community than it is in the white—and far more so than some secular black intellectual critics suggest.[25] Whether this reality is continuing as strongly today as in the past is less clear. So is whether the future will be the same. There are doubts, but they do not alter the relative strength of religion among blacks as a whole compared to the white community.[26] Diversity is common within the black church. One important example is the number of black denominations. Most blacks are either Methodists or Baptists, by far the majority being Baptists. Three Baptist denominations dominate: the first and much the largest is the National Baptist Convention USA: second is the National Baptist Convention of America; third is the Progressive National Baptist Convention. Each of these conventions (the characteristic Baptist word for a national organization of independent churches) has over two million members, and the National Baptist Convention has more than three times that number. The Methodists trail far behind, but the African Methodist Episcopal Church has about a million members, and the C.M.E. church has somewhat fewer than that. In addition to the black Methodist and Baptist groups, there are numerous other denominations and many, many independent black churches. The two largest secondary denominations are the Church of God in Christ

24. The following is, in part, based on an adaption of Fowler, *Religion and Politics in America,* ch. 12; for an able overview, see Sydney Ahlstrom, *A Religious History of the American People* (Garden City, NY: Doubleday, 1975), vol. 2, ch. 62.

25. See, for example, Adolph Reed, Jr., *The Jesse Jackson Phenomenon* (New Haven, CT: Yale University Press, 1986), ch. 4.

26. "Rethinking Evangelization of Black Families," *Our Sunday Visitor,* 24 August 1986, p. 3.

and the larger National Primitive Baptist Church of the U.S.A., which has almost two million members.[27]

Obviously, membership figures are slippery things, and we can place no great reliance on claims of membership in any church. But the general points remain true: blacks belong to black churches; and these churches exist as a number of separate denominations, some larger than others, with many independent churches. Among these latter are the storefront churches, which dot black neighborhoods in every major city and many small towns.

Not every black attends a black church, and there are blacks in denominations that are overwhelmingly white. This is notably true in the United Methodist Church, cousin of black Methodism, which at the local level has sometimes welcomed blacks. However, the gap in tradition between the black churches and white denominations such as the United Church of Christ, the various Lutheran churches, or the Episcopal Church is obvious, and their numbers of black communicants are very small. Of all the predominantly white churches, the Roman Catholic Church has attracted the most blacks. Although only about one-half of 1 percent of Catholic priests and sisters are black (and only 1 percent of seminarians), perhaps 15 percent of black Christians are Roman Catholics in the United States, a significant group even if they represent only about 3 percent of all American Catholics.[28]

It was in the 1960s, a remarkable decade of change for black people, that the modern black church was born. The mobilization of black churches, black clergy, and the black laity behind the cause of civil rights was the religious event of the 1960s. One crucial part of the story was the emergence of black clergymen as forces for change in their churches and communities. Most often the clergy—and sometimes the laity—entered into dialogue with themselves and others about what they wanted at their local level, and then they acted. This local work was usually the arena where change happened most concretely. The National Committee of Negro Churchmen, Martin Luther King, Jr., and young radicals shouting "black power" were usually far away, though all of them had their role in stimulating local black churches to action. On the other

27. Constant H. Jacquet, Jr., ed., *Yearbook of American and Canadian Churches, 1985* (Nashville: Abingdon, 1985), pp. 229-35; Leo Rosten, ed., *Religions of America* (New York: Simon and Schuster, 1975), p. 375.

28. Joe R. Feagin, "Black Catholics in the United States: An Exploratory Analysis," in *The Black Church in America,* ed. Hart M. Nelsen et al. (New York: Basic Books, 1971), pp. 246ff.; Mary S. Gordon, "Black Religious Gather, Ask 'Specific Needs' Be Recognized," *National Catholic Reporter,* 28 August 1981; Michael P. Harris, "A First for Black Catholics," *Time,* 28 March 1988, p. 71.

hand, the question of what the local black church was going to do to improve conditions was right at hand. Over the decade of the 1960s, local black churches in the North and the South tested and entered the political currents.

This was a revolution. The black church had had a long history in the United States of protective caution, which was not the only strategy but mainly what happened. Black churches lacked political and monetary resources to do things much differently, and they were rarely eager to draw attention and provoke white hostility. Moreover, much of black religion was inner-focused and concentrated much more on changing individuals and preparing for heaven than on political action in this world.[29] The revolution in the black church of the 1960s did not carry all before it, and its successes came only after a tremendous internal struggle over political action. There was initially an enormous resistance. The best and most widely known example was the National Baptist Convention USA. Its powerful leader, Rev. Joseph H. Jackson, objected to black clergy or churches adopting the role of political involvement. In the end, though, controlling the membership proved difficult. In the Baptist tradition decentralization was the reality, and black churches more and more went their own way.[30]

The militancy that spread among black clergy was the key. In the earlier 1960s it was unevenly evident, but it grew steadily with time. Not surprisingly, it became popular first among black clergy in white liberal denominations, North and South, and among younger black clergy. Yet it spread far beyond them. Dr. Martin Luther King, Jr., was the symbol and the reality of the new mood of the clergy. He was increasingly supported by black ministers and priests in places big and small, prominent and forgotten. Indeed, the later 1960s was a golden age for the black clergyman in terms of political influence and activity. He was often in the front lines and often won wide respect for his service.[31]

29. Leon Litwack, *Been in the Storm so Long* (New York: Viking, 1980); Charles V. Hamilton, *The Black Preacher in America* (New York: William Morrow, 1972), ch. 2; E. Franklin Frazier, *The Negro Church in America* (New York: Schocken, 1970); G. Myrdal, "The Negro Church: Its Weakness, Trends and Outlook," in *The Black Church in America*, pp. 257-64; Hadley Contril and Muzafer Sherif, "The Kingdom of Father Divine," in *The Black Church in America*, pp. 175-93.

30. Hamilton, *The Black Preacher*, ch. 5 and pp. 26-27, 173-81, 127-33; C. Eric Lincoln, *The Black Church since Frazier* (New York: Schocken Books, 1970), chs. 2, 4; Gayraud S. Wilmore, *Black Religion and Black Radicalism: An Examination of the Black Experience in Religion* (Garden City, NY: Doubleday, 1972), chs. 1-7; see also Fowler, *Religion and Politics in America*, ch. 12.

31. Martin Luther King, Jr., "Letter from Birmingham Jail," in *The Black*

Some religious blacks still resist a political church. Those black churches—and there are many—that resemble "sects" in their self-conscious tension with a sinful environment are much more likely to be conservative regarding political involvement, just as they were less willing to back King and the civil rights movement in the 1960s. On the other hand, the increasing "church" side of black religion has given strong support for civil rights and an involved clergy. Less removed from the larger society, this branch of black religion has acted much more aggressively to change America. Yet this division was sharper in the 1960s than it is today since most blacks now accept a politically active role for their church and its leaders.[32]

Similar shock waves hit the white church as their few black clergy and laity began insisting on changes. In the more liberal Protestant denominations there was often considerable support at the top for black activism, which sometimes helped; among fundamentalist and evangelical denominations the problems were often terrible. Nevertheless, in the end the battle for activism among religious blacks within both white and black churches was won.

The shift to an acceptance of the legitimacy and, indeed, the importance of the black church's taking social and political action does not mean that the actions it frequently took twenty years ago and takes today may be seen as a serious challenge to the American liberal order. There is a crucial distinction between the radical shift toward politics and a shift toward radical politics. Yet there is no question that an impulse toward radicalism in black religious circles existed and went beyond the turn to politics itself. The emergence of militant black theologians in the 1960s was its vanguard. Young and not so young black theologians sought to lead blacks to a new Christian life that would involve active struggle for dramatically changed life conditions. One step, they insisted, was the discovery of a God who loved tough-minded, aggressive Christians working for a new life rather than passive, pietistic Christians who accepted their lot.[33]

Church in America, pp. 292-98; Ronald L. Johnstone, "Negro Preachers Take Sides," in *The Black Church in America,* pp. 275-86; Hart M. Nelsen and Anne K. Nelsen, *The Black Church in the Sixties* (Lexington, KY: University of Kentucky Press, 1975), pp. 136-37, 123.

32. Gary T. Marx, "Religion: Opiate or Inspiration of Civil Rights Militancy among Negroes?" *American Sociological Review* 32 (February 1967): 64-72; Stuart R. Rothenberg and Frank Newport, *The Evangelical Voter: Religion and Politics in America* (Washington, DC: Institute for Government and Politics, 1984), pp. 123-125.

33. For a good selection, see James J. Gardiner and J. Deotis Roberts, eds., *Quest for a Black Theology* (Philadelphia: Pilgrim, 1971).

By far the most important liberation voice was that of James Cone. In his articles and books in the 1960s and 1970s, Cone bitterly denounced the United States as a hopelessly racist society and insisted that "the essence of the gospel is the liberation of the oppressed from sociopolitical humiliation for a new freedom in Jesus Christ."[34] Cone dismissed those who disagreed as victims of ignorance at best or racism at worst: "I do not see how anyone can read the Scriptures and conclude otherwise."[35]

The Bible was thus a book for blacks who suffered, who wanted liberation, and who sought to get to that goal less with philosophy than action. It was in this context that Cone made his famous argument that God is black. If God is about suffering and liberation, Cone suggests, then in America God has to be black. Cone granted that God or Jesus is transcendent and supersedes any historical time or particular people; yet he was both transcendent and involved, and in his involvement he certainly had to be black. He was with the black people in their suffering.

Cone was quite prepared to follow black power in an endorsement of violence. As far as he was concerned, what counted was the relationship of means to ends: if violence was appropriate to legitimate ends, then it was justified. This is the view that most Christians have held over the centuries since Augustine, but it was not the view among leading change-oriented black clergy, above all Martin Luther King, Jr. No wonder Cone's sympathies did not run toward the orthodox civil rights movement. Some black thinkers have insisted that they must pursue a path that will lead toward reconciliation with whites as a crucial part of their Christianity, but Cone was reluctant to follow this path. He insisted that there is no reconciliation without liberation, and true reconciliation necessarily involves the liberation of the black oppressed. Then and only then can there be authentic reconciliation.[36]

Cone got a serious hearing among black Christian leaders and mainline Protestant thinkers in the late 1960s and early 1970s. He spoke in language that was sophisticated enough in that age of great discontent to have some appeal. After all, the 1960s saw many mainline white Protestant clergy also emphasizing Christ's commitment to social change, the poor, and the oppressed. Some could even identify with Christ as a black

34. James Cone, *God of the Oppressed* (New York: Seabury, 1975), pp. 218, 51, and ch. 2.

35. *Ibid.*, p. 51.

36. *Ibid.*, pp. 211-21, 206-12, 240-43, and, more generally, chs. 5-6, 8, 10.

man in symbolic terms. There was, however, considerable uneasiness at the exclusivity of identifying Christ only with blacks, as if there were no other suffering peoples and no other kinds of oppression. There was also a sense that Cone spoke too little of love and reconciliation.

There is, however, scant evidence that Cone or other radicals altered any doctrines in the typical black Baptist or Methodist church. They had always seen God as an ally of the oppressed and did not believe that he resisted social change; but grand notions about God's symbolic or actual blackness and sympathy for black power or violence hardly became normal church fare. Views such as Cone's fell outside the main body of black Christians. These views were radical, but they achieved no popular resonance.[37]

There have been those within the evangelical and fundamentalist center of black Christianity who have written and spoken for a more militant black Christianity whose word has received wide respect. They have shared Cone's feeling that white America has badly mistreated blacks; that the white evangelical record of social justice programs and Christian love toward blacks is disgraceful; that simple racism and excuses about the dangers of internal communism have allowed too many white Christians to fail to assist blacks. At the same time, there has been some uneasiness about Cone's approach to Christianity: it seemed to start with the black experience in the United States rather than with God, and it left out the gospel of reconciliation even as it appropriately stressed black militance.

Two of the most influential black evangelicals in recent years have been Tom Skinner and John Perkins. Skinner has some sympathies for black power and insists that being a Christian does not require any black person to give up being black. This is not possible, nor is it what Christ expected or wanted. On the other hand, Skinner is an integrationist: he wants a society where blacks and whites live together, and he has made no bones about it. Black power may have its uses on the way to integration, but only if the question is constantly asked, is black (or, for that matter, any) power employed in the service of Christ? Power loose from Christ is too dangerous. Predictably, Skinner applauds Martin Luther King, Jr., as the exemplar of the kind of Christian he has in mind. King was in tune with "the tough radical Jesus," as he should be; but he also knew of the other missions of Christianity. Moreover, King was fully aware of the reality of sin and the impossibility of utopia. He was a radi-

37. For a somewhat different view of present and past, see Peter J. Paris, *The Social Teaching of the Black Churches* (Philadelphia: Fortress, 1985).

cal realist open to the several sides of Christianity, and Skinner fully approves.[38]

John Perkins has been another widely admired black evangelical. While Skinner has concentrated on urban ghettos and street ministries in places such as Newark and Brooklyn, Perkins' base has been in rural Mississippi. Perkins went through the turbulent and violent civil rights era, suffering familiar and terrible personal costs. He emerged determined to work in his local terrain for Christ and for economic improvement among blacks (cooperatives are crucial for him). His engaging book *Let Justice Roll Down* recounts his experiences in the 1960s and his Christian discovery and the witness that followed. Later books, such as *A Call to Wholistic Ministry,* report on his more recent ministry, called the Voice of Calvary, which struggles to help poor blacks out of "their deep state of despair and poverty" and in the process fleshes out the gospel of Christ.[39]

Overall in the black church the talk has quieted, black power inflames few passions, and denouncing white racists does not now seem much of a step toward change. Religious blacks' commitment to political action to help the black cause is now firmly established. Its final institutional victory came in 1982, when Rev. T. J. Jamison succeeded to the presidency of the National Baptist Convention USA, by far the largest group of black churches in America. Jamison publicly affirmed the policy of black religion's involvement in political and social reform, and in the process he both rejected the N.B.C.'s cautious past and confirmed the reality of the drift of black religion in America.[40] But radical action in which the world of black religion directly challenges the American liberal order is rare. The politics of the black church is almost entirely a politics of integration, a call to allow blacks their share within liberalism.

This direction is even reflected in the history of the Black Muslims, the most recent incarnation of the longtime radical separatist side of

38. See *Tom Skinner Associates 15th Anniversary* booklet, 1979; Tom Skinner, *Black and Free* (Grand Rapids: Zondervan, 1970); Tom Skinner, *How Black Is the Gospel?* (Philadelphia: Lippincott, 1970); Tom Skinner, "Black Power," *The Other Side,* January-February 1972, pp. 7-11, 46-47.

39. John Perkins, *Let Justice Roll Down* (Glendale, CA: Regal, 1976); John Perkins, *A Call to Wholistic Ministry* (St. Louis: Open Door, 1980); Will Norton, Jr., "John Perkins: The Stature of a Servant," *Christianity Today,* 1 January 1982; Will Norton, Jr., "John Perkins, the Prophet," *Christianity Today,* 1 January 1982.

40. Richard N. Ostling, "Moving into the Mainstream," *Time,* 19 September 1983.

black religion in the United States. The Black Muslim movement, now known as the American Muslim Mission, was exposed to wide public knowledge in the 1960s as one more sign, it was said, that blacks were rebelling in the United States. At that time there was considerable discussion in the white and black communities of the Muslims' alleged sympathy for violence, their hostility to whites, their support for a separate black state, and their troubled relations with the "official" Middle East version of Islam. There was also considerable speculation about how many Black Muslims there were and how fast they were growing.

It is doubtful that the Black Muslim movement had more than 100,000 members at its height in the 1960s, though some figures ranged up to 250,000. Neither number comes close to its much smaller membership today, and it remains true that the biggest single problem the Muslims face is opposition from the bulk of black people. Yet the Muslims are a flourishing group, especially in the major cities of the United States, one with its own world of belief, ritual, organization, and institutions.

The Muslims claim to be followers of Muhammad, the prophet of Allah. According to them, Allah chose blacks as his divine servants and the leaders of the Nation of Islam as special messengers to global blacks. In this view, Allah was black and loved and honored blacks; through the 1960s, a central doctrine held that white men were "devils" whose time of rule and oppression would one day end terribly. Meanwhile, blacks were supposed to avoid whites—avoid contact with the devil—as they served Allah. It followed that efforts to build and support black institutions were essential, so that social and economic separatism could be achieved. In the long run, blacks were also to separate from whites politically, though whether that was to be in a distinct nation or as a separate section of the American nation was not always clear.

The concrete Muslim program of transforming religion into action, however, is what has really counted and what has brought Muslims respect. Theirs is a religion that helps people in a world less impressed with promises than performance, especially the disillusioned world of the lower-class black, who has always been a central target for Muslim recruitment. Muslim efforts to translate their faith into life have centered on the school and the home. Muslims run a number of schools (the first was formed in 1932) as part of their objective to save the youth, especially ghetto youth. Just as in Muslim homes, the emphasis at school is on an ethical life: it restricts sex to the married, and those who deviate are disgraced; it insists on discipline, children disciplined at home and in school and women disciplined in the service of their husbands or fathers. The emphasis is on cleanliness, neatness, demure dress, and deportment.

It emphasizes earning one's own way; following Muslim rituals and ceremonies; and pulling oneself together in a life of decency and religion. That all of this is in obvious contrast to some aspects of ghetto life is no accident, of course; but it is also meant to contrast with middle-class life, white and black.

Muslims frightened some of the general public in the United States when they were "discovered" in the 1960s; but they were always more internally divided, less popular with most blacks, and more ensnared in their own problems than the general public knew. Their centralized system of organization led to many problems, the most famous being the defection of Malcolm X in 1964; their apparent militance provoked antagonism from both whites and blacks; their separatist style won some admiration but also considerable antagonism from blacks. Not only middle-class blacks but also the official rulers of world Islam spurned the Black Muslims. The latter saw them as impostors who believed obviously heretical things, such as that whites were devils and that blacks would inherit the earth.[41]

From a contemporary perspective, much has changed in the Muslim movement. It has not only lost its media chic, it has lost membership (though how much is not known outside the faith), and it has a new leader who is guiding it over some of the difficult shoals it encountered in the 1970s. The movement has edged closer to the wider Islamic faith and life, though it has not yet won acceptance. It has laid aside its rhetoric of the evil nature of whites, the special place for blacks, and the rest of its once seemingly racist vocabulary; insofar as such rhetoric remains, its spokesmen say, it is now only symbolic. The temples are no longer closed permanently to all outsiders, though one still cannot walk in off the street. Financial openness has increased. Above all, the demand—whatever it meant—for a black separatist state has come to an end.

All of this sounds like the Black Muslims have moved in the familiar progression from sect to church, from a religion of opposition to a religion of accommodation or even conformity. The pattern is classic, but how applicable it is in this instance is less clear. The Black Muslim movement is also suffering from schism, which may be suggestive. The emergence of Louis Farrakhan during the 1984 presidential election campaign alerted many for the first time that the former Black Muslim movement had split. Rev. Farrakhan's Nation of Islam, despite his once

41. C. Eric Lincoln, *The Black Muslims in America* (Boston: Beacon, 1973); Lincoln, "The Black Muslims as a Protest Movement," in *The Black Church in America*, pp. 210-24.

highly publicized activities on behalf of Jesse Jackson, insists that it represents the traditional and separatist impulse of the Black Muslim movement of old, now being "sacrificed" by the movement of the American Muslim Mission. Perhaps this is true, but the much larger American Muslim Mission is hardly just another American church. And yet the first steps appear to have been taken.[42]

As the Muslims accept more of the larger society, they may come to play a role in the larger political arena. After all, they represent a disciplined and determined proportion of the black community and thus have some political resources that they presently do not use. As they ease into American life a bit more, we may hear a good deal of the Muslims in politics, though how radical they will be is doubtful. They will then underscore what is otherwise true: that black religion is the most activist sector of American religion.

The black clergyman is central in modern religious-political activism. Black Christians tend to expect their preacher to be a strong figure, and he is commonly one of the leaders of the black community in every town and city. While his name does not necessarily get into the paper, his influence is widely acknowledged. Many black clergymen endorse issues and even candidates right from the pulpit. They cannot be lightly flicked away if the national church headquarters or local whites are unhappy with them. They are at the center of the stage, and if their local church people back them, they are secure.

Today black ministers are often in political office, leading campaigns, actively endorsing candidates. Among the more famous examples are the Rev. Andrew Young and the Rev. Jesse Jackson, both former aides to Martin Luther King, Jr. Andrew Young achieved considerable publicity in his role as ambassador to the United Nations during the Carter administration, and he is now the mayor of Atlanta. Jesse Jackson, of course, is at the moment the most prominent black politician in the United States, well known for his campaign for the Democratic nomination for president in 1984 and 1988, and for his controversial efforts in Chicago to obtain jobs, political influence, and generally better living conditions for blacks through his organization PUSH (People United to Save Humanity). Jackson has long been at the center of controversy: even critics who wish him well contend that he is better at articulating concerns than at detailed organization and actual accomplishment. But Jackson is an unmistakable force for re-

42. E. R. Shipp, "Candidacy of Jackson Highlights Split among Black Muslims," *New York Times,* 27 February 1984; James Emerson Whitehurst, "The Mainstreaming of the Black Muslims: Healing the Hate," *Christian Century* 97 (27 February 1980): 225-29.

ligion in politics and not at all discordant with a common leadership style among black clergy. Surveys show that black Christians usually want clergy who will lead, and they do not object to those who lead, as Jackson does, with a memorable style.[43]

Today politics is integral to most (but not all) of the black church. The revolution is completed, and yet the result has not been at all radical. Campaigning for Jesse Jackson for president, for an expanded welfare state, and for a vague notion of world peace simply does not add up to radicalism by any definition. The public face of black religion has altered enormously in the last twenty years or so. But that alteration has not been a move toward radical rejection of liberal values or institutions. If any-thing, it has been a determined decision to join in the liberal society and get from it what one can, from "rights" to jobs, just like any other partic-ipant in the pluralist competition. To be sure, sometimes there is talk of "Resurrection" and "the Cross," perhaps some radical-sounding quota-tions about "economic violence." But they are not evidence of radical-ism—just a different cultural style than that used by dominant intellectual and media elites. Beneath the biblical language appears to lie no far-reach-ing transformative ethic, but rather the ongoing demand for black en-trance into liberal America—jobs, rights, opportunities, and respect.

There is certainly the possibility of a challenge to the liberal order from much of organized black religion in the United States. The legiti-macy of political action is widely accepted in the black church, among laity as well as clergy; there is much less lay resistance to it than in white Protestant or Catholic circles. But what is missing is a commitment to a theological or ideological analysis and program that reject liberal Amer-ica, as opposed to rejecting present divisions of the economic pie or ra-cism. The ideas of radical black theologians in the 1960s and 1970s did not penetrate to the local church. Liberal culture proved far more attrac-tive—and remains so.

The "Cults"

PERHAPS THE MOST OBVIOUS CANDIDATE for genuine radicalism in American religion is the world of the so-called cults. They would seem to be self-evident centers of radical opposition to liberal America's moral-

43. Barbara A. Reynolds, *Jesse Jackson: The Man, the Movement, the Myth* (Chicago: Nelson-Hall, 1975); Reed, *The Jesse Jackson Phenomenon;* Thomas Landess and Richard Quinn, *Jesse Jackson and the Politics of Race* (Ottawa, IL: Green Hill, 1985).

ity, individualism, and institutions, including the church and government. And, at least in the 1970s, hardly a radical era otherwise in the United States, cults appeared to be on the march.

The realm of the cults is always shifting and evolving. Any attempt to impose neat definition boundaries on this realm would be an exercise in illusion. The very term *cults* is a dubious choice, because it is a word that activates popular prejudice. However, for a large proportion of the cult analysts today, generally conservative Christian writers, *cults* is exactly the right word because it properly denotes something sinister.[44] Those not interested in terminological quarrels or who just want to get on with their discussions go along and use the common term *cults* also.[45] Some writers in the 1970s preferred more "neutral" terms such as *new religions* or *alternative religions*.[46] These made sense, though some cults are not new religions and some alternative religions are not cults. Moreover, these terms simply failed the test of ordinary usage—and still do. *Cults* is the reigning term, though some groups often called cults, such as the Mormons and Jehovah's Witnesses, now really qualify as alternative religions.

There are two ordinary paths to a definition of cults. One consists of naming groups commonly called cults. In this view, cults are nothing more than groups people say are cults, sometimes organized into varieties, sometimes just listed one after another without analytic framework.[47] Hare Krishna always gets a lot of attention, as does Meher Baba and, of course, the Unification Church (the Moonies). Also popular on

44. E.g., Walter Martin, *The Kingdom of the Cults* (Minneapolis: Bethany, 1985); Anthony A. Hoekema, *The Four Major Cults* (Grand Rapids: Eerdmans, 1963).

45. E.g., J. Gordon Melton and Robert L. Moore, *The Cult Experience: Responding to the New Religious Pluralism* (New York: Pilgrim, 1982). David G. Bromley and Anson Shupe complain about the term *cults* but use it regularly in *Strange Gods: The Great American Cult Scare* (Boston: Beacon, 1981), pp. 56-57 and *passim*.

46. E.g., Irving I. Zaretsky and Mark P. Leone, "The Common Foundation of Religious Diversity," in *Religious Movements in Contemporary America,* ed. Irving I. Zaretsky and Mark P. Leone (Princeton: Princeton University Press, 1974), pp. x-xxxvi; Jacob Needleman, *The New Religions* (Garden City, NY: Doubleday, 1970), ch. 1; Melton and Moore, *The Cult Experience,* pp. 15, 17.

47. Melton and Moore, *The Cult Experience,* pp. 19-20 and Appendix A has both; Ronald Enroth et al., *A Guide to Cults and New Religions* (Downers Grove, IL: InterVarsity Press, 1983) is an example of a straightforward presentation of a "list."

and, of course, the Unification Church (the Moonies). Also popular on the lists are the sensational People's Temple of Jim Jones, the Divine Light Mission, and the Children of God movement. More mysterious are Scientology, spiritualist groups, and that perennial spawner of fantasy, Satanism. While this list could be expanded almost indefinitely, the main groups come up again and again. The actual universe meant by "the cults" is well known.[48]

The other approach to this universe is more definitional, seeking to examine what cults have in common. Predictably, there are a host of competing candidates, but since these have the potential to sidetrack my purposes, I will offer a standard definition and proceed.[49] By a cult I mean a tight communal group that is united by an unconventional religion and is physically or psychologically in some tension with the rest of society.

48. E.g., on Hare Krishna: J. Stillson Judah, "The Hare Krishna Movement," in *Religious Movements in Contemporary America,* pp. 463-78; Bromley and Shupe, *Strange Gods,* ch. 2; Daniel Cohen, *The New Believers: Young Religion in America* (New York: M. Evans, 1975), sec. 2. On Meher Baba: Needleman, *The New Religions,* ch. 3; Dick Anthony and Thomas Robbins, "The Meher Baba Movement: Its Effect on Post-Adolescent Social Alienation," in *Religious Movements in Contemporary America,* pp. 479-511. On the Moonies: Eileen Barker, *The Making of a Moonie: Choice or Brainwashing* (New York: Basil Blackwell, 1984); Irving Louis Horowitz, ed., *Science, Sin and Scholarship: The Politics of Reverend Moon and the Unification Church* (Cambridge: M.I.T. Press, 1978); Cohen, *The New Believers,* sec. 1; Bromley and Shupe, *Strange Gods,* ch. 2. On Jim Jones: Bromley and Shupe, *Strange Gods,* ch. 2; Cohen, *The New Believers,* sec. 1. On Divine Light: Cohen, *The New Believers,* sec. 2; Bromley and Shupe, *Strange Gods,* ch. 2. On Children of God: Bromley and Shupe, *Strange Gods,* ch. 2; Cohen, *The New Believers,* sec. 1. On Mormonism: Hoekema, *The Four Major Cults;* Martin, *The Kingdom of the Cults,* ch. 6. On Jehovah's Witnesses: Lee R. Cooper, "Publish or Perish: Negro Jehovah's Witness Adaptation in the Ghetto," in *Religious Movements in Contemporary America,* pp. 700-21; Hoekema, *The Four Major Cults;* Martin, *The Kingdom of the Cults,* ch. 4. On scientology: Bromley and Shupe, *Strange Gods,* ch. 2; Martin, *The Kingdom of the Cults,* ch. 14. On spiritualism: June Macklin, "Belief, Ritual, and Healing: New England Spiritualism and Mexican-American Spiritualism Compared," in *Religious Movements in Contemporary America,* pp. 383-417. On Satanism: Edward J. Moody, "Magical Therapy: An Anthropological Investigation of Contemporary Satanism," in *Religious Movements in Contemporary America,* pp. 355-82; Cohen, *The New Believers,* sec. 3.

49. Three interesting discussions are in John Wilson, *Religion in American Society* (Englewood Cliffs, NJ: Prentice-Hall, 1978), pp. 139, 94-99, ch. 8; Willa Appel, *Cults in America: Programmed for Paradise* (New York: Holt, Rinehart and Winston, 1983), p. 4; Melton and Moore, *The Cult Experience,* pp. 15, 17.

sorted and seemingly disparate individual cults, or alternative religions, and therefore will serve.

The question is this: are cults a radical force in American religion? Have we at last found in them the hitherto missing place of radical religion in the United States? The answer is an emphatic yes if one reads some of the frightened and angry books on cults that appeared regularly in the 1970s. Moreover, there is no doubt that those who joined the 1970s-style cults were aligning themselves with groups originated by alienated radicals. In fact, a large proportion of the joiners are young people who are self-consciously radical in their alienation from contemporary liberal society.[50]

What disturbs critics more is the *nature* of many cults, which they see as deeply radical. Cults, they charge, are highly authoritarian, are devoted to brainwashing, and persistently attack societal institutions. Assertions of obsession with fanatical leaders are always controversial, as are the routine accusations of the brainwashing of converts. The groups in this portrait emerge as worthy imitators of the Maoists in their heyday of indoctrination and Hitler's SS in its.[51] The implicit and sometimes explicit objection here is that cults deny liberal freedom and that the individual with free choice disappears in a cult, is lost in a despot-ruled group of robots.

Defenders of the cults—rarely members or even fellow-travelers—understand these charges very well. But they are equally quick to insist that the cults are not radical from a shared liberal framework. They urge us not to fall for the cult scare "hoax." Yes, the cults have leaders; but they are mostly not the all-powerful, greedy, evil creatures the media portray. These defenders maintain that brainwashing is a myth, and they insist that the case for deception and mind control by cults is wildly exaggerated by anticultists. Moreover, they ask, who should speak for freedom? Should anticultists speak for it, those who sometimes legitimate deprogramming, an obvious exercise in the denial of human freedom and individual choice? Cult defenders say that anticultists are a new

50. For example, Appel, *Cults in America,* pp. 64-66; Ivan Doress and Jack N. Porter, "Kids in Cults," in *In Gods We Trust: New Patterns of Religious Pluralism in America,* ed. Thomas Robbins and Dick Anthony (New Brunswick, NJ: Transaction Books, 1981), pp. 297-302; Trudy Solomon, "Integrating the 'Moonie' Experience: A Survey of Ex-Members of the Unification Church," in *In Gods We Trust,* pp. 275-94; John Lofland, *Doomsday Cult: A Study of Conversion, Proselytization, and Maintenance of Faith* (New York: Irvington, 1977).

51. For example, Appel, *Cults in America,* chs. 3, 5, 6, and pp. 165-66.

form of "bigotry" when they claim to honor freedom while actually pro-faning it.[52]

The theory that the cults are an attack on the liberal institutions of the United States emphasizes the alternative model of organized life that each represents—which is an implicit, and often explicit, critique. Cult critiques are often selective, faulting some institutions—the Christian churches, for instance—more than others. Those others, often our government and our mixed capitalist economy, are arguably a good deal more important in our liberal order. Everyone concedes that the new cults of the 1970s caused severe family tensions, though older alternative religions such as the Mormons are extremely "pro-family" if one is within their confines. Actually, there is rarely any inherent opposition to family itself; it happens mostly when children and their families divide over cults.[53]

Moreover, even if the overall mood is somehow critical of liberal America as a place where the true faith—however defined—cannot flourish, the tendency of the cults to concentrate on withdrawal in one sense or another, rather than an all-out attack on liberal institutions and culture backed up by political engagement, drains radical energies from the cults. From this angle, cults are a kind of safety valve that draws off potentially potent radical force.[54] Cults "translate the individual's enthusiasm for change into a kind of change that will be tolerated. As a result, the majority of these groups sustain the social order; they do not challenge it. They are conservative, although often in a radical guise."[55]

Another perspective argues that joining a cult has normally been equally nonradical. Especially if young people joined one of the 1970s cults, the rebellion from their normal environment usually had a few long-term implications. According to this view, they were simply going through a stage of life, and chance led them to do so with a cult. Adolescent rebellion was at work, and few ended up in cults as their personal development proceeded. Nothing radical here, just a somewhat unconventional form of an age-old and necessary process, the separation of

52. Two good examples of critics of the anticult mood are Melton and Moore, *The Cult Experience,* pp. 36-46, 85; and Bromley and Shupe, *Strange Gods,* chs. 5, 7, pp. 124-127, 3-4, 204.

53. E.g., Bromley and Shupe, *Strange Gods,* pp. 70, 71, 77, 89-90.

54. Rodney Stark and William Sims Bainbridge, *The Future of Religion: Secularization, Revival and Cult Formation* (Berkeley: University of California Press, 1985), ch. 15.

55. Zaretsky and Leone, "The Common Foundation of Religious Diversity," in *Religious Movements in Contemporary America,* p. xxxv.

young people from their families as they move toward becoming integrated, independent personalities.[56]

These arguments are plausible and diminish the prima facie radicalness that some cults' lifestyle suggests. But the "they are not radical" disposition can be carried too far. One example is the claim that the cults are not radical because they are actually most concerned with practical help for people now. In this perspective, to be radical either involves not being primarily concerned with helping people or not being so *now*. By this test Marx was no radical; nor was Jesus. The issue is, what changes are required to help people? If they are sweeping, one may be a radical—and by this standard the cults are radical.[57]

More to the point is the cults' consistent emphasis on community, though not necessarily a separated community except in the newer cults. This emphasis on community, on the group's conformity to its norms rather than outside values—especially the larger liberal culture's values—is in fact the prime and distinguishing radical feature of cults. *Community* is a radical word in liberal cultures if it is meant as a commitment to a single group's values over the individual and over time. Community in the sense of an assorted number of group associations at one time or over a lifetime,[58] or as detached adherence to one or another "lifestyle," are expressions of *liberal individualism* in America.[59] Commitment to a cult over a lifetime is something different. This radical affirmation by cults of the culture-denying community value is undoubtedly one important reason so few Americans stay with cults. Cults ask too much of members in our culture. Cults do not really want anarchic, rebellious late-adolescents; they want people who are seriously prepared to opt for community, a community built around a serious and strict system of meaning at that.[60]

Though cults are in their complex way a challenge to liberal Amer-

56. For example, Melton and Moore, *The Cult Experience,* pp. 53-54; Appel, *Cults in America,* pp. 58-59.

57. Both arguments are in Zaretsky and Leone, "The Common Foundation of Religious Diversity," p. xxxv.

58. A basic description of America's communal pattern is in Herve Varenne, *Americans Together: Structured Diversity in a Midwestern Town* (New York: Columbia University Press, 1977).

59. Robert Bellah et al., *Habits of the Heart: Individualism and Commitment in American Life* (Berkeley: University of California Press, 1985), pp. 72-73.

60. For some emphasis on cults and community, see Appel, *Cults in America,* pp. 11, 13-14, 64-11; Melton and Moore, *The Cult Experience,* pp. 4-5, 27, 125, 31-35; Anthony and Robbins, "The Meher Baba Movement," in *Religious Movements in Contemporary America,* pp. 479-511, 73.

ica, their challenge is empty when one goes from theory to practice. The fact is that few cults have many followers. Students of cults know that cults do not have more than 200,000 adherents, and most estimates put the number much lower. Moreover, they diminished in size in the 1980s. Such celebrated groups as Hare Krishna and the Moonies, never very large despite all the publicity and scare stories, have fallen to below 5,000 members each in the United States.[61]

Their numbers are few, and their cooperation with each other varies from slight to none. Moreover, they do not last very long, on the whole. While sects do tend to recruit from the relatively disadvantaged in society, often people in self-conscious tension with the larger society, they do not flourish much beyond the first generation. They rarely grow much, and most, in fact, do not develop over time into larger groups, much less churches. As generations turn, the tension between the cult and the larger society tends to decrease—and with it the cult. If the tension does not decrease, then the cult does not grow either; its radicalness stands in its way. Most cults fade away either literally or into stagnant and forgotten backwaters of no growth or influence.[62] And, on the whole, they make no effort to strike at the larger culture except through example, often an example displayed from a distance at that. In this sense, their radicalness is distinctly nonengaged—and because of that somewhat toothless. If it is still true that the "new religions are at odds with the values, lifestyles, and aspirations of the majority of contemporary Americans . . . [they] condemn and reject the way most of us live . . . [and] seek to recruit and reshape anyone who will listen to them,"[63] what does this radicalness matter in society as a whole? The Sojourners community is intensely political in comparison with most cults. Cults lack a political agenda; they have only a privatist conversion agenda, which not only has not succeeded but is succeeding less and less.

The major exception is probably the Unification Church—the Moonies. They reflect the characteristics of a cult in almost all ways, including a strict sense of separation and alienation. But the objective of the group is not a withdrawal into a society of isolated "purity." Well more than most such groups, the Unification Church casts one eye outward and seeks to "communalize the whole society."[64] It neither shuns

61. Melton and Moore, *The Cult Experience,* pp. 26-27.

62. Stark and Bainbridge, *The Future of Religion,* ch. 6.

63. Thomas Robbins, Dick Anthony, Madeline Doucas, and Thomas Curtis, "The Last Civil Religion: Reverend Moon and the Unification Church," in *Science, Sin and Scholarship,* p. 67; Bromley and Shupe, *Strange Gods,* p. 4.

64. Robbins et al., "The Last Civil Religion," pp. 47-73.

politics nor approves it as an afterthought; politics is central for the Unification Church. And this more than anything else is why so much scrutiny and criticism has deluged this group.[65]

But the Unification Church and similar groups, as well as radical Christian communities such as Sojourners, are all similar in sharing limited popular appeal. However much they are a challenge in theory, in the actual gritty culture at present—or in prospect—they constitute no challenge to liberal culture or institutions. Thus, while there are radical cults and radical Christian groups that sharply disagree with our liberal society and its values, their practical significance at present is nil. Their numbers and resources are too few, which, in this case, is actually to say that their appeal is very weak. Liberalism and radical religion in America simply are not public enemies. They are different roads, but they do not crisscross, much less struggle with each other for the basic right of way. This may change, of course, though there is little sign that the American church-going public is eager to listen to the prophets heralding such a change.

65. A good discussion of this issue and others regarding the Unification Church in general is Robbins et al., "The Last Civil Religion," pp. 111-25; Marianne Lester, "Profits, Politics, Power: The Heart of the Controversy," in *Science, Sin and Scholarship,* pp. 155-59; Frank Baldwin, "The Korea Lobby," in *Science, Sin and Scholarship,* pp. 160-74; Ann Crittenden, "Moon's Sect Pushes Pro-Seoul Activities," in *Science, Sin and Scholarship,* pp. 176-91.

CHAPTER NINE

Conclusion

IN SO MANY REALMS OF AMERICAN LIFE TODAY it seems as though religion does not exist. Liberal culture seems completely triumphant. Moreover, the vestiges of religious culture that do remain as memories of the past are increasingly under fire. The public school is "free" of religion today, joining the workplace. Sports, rock music, and most certainly the shopping center are hardly places today where one is likely to meet religion.

It is true that religion has raised its head in the public realm recently and runs against the trend; it has occupied more of the political agenda in the last decade than at any time in the last fifty years. But while this may seem to be a sign of religion's health in the United States, one wonders. Perhaps the opposite is true: perhaps the reappearance of religion in public controversy is a sign of weakness, an expression of desperateness, the last, bitter struggle of a slowly dying subculture.

However, against such an analysis, which suggests a declining fate for religion in our liberal culture, we have our statistics regarding religious belief and church membership in the American population. We have seen how pervasive religious belief is in the United States and how most adult people affiliate with one or another form of organized religion. This is unquestionably an age of belief and commitment in America's diverse and complex world of religion. We do not lack straws in the wind, but they blow in every direction. To predict the future of religion in the United States would, therefore, be bold and perhaps foolish. It is, however, safer to suggest that its future will be deeply affected by its relationship with the larger liberal culture. And I would argue that it may well be that the future of liberal culture itself will in turn be affected significantly by its relationship with religion. Each has been very important to the other over the past three hundred years, and they seem almost destined to continue thus.

In this book I have explored the relationship between religion and liberalism in American culture. The common view, which deserves respect, is that religion has been an integral part of our history and remains so today. While it comes in many forms, the consistent theme is that religion serves liberal culture quite directly. In some versions, as we have observed, religion has operated as a source of American liberal values; in others, it has generated their public rationale (civil religion); in still others, religion has provided a foundation of belief and morality upon which liberalism unconsciously rests (de Tocqueville).

The list of suggested possibilities is long, and rarely is one idea proposed to the exclusion of all others. They all involve patterns of intermixing religion and liberalism that are complex and difficult to disentangle. Few of them seem wise to ignore. To be sure, the bulk of observers do not think that religion in America makes a significant contribution to the substance and direction of contemporary liberalism. They see it as clearly a junior partner now. Indeed, this is its own self-image. What remains the same, however, is the idea that going to church on Sunday and much of the rest of religion in America works to support the American way. Religion is an integral part of the American way, just as much as are the First Amendment, "getting ahead," and the celebration of individualism.[1] The intentions of religious leaders or groups—and indeed of those who have power in American culture—are not the issue. What actually happens is the issue. Proponents of this interpretation insist that the reality is a close and supportive interaction between religion and our culture.

Against this conventional view, whose richness I have tried to honor in the book, is a contrasting view of the contemporary image of religion in our society. From this perspective, religion in the United States is increasingly in revolt against liberal culture, or at least challenges it and is often in conflict with it. Noting the work of angry fundamentalists, activist liberal Protestants, separatist cults, and "prophetic" Catholic bishops, some analysts suggest that it would be difficult to confuse the contemporary situation with strong support for the liberal order. They suggest that those who disagree must have in mind a process that is a good deal deeper, or more mysterious, than the usual image of the closeness of religion and liberalism. And those who disagree must also have a large capacity to ignore the substantial contemporary evidence of conflict.[2]

There is as yet little developed theory that undertakes to explain the current undeniable signs of tension between parts of organized religion and contemporary liberalism. While hardly unprecedented in American

1. See my interpretation of these perspectives in detail in chapters 4 and 5.

2. This thesis is explored in chapters 6, 7, and 8.

history, the tension is unusual, especially in the last half-century, and we need to know much more about its origins, its patterns, and its future. Its existence cannot but impress students who have been schooled in American history, which often enough has reflected direct support for our liberal order from most of religion, organized or unorganized.

My argument in this book has been that we should not slight these indicators of tension in our day, even though they are young and their future is uncertain. I insist, though, that their sound is not a good measure of their fury, and that the depth of their attack on liberal culture is modest. Often it represents more a struggle to recall America to one version or another of "true" American values (liberalism) than a serious attack on liberal values or culture at their roots. I have also argued that we should not confuse the occasionally "radical" proclamations of religious elites with lay attitudes, nor igore the multitude of often conflicting directions of religious politics, the frequent political ineffectiveness of religious groups, and the resistance of the larger culture to their messages. Overall, the new mood of tension between some aspects of American religion and features of our liberal culture should be noted, but with due skepticism about any interpretation suggesting that we can best understand religion and liberalism today as antagonists. We are not there now; indeed, we are very far from there.

What I contend is that religion and liberalism, in fact, are as close together as they have ever been in American life. But if the signs of conflict are still superficial, there is also little basis for interpreting religion as a direct handmaiden of liberal culture. In American history this was often an apt metaphor—and at some points still is. But more often now, the nature of the closeness of religion and our culture is different. Religion still serves liberalism; but it does not serve it so much by rationalizing capitalism, providing the materials for a civic religion, endorsing liberal values and practices, and the rest, so much as it serves by offering a temporary *compensation* for the limitations of liberalism.

Religion provides a world where people may find some of what contemporary liberalism is so silent about (though not always by any means, and not for everyone). Many find meaning, values, and community in religion. This is a trinity that liberal culture does not provide for many modern Americans but one that many people obviously seek— sometimes desperately. Team sports appear to be one chosen means for help in these areas in the United States.[3] Religion is another, operating

3. For a fascinating discussion of sports in this context see Allen Guttmann, *From Ritual to Record: The Nature of Modern Sports* (New York: Columbia University Press, 1978), ch. 6 and pp. 134-36.

to fill up the empty spaces left by liberal culture without, on the whole, challenging liberalism in theory or in the culture. In this it performs no mean service, however unintended it may be in many instances, indeed however regretted by those in America who wish religion would provide a sharp edge for change in the society.

My argument points both to a possible explanation for the enduring strength of religion in our "modern" culture (unexpected in some circles), while opening both religion and liberalism in the nation to a fresh angle of interpretation. It has turned out that religion is basically supportive of our liberal order, but in a backhanded—though central—fashion.

This analysis implies that were religion to weaken, we could expect major consequences for liberalism and liberal culture in this country. The decline of religion might very well show liberalism's problems with meaning and with the encouragement of community. Its insufficiency for crucial human needs might emerge in a most unpleasant and even explosive fashion.

In light of this possibility it is ironic to note the virtual absence of religion in the writings of leading liberal theorists in our time. Such voices as John Rawls, Robert Dahl, Robert Nozick, and a host of others simply pass by the subject. Those who do not ignore religion act as if religion is a matter of the past. Its current absence may be regretted perhaps, as with Daniel Bell, or not regretted at all, but the fact of its absence is a given.[4]

Critics of liberalism make the same mistake that they have for a long time. In her illuminating book *The Radical Persuasion,* Aileen Kraditor remarks how turn-of-the-century Marxist opponents of liberal America simply would not acknowledge the complex role of ethnic and religious ties in worker self-definitions and thus seriously misunderstood the working class and mispredicted its behavior.[5] In like fashion, leftist critics today are largely secularists and, except for routine denunciations of something termed "the religious right," do not take religion seriously in the American equation.[6] Even so sympathetic an observer as Michael

---

4. Daniel Bell, *The Cultural Contradictions of Capitalism* (New York: Basic Books, 1978); Don Herzog, *Without Foundations: Justification in Political Theory* (Ithaca, NY: Cornell University Press, 1985).

5. Aileen Kraditor, *The Radical Persuasion, 1890–1917* (Baton Rouge: Louisiana State University Press, 1981).

6. Some examples of leftist critics who do not take religion seriously except for critics of the "religious right" are Richard Flacks, "The Left in Search of the People," *Working Papers for a New Society,* 8 (February 1981), and George Vickers, "A Guide to the Sectarian Left," *The Nation,* 17 May 1980.

Harrington, while acknowledging religion's existence, refuses to consider that it is a serious factor in American life any longer.[7]

It is also ironic to note just how hard so many unwary secular liberals struggle to drive religion not just from the public square, but from every corner of American life. This effort might make sense as a strategy for genuine radicals seeking to destroy liberalism or the United States as we know it. But it does not make much sense for the supposed friends of liberalism, given liberalism's reliance on religion.[8]

Sometimes the motivation to eliminate religion, or its force, appears to flow from a sense that intermingling religion with liberalism somehow corrupts liberalism. "Nonrational" or "irrational" elements do not belong. Yet we have seen that historic liberalism depended on religion at its beginning and for long afterwards. Very often the motivation is simply fear of religion, or some portion of organized religion: public Christianity as a threat to tolerance for Jews and atheists; assorted religious activists as a threat to liberal abortion policy, or feminism, or the public schools, or whatever.

At another level, there is a well-understood concern over the uneasy relations among religious groups and over how religion in America interacts with nonreligious elements in our diverse society. Public peace is the goal, and disputes deriving from religious energy, or fanaticism, have torn many a culture apart.[9] This is no small concern, and it is one only a fool would dismiss. But it cannot be pursued singlemindedly by the friends of liberalism. Religion is also important to liberalism in the United States.

If I am correct, my analysis raises important questions for liberalism. On the one hand, it points directly to problems in contemporary liberalism by underscoring the concern of much contemporary political thinking, which emphasizes liberalism's difficulties in ensuring a basis for political values as well as an environment in which to foster community. One thinks immediately of such useful works as *Habits of the Heart* by Robert Bellah and his colleagues, *The Naked Public Square* by Richard John Neuhaus, and, at a more formal philosophical level, *Without Foun-*

7. Michael Harrington, *The Politics at God's Funeral: The Spiritual Crisis of Western Civilization* (New York: Penguin, 1983).

8. This is a delicate business since few in the United States are willing to admit an animus toward religion. There clearly are such organized groups, such as the Freedom from Religion Foundation; but others who have self-consciously tried to drive religion out of the public square contend that they approve of religion in private, examples being the People for the American Way and the American Jewish Committee.

9. A characteristic expression is the editorial "Oh So Sure They're Right," *New York Times*, 9 September 1984.

PRIVATE /PUBLIC

dations by Don Herzog.[10] They confirm the implication of this study that liberalism is in trouble in its modern versions because in theory, and perhaps in practice, it no longer has a basis for values or community. Where I would differ is on the frequent intellectualist assumption that this basis is, in fact, missing or even weak in the United States simply because it is missing or weak in modern liberalism. Frankly, I believe that they have often confused elite intellectual culture with American culture as a whole.

It follows from this observation that the camps of both liberalism's critics and its sympathizers exaggerate the crisis of value and community that they discern in America. There may appear to be a crisis of dramatic importance among selected intellectuals in Cambridge, Massachusetts, or Berkeley, California; but the crisis is not as evident among the population at large. For many, religion continues to contain a source of *meaning* and *values* and, along with other activities, fills up the empty spaces of life in a liberal society with *community* (or at least the hope of community). If there is a dramatic crisis, it is more one for contemporary liberal theory in its intellectual, secular forms than for liberal culture as a whole.

To be sure, this is a matter of degree. We have seen in study after study of religious people in the United States how much religion is a retreat from or a compensation for what they do not discover in the larger culture. And the turn to activism by many differing religious groups can hardly be read as a statement of enthusiasm for the directions of current culture.

One might conclude that my analysis directs us to the goal that Bellah and his associates challenge modern American political thinking to pursue: serious reformulation of liberalism as we know it to address questions of meaning and community. Many contemporary intellectuals obviously share this goal and are attempting the challenge.[11] But I wonder how urgent this need is. The culture itself may have worked out its own means of dealing with the deficiencies of liberalism in good part through the role religion plays in many citizens' lives. Yet, if a reduced level of concern—even for liberalism in theory—may be appropriate, still liberalism as it applies in the American context should be reformulated. Accuracy is required: we need an acknowledgment that American liberalism is a halfbreed in practice, not the sole faith of a people.

10. Robert Bellah et al., *Habits of the Heart: Individualism and Commitment in American Life* (Berkeley: University of California Press, 1985); Richard John Neuhaus, *The Naked Public Square: Religion and Democracy in America* (Grand Rapids: Eerdmans, 1984); Don Herzog, *Without Foundations*.

11. A prominent example is Michael Sandel in his *Liberalism and the Limits of Justice* (Cambridge: Cambridge University Press, 1982).

Liberalism apparently can only exist, in the United States at any rate, with another, often misunderstood and not clearly liberal, supporting player: that player is religion, organized and unorganized. Instead of seeing this as a failure of modern liberalism or as indicative of the failures of modern liberalism, we should see it as indicative of strength. Perhaps it shows liberalism's continuing ability to be flexible and adaptive and to substitute other traditions and experiences for the gaps in its own adequacy as a living theory.

More relevant at the moment is the fact that religion in America today is not weak by any means. Even its underachievement in political terms derives more from its diversity than from its weakness among the population at large. Liberalism's reliance on religion is currently not at stake. Though many liberal theorists will not grant this reality, liberalism continues to get substantial—if indirect—reinforcement from religion in the United States.

It is the other side of the coin that might more plausibly attract our attention. That is, what are the problems posed for *religion* in our society if it abandons its indirect support of liberalism and engages liberalism in a frontal attack? The air is full of religious dissent over liberal culture, and the trend line is unmistakable.[12] Those who view themselves as allies of religion (of religion in the United States in particular) should ponder the implications. I have in mind the consequences for the health of religion itself. After all, for all of my emphasis on the dependence of liberalism on religion, their relationship is not a one-way street—not at all. Liberalism supports religion in the United States even as it is sustained by religion. To cite one obvious example: liberal political values expressed through the First Amendment and in Supreme Court decisions have often protected and nourished the free exercise of religion.[13]

I wonder specifically about the decline of religion's appeal—at least organized religion's appeal—if it shifts to attack the culture and society. If more of organized religion begins to insist that its followers choose between its vision of the holy life and contemporary society, how many Americans would select religion? One suspects that liberal culture would overwhelm the attraction of organized religion for many people, perhaps for most people, in the United States. No doubt many activist religious leaders at present, for example many liberal Protestant voices, expect substantial losses among the supposedly faithful as they press toward what

12. Chapters 6, 7, and 8 examine the mood of criticism of the culture from American religion.
13. The idea that religion needs liberalism, and this specific example, are nicely expressed in William A. Galston, "Public Morality and Religion in the Liberal State," *Political Science* 19 (Fall 1986): 807-24.

they see as a living faith. More than a few activists and commentators, as we know, believe that the process has already begun.

Some activists almost welcome these numerical declines, suggesting that the departure of casual believers strengthens the faithfulness and determination of those who remain.[14] That it also deepens their isolation and inability to reach the larger population is the rarely mentioned other side of the coin. It is true enough, however, that a devoted religious believer cannot make numbers the test of anything important when he or she is called to acknowledge and live the truth. The consequences of such discipleship must be what they will be.

Welcomed or not, there will be costs if American churches and religions demand that their followers break from their compromise with the liberal order. At the moment, this possibility is remote: neither liberalism nor religion in America is likely to suffer any noticeable costs from conflict and potential disentanglement. The reason is simply that no disentanglement appears on the horizon. For better or for worse, the rather remarkable relationship between religion and liberalism that I have described sails serenely on. Neither secular intellectuals nor religious activists will sink it quickly or easily.

14. See, e.g., William R. Hutchison, "Past Imperfect: History and the Prospect for Liberalism (I)," *Christian Century*, 1-8 January 1986, pp. 11-15.

BIBLIOGRAPHY

Ahlstrom, Sydney. *A Religious History of the American People*. 2 vols. Garden City, NY: Doubleday, 1975.

―――. "Theology in America: A Historical Survey." In *Religion in American Life*, vol. 1, edited by James Ward Smith and A. Leland Jamison, 232-321. Princeton: Princeton University Press, 1961.

Alexander, Charles P. "An Unwavering Voice for the Poor." *Time*, 14 October 1985, 68.

Alexander, John F. "Editorial." *The Other Side*, July-August 1975, 63.

―――. "Politics, Repentance and Vision." *The Other Side*, March-April 1974, pp. 2-4, 52-54.

Ames, Michael. "Ideological and Social Change in Ceylon." In *The Protestant Ethic and Modernization: A Comparative View*, edited by S. N. Eisenstadt, 271-88. New York: Basic Books, 1968.

Anderson, Jervis. "Standing out There on the Issues: Bishop Paul Moore, Jr." *New Yorker*, 28 April 1986.

Andreski, Stanislav. "Method and Substantive Theory in Max Weber." In *The Protestant Ethic and Modernization: A Comparative View*, edited by S. N. Eisenstadt, 46-63. New York: Basic Books, 1968.

Anthony, Dick, and Thomas Robbins. "The Meher Baba Movement: Its Effect on Post-Adolescent Social Alienation." In *Religious Movements in Contemporary America*, edited by Irving I. Zaretsky and Mark P. Leone, 479-511. Princeton: Princeton University Press, 1974.

―――. "Spiritual Innovation and the Crisis of American Civil Religion." In *Religion and America: Spirituality in a Secular Age*, edited by Mary Douglas and Steven Tipton, 229-48. Boston: Beacon, 1982.

Appel, Willa. *Cults in America: Programmed for Paradise*. New York: Holt, Rinehart and Winston, 1983.

Baldwin, Frank. "The Korea Lobby." In *Science, Sin and Scholarship: The Politics of Reverend Moon and the Unification Church*, edited by Irving Louis Horowitz, 160-74. Cambridge: M.I.T. Press, 1978.

Barker, Eileen. *The Making of a Moonie: Choice or Brainwashing.* New York: Basil Blackwell, 1984.

Baudrillard, Jean. *In the Shadow of the Silent Majorities . . . Or the End of the Social and Other Essays.* New York: Semiotexts, 1983.

Beatty, Kathleen Murphy, and Oliver Walter. "Religious Beliefs and Practice: New Forces in American Politics?" Paper presented at the annual meeting of the American Political Science Association, 1982.

———. "Religious Preference and Practice: Reevaluating Their Impact on Political Tolerance." *Public Opinion Quarterly* 48 (Spring 1984).

Bell, Daniel. *The Cultural Contradictions of Capitalism.* New York: Basic Books, 1978.

———. "The Return of the Sacred? The Argument on the Future of Religion." *British Journal of Sociology* 28 (December 1977): 419-49.

Bellah, Robert N. *Beyond Belief.* New York: Harper and Row, 1970.

———. *The Broken Covenant: American Civil Religion in Time of Trial.* New York: Seabury, 1975.

———. "Civil Religion in America." In *American Civil Religion,* edited by Russell Richey and Donald Jones, 21-44. New York: Harper and Row, 1974.

Bellah, Robert N.; Richard Madsen; William M. Sullivan; Ann Swidler; and Steven M. Tipton. *Habits of the Heart: Individualism and Commitment in American Life.* Berkeley: University of California Press, 1985.

Benson, Peter L., and Dorothy L. Williams. *Religion on Capitol Hill: Myths and Realities.* New York: Harper and Row, 1982.

Bercovitch, Sacvan. *The Puritan Origins of the American Self.* New Haven: Yale University Press, 1975.

Berger, Joseph. "U.S. Bishops Laud Economic Letter." *New York Times,* 14 November 1985.

Berger, Peter L. "From the Crisis of Religion to the Crisis of Secularity." In *Religion and America: Spirituality in a Secular Age,* edited by Mary Douglas and Steven Tipton, 14-24. Boston: Beacon, 1983.

———. "Religion in Post-Protestant America." *Commentary,* May 1986, 41-46.

Bibellini, Rosino, ed. *Frontiers of Theology in Latin America.* Maryknoll, NY: Orbis, 1979.

"The Bishops' Pastoral on the U.S. Economy: Reaction to the First Draft." *Overview,* February 1985, 1-6.

Black, David. "Religion: A Witness to Theology's Changing Face." *The Virginian-Pilot and the Ledger-Star,* 5 July 1986.

Briggs, Kenneth A. "Church Groups Protest." *New York Times,* 11 January 1984.

———. "Leader of Catholic Bishops Drafts Statement Opposing Partisanship." *New York Times,* 9 August 1984.

Bromley, David G., and Anson Shupe, eds. *New Christian Politics.* Macon, Georgia: Mercer University Press, 1984.

———. *Strange Gods: The Great American Cult Scare.* Boston: Beacon, 1981.

Brown, Robert McAfee. *Theology in a New Key: Responding to Liberation Themes.* Philadelphia: Westminster, 1978.

Buell, E. H., Jr. "An Army That Meets Every Sunday? Popular Support for the Moral Majority in 1980." Paper presented at the annual meeting of the Midwest Political Science Association, 1983.

Buursma, Bruce. "Bishops Decry U.S. Economic Order." *Wisconsin State Journal,* 7 June 1986.

Camara, Dom Helder. *Spiral of Violence.* London: Sheed and Ward, 1971.

Campagna, Bob, and Susan K. Delbner. "Faith and Resistance in Missouri." *Sojourners,* June 1986, 11.

Campbell, Thomas C., and Yoshio Fukuyama. *The Fragmented Layman: An Empirical Study of Lay Attitudes.* Philadelphia: Pilgrim Press, 1970.

Camus, Albert. *The Plague.* New York: Alfred A. Knopf, 1960.

Cantril, Hadley, and Muzafer Sherif. "The Kingdom of Father Divine." In *The Black Church in America,* edited by Hart M. Nelson, Raytha L. Yokley, and Anne K. Nelson, 175-93. New York: Basic Books, 1971.

Caplow, Theodore, et al. *All Faithful People: Change and Continuity in Middletown's Religion.* Minneapolis: University of Minnesota Press, 1983.

Castelli, Jim. *The Bishops and the Bomb: Waging Peace in a Nuclear Age (with text of the Bishops' 1983 Pastoral).* Garden City, NY: Doubleday-Anchor, 1983.

"Catholic Bishops and American Economics: A Survey of Comment, and Some of Our Own." *Religion and Society Report,* March 1985, B1-B10.

"The Catholic Priesthood." *Overview* 19 (no. 10): 1-8.

"Catholics Urged to Press Views." *New York Times,* 10 August 1984.

"Challenge of Peace: God's Promise and Our Response." *Catholic Herald,* 7 April 1983, 1-28.

The Christian as Citizen. Carol Stream, IL: Christianity Today Institute, 1985.

"Church vs. *Contra* Aid." *Christian Century,* 9 April 1986, 353-54.

Cleage, Albert B., Jr. "Coming in out of the Wilderness." In *The Black Church in America,* edited by Hart M. Nelsen, Raytha L. Yokley, and Anne K. Nelsen, 355-64. New York: Basic Books, 1971.

Clebsch, William. *From Sacred to Profane: The Role of Religion in American History.* New York: Harper and Row, 1968.

Clecak, Peter. *Crooked Paths: Reflections on Socialism, Conservatism, and the Welfare State.* New York: Harper and Row, 1977.

Coffin, William Sloan, Jr. *Once to Every Man.* New York: Atheneum, 1977.

Cohen, Daniel. *The New Believers: Young Religion in America.* New York: M. Evans, 1975.

Collum, Danny. "Trident Resistance Actions North and South." *Sojourners,* March 1986, 12.

Cone, James. *God of the Oppressed.* New York: Seabury, 1975.

The Connecticut Mutual Life Report on American Values in the '80s: The Impact of Belief. Hartford: Connecticut Mutual Life Insurance Co., 1981.

Cooper, Lee R. "Publish or Perish: Negro Jehovah's Witness Adaptation in the Ghetto." In *Religious Movements in Contemporary America,* edited by Irving I. Zaretsky and Mark P. Leone, 700-721. Princeton: Princeton University Press, 1974.

Cord, Robert L. *The Separation of Church and State: Historical Fact and Current Fiction.* New York: Lambeth, 1982.

Crews, Frederick. "In the Big House of Theory." *New York Review of Books,* 29 May 1986.

Crittenden, Ann. "Moon's Sect Pushes Pro-Seoul Activities." In *Science, Sin and Scholarship: The Politics of Reverend Moon and the Unification Church,* edited by Irving Louis Horowitz, 175-91. Cambridge: M.I.T. Press, 1978.

Curry, Thomas J. *The First Freedoms.* New York: Oxford University Press, 1986.

Davis, Lori. "Elites Don't Understand." *Moral Majority Report,* 22 February 1982.

Delloff, Linda-Marie. "In Spirituality and in Service: The NCC." *Christian Century,* 29 May 1985, 547-48.

De Soto, William. "Religious Interest Groups in Madison." Unpublished paper, 1985.

de Tocqueville, Alexis. *Democracy in America.* Vol. 2, Bk. 1, ch. 5. New York: Vintage, 1957.

Dolan, Jay P. *The American Catholic Experience: A History from Colonial Times to the Present.* Garden City, NY: Doubleday, 1985.

Dolan, Jay P., and David C. Leege. "A Profile of American Catholic Parishes and Parishioners: 1820s to the 1980s." *Notre Dame Study of Catholic Parish Life.* Report No. 2 (February 1985): 1-8.

Doner, Colonel V., ed. *The Christian Voice Guide: Strategies for Reclaiming America.* Pacific Grove, CA: Renod, 1984.

Doress, Ivan, and Jack N. Porter. "Kids in Cults." In *In Gods We Trust: New Patterns of Religious Pluralism in America,* edited by Dick Anthony and Thomas Robbins, 297-302. New Brunswick, NJ: Transaction Books, 1981.

Douglas, Mary, and Steven Tipton, eds. *Religion and America: Spirituality in a Secular Age.* Boston: Beacon, 1983.

Dunn, John. *Locke.* Oxford: Oxford University Press, 1984.

Dupre, Louis. "Spiritual Life in a Secular Age." In *Religion and America: Spirituality in a Secular Age,* edited by Mary Douglas and Steven Tipton, 3-13. Boston: Beacon, 1983.

Edsall, Thomas B. "Bush Isn't Just Pandering to Conservatives, He's Splitting Them." *Washington Post National Weekly Edition,* 10 March 1986.

Edwards, D. "Key Posts Please Conservatives." *Moral Majority Report,* 16 March 1981.

Edwards, Mark. "Liberals Using PAW to Pave the Way for Kennedy to Run for President." *Moral Majority Report,* 19 October 1981.

Eisenach, Eldon J. *Two Worlds of Liberalism: Religion and Politics in Hobbes, Locke, and Mill.* Chicago: University of Chicago Press, 1981.

Eisenstadt, S. N., ed. *The Protestant Ethic and Modernization: A Comparative View.* New York: Basic Books, 1968.

———. "The Protestant Ethic Thesis in an Analytical and Comparative Framework." In *The Protestant Ethic and Modernization: A Comparative View,* edited by S. N. Eisenstadt, 3-45. New York: Basic Books, 1968.

Elazar, Daniel. "The American Cultural Mix." In *The Ecology of American Political Culture,* edited by Daniel J. Elazar and Joseph Zikmund, 13-42. New York: Crowell, 1975.

———. *Community and Polity: The Organizational Dynamics of American Jewry.* Philadelphia: Jewish Publication Society, 1976.

Enroth, Ronald, et al. *A Guide to Cults and New Religions.* Downers Grove, IL: InterVarsity Press, 1983.

Evans, Robert A. "Recovering the Church's Transforming Middle: Theological Reflections on the Balance between Faithfulness and Effectiveness." In *Understanding Church Growth and Decline, 1950–1978,* edited by Dean R. Hoge and David A. Roozen, 288-314. New York: Pilgrim Press, 1979.

"Excerpts from Draft of Bishops' Letter on the U.S. Economy." *New York Times,* 12 November 1984.

Falwell, Jerry. *Listen America*. Garden City, NY: Doubleday, 1980.

"Falwellians' Force Is Hard to Resist." *Milwaukee Journal*, 25 October 1983.

Feagin, Joe R. "Black Catholics in the United States: An Exploratory Analysis." In *The Black Church in America*, edited by Hart M. Nelsen, Raytha L. Yokley, and Anne K. Nelsen, 246ff. New York: Basic Books, 1971.

Fischoff, Ephriam. "The Protestant Ethic and the Spirit of Capitalism: The History of a Controversy." In *The Protestant Ethic and Modernization: A Comparative View*, edited by S. N. Eisenstadt, 67-86. New York: Basic Books, 1968.

Fitzgerald, Frances. "A Disciplined Charging Army." *New Yorker*, 18 May 1981.

Flacks, Richard. "The Left in Search of the People." *Working Papers for a New Society* 8 (February 1981).

Fowler, Robert Booth. *Believing Skeptics: American Political Intellectuals, 1945–1964*. Westport, CT: Greenwood, 1978.

———. *A New Engagement: Evangelical Political Thought, 1966–1976*. Grand Rapids: Eerdmans, 1982.

———. "Religion and Liberalism in the United States." In *The Liberal Future in America: Essays in Renewal*. Westport, CT: Greenwood Press, 1985.

———. *Religion and Politics in America*. Metuchen, NJ: Scarecrow Press, 1985.

Frady, Marshall. *Billy Graham: A Parable of American Righteousness*. Boston: Little, Brown, 1979.

Franz, Deltun. "Channeling War Taxes to Peace." *Sojourners*, March 1977, 21-33.

Frazier, E. Franklin. *The Negro Church in America*. New York: Schocken, 1970.

Freud, Sigmund. *The Future of an Illusion*. Garden City, NY: Doubleday, 1964.

Fromm, Erich. *Escape from Freedom*. New York: Avon, 1965.

Gallup, George, Jr., and David Poling. *The Search for America's Faith*. Nashville: Abingdon, 1980.

Galston, William A. "Public Morality and Religion in the Liberal State." *Political Science* 19 (Fall 1986): 807-24.

Gardiner, James J., and J. Deotis Roberts, eds. *Quest for a Black Theology*. Philadelphia: Pilgrim, 1971.

Garrison, Vivian. "Sectarianism and Psychosocial Adjustment: A Controlled Comparison of Puerto Rican Pentecostals and Catholics." In *Religious Movements in Contemporary America*, edited by Irving I. Zaretsky and Mark P. Leone, 298-329. Princeton: Princeton University Press, 1974.

Gaustad, Edwin Scott. "Did the Fundamentalists Win?" In *Religion and America: Spirituality in a Secular Age*, edited by Mary Douglas and Steven Tipton, 169-78. Boston: Beacon, 1983.

————. *Dissent in American Religion.* Chicago: University of Chicago Press, 1973.

Gerth, H. H., and C. Wright Mills. "A Biographical View." In *From Max Weber,* 3-31. New York: Oxford University Press, 1958.

Gerth, H. H., and C. Wright Mills, eds. *From Max Weber.* New York: Oxford University Press, 1958.

"Getting Ready for the Hero." *Sojourners,* January 1986.

Gish, Art. "Simplicity." *The Other Side,* May-June 1973, 14-16.

Glock, Charles, et al. *To Comfort and to Challenge: A Dilemma of the Contemporary Church.* Berkeley: University of California Press, 1967.

Golden, Penny, and Mitchell McConnell. *Sanctuary: The New Underground Railroad.* Maryknoll, NY: Orbis, 1986.

Goldman, Ari L. "Church Council Urged to Change." *New York Times,* 16 May 1985.

Gordon, Mary S. "Black Religious Gather, Ask 'Specific Needs' Be Recognized." *National Catholic Reporter,* 28 August 1981.

"Graham Lauds Moral Majority." *Moral Majority Report,* 16 February 1981.

Greeley, Andrew M. *American Catholics since the Council: An Unauthorized Report.* Chicago: Thomas More, 1985.

————. *The Denominational Society.* Glenview, IL: Scott, Foresman, 1972.

————. "A 'Radical' Dissent." In *Challenge and Response: Critiques of the Catholic Bishops' Draft Letters on the U.S. Economy,* edited by Robert Royal, 33-47. Washington, DC: Ethics and Public Policy Center, 1985.

————. "Religious Musical Chairs." In *In Gods We Trust: New Patterns of Religious Pluralism in America,* edited by Thomas Robbins and Dick Anthony, 101-26. New Brunswick, NJ: Transaction Books, 1981.

Greeley, Andrew M., and Mary Greeley Durkin. *How to Save the Catholic Church.* New York: Viking, 1984.

Guth, James L. "The New Christian Right." In *The New Christian Right: Mobilization and Legitimization,* edited by Robert C. Liebman and Robert Wuthnow, ch. 2. New York: Aldine de Gruyter, 1983.

————. "The Politics of Preachers: Southern Baptist Ministers and Christian Right Activism." In *New Christian Politics,* edited by David G. Bromley and Anson Shupe, 235-49. Macon, GA: Mercer University Press, 1984.

————. "The Politics of the 'Evangelical Right': An Interpretive Essay." Paper presented at the American Political Science Association, 1981.

————. "Southern Baptist Clergy: Vanguard of the Christian Right?" In *The*

New Christian Right: Mobilization and Legitimization, edited by Robert C. Liebman and Robert Wuthnow, ch. 6. New York: Aldine de Gruyter, 1983.

Gutiérrez, Gustavo. *A Theology of Liberation.* Maryknoll, NY: Orbis, 1973.

Hadden, Jeffrey K. *The Gathering Storm in the Churches.* Garden City, NY: Doubleday, 1969.

————. "Televangelism and the Future of American Politics." In *New Christian Politics,* edited by David G. Bromley and Anson Shupe, 151-64. Macon, GA: Mercer University Press, 1984.

Hall, John R. "The Apocalypse at Jamestown." In *In Gods We Trust: New Patterns of Religious Pluralism in America,* edited by Thomas Robbins and Dick Anthony, 171-90. New Brunswick, NJ: Transaction Books, 1981.

Hall, Thomas Cuming. *The Religious Background of American Culture.* Boston: Little, Brown, 1930.

Hall-Williams, Steven. "Pledge Says 'No' to *Contra* Aid." *Sojourners,* June 1986, 10.

Hamilton, Charles V. *The Black Preacher in America.* New York: William Morrow, 1972.

Hammond, Phillip E. "Another Great Awakening?" In *The New Christian Right: Mobilization and Legitimization,* edited by Robert C. Liebman and Robert Wuthnow, ch. 11. New York: Aldine de Gruyter, 1983.

Hanna, Mary T. *Catholics and American Politics.* Cambridge: Harvard University Press, 1979.

————. "From Civil Religion to Prophetic Church: American Bishops and the Bomb." Unpublished paper.

Harding, Vincent. "In the Company of the Faithful." *Sojourners,* May 1985, 14-21.

Harper, Charles L., and Kevin Leicht. "Explaining the New Religious Right: Status Politics and Beyond." In *New Christian Politics,* edited by David G. Bromley and Anson Shupe, 101-10. Macon, GA: Mercer University Press, 1984.

Harrington, Michael. *The Politics at God's Funeral: The Spiritual Crisis of Western Civilization.* New York: Penguin, 1983.

Harris, Michael P. "A First for Black Catholics." *Time,* 28 March 1988, p. 71.

Harrison, Ira. "The Storefront Church as a Revitalization Movement." In *The Black Church in America,* edited by Hart M. Nelsen, Raytha L. Yokley, and Anne K. Nelsen, 240-45. New York: Basic Books, 1971.

Hartz, Louis. *The Liberal Tradition in America.* New York: Harcourt, Brace and World, 1955.

Heimert, Alan. *Religion and the American Mind: From the Great Awakening to the Revolution.* Cambridge: Harvard University Press, 1966.

Henry, Carl F. H. "Church and State: Why the Marriage Must be Saved." In *The Christian as Citizen,* 9-13. Carol Stream, IL: Christianity Today Institute, 1985.

Hertzberg, Arthur. "The Triumph of the Jews." *New York Review of Books.* 21 November 1985.

Hertzke, Allan. *Representing God in Washington: The Role of Religious Lobbies in the American Polity.* Knoxville: University of Tennessee Press, 1988.

"The Hiroshima Decision." *Sojourners,* August-September 1985.

Hitchcock, James. *The Decline and Fall of Radical Catholicism.* New York: Herder and Herder, 1971.

Hoekema, Anthony A. *The Four Major Cults.* Grand Rapids: Eerdmans, 1963.

Hoffman, Thomas John. "Religion and Politics: An Empirical Inquiry." Ph.D. dissertation, University of Arizona, 1982.

Hoge, Dean R. *Converts, Dropouts, Returnees: A Study of Religious Change among Catholics.* New York: Pilgrim Press, 1981.

———. "National Contextual Factors Influencing Church Trends." In *Understanding Church Growth and Decline, 1950–1978,* 94-122. New York: Pilgrim Press, 1979.

———. "A Test of Theories of Denominational Growth and Decline." In *Understanding Church Growth and Decline, 1950–1978,* 179-97. New York: Pilgrim Press, 1979.

Hoge, Dean R., and David A. Roozen. "Research on Factors Influencing Church Commitment." In *Understanding Church Growth and Decline, 1950–1978,* 42-68. New York: Pilgrim Press, 1979.

———. "Some Sociological Conclusions about Church Trends." In *Understanding Church Growth and Decline, 1950–1978,* 315-33. New York: Pilgrim Press, 1979.

Horowitz, Irving Louis. "The Politics of New Cults: Non-Prophetic Observations on Science, Sin and Scholarship." In *In Gods We Trust: New Patterns of Religious Pluralism in America,* edited by Thomas Robbins and Dick Anthony, 161-70. New Brunswick, NJ: Transaction Books, 1981.

———. *Science, Sin and Scholarship: The Politics of Reverend Moon and the Unification Church.* Cambridge: M.I.T. Press, 1978.

Hume, David. *The National History of Religion.* Oxford: Oxford University Press, 1976.

Hunter, James Davison. *American Evangelicalism: Conservative Religion and the Quandary of Modernity.* New Brunswick, NJ: Rutgers University Press, 1983.

————. *Evangelicalism: The Coming Generation.* Chicago: University of Chicago Press, 1987.

————. "The Liberal Reaction." In *The New Christian Right: Mobilization and Legitimization,* edited by Robert C. Liebman and Robert Wuthnow, ch. 8. New York: Aldine de Gruyter, 1983.

Hutchison, William R. "Past Imperfect: History and the Prospect for Liberalism (I)." *Christian Century,* 1-8 January 1986, 11-15.

Ignatieff, Michael. *The Needs of Strangers.* New York: Penguin, 1986.

"In Defense of Creation: The Nuclear Crisis and a Just Peace." *Christian Century,* 14 May 1986, 481.

Isaac, Rael Jean. "Do You Know Where Your Church Offerings Go?" *Reader's Digest,* January 1983, 120-25.

Jackson, Dave, and Neta Jackson. "Living in Community, Being the Church." *The Other Side,* May-June 1973, 8-13.

Jaffe, Frederick S., et al. *Abortion Politics: Private Morality and Public Policy.* New York: McGraw-Hill, 1981.

Johnstone, Ronald L. "Negro Preachers Take Sides." In *The Black Church in America,* edited by Hart M. Nelsen, Raytha L. Yokley, and Anne K. Nelsen, 275-86. New York: Basic Books, 1971.

Jones, Phillip Barron. "An Examination of the Statistical Growth of the Southern Baptist Convention." In *Understanding Church Growth and Decline, 1950–1978,* edited by Dean R. Hoge and David A. Roozen, 160-78. New York: Pilgrim Press, 1979.

Judah, J. Stillson. "The Hare Krishna Movement." In *Religious Movements in Contemporary America,* edited by Irving I. Zaretsky and Mark P. Leone, 463-78. Princeton: Princeton University Press, 1974.

Kann, Mark E. *The American Left: Failures and Fortunes.* New York: Praeger, 1982.

Kant, Immanuel. *Religion within the Limits of Reason Alone.* New York: Harper and Row, 1960.

Kelley, Dean M. "Commentary: Is Religion a Dependent Variable?" In *Understanding Church Growth and Decline, 1950–1978,* edited by Dean R. Hoge and David A. Roozen, ch. 15, pp. 338-39. New York: Pilgrim Press, 1979.

————. *Why Conservative Churches Are Growing.* New York: Harper and Row, 1972.

Kelly, George Armstrong. *Politics and Religious Consciousness in America.* New Brunswick, NJ: Transaction Books, 1984.

Kennedy, Eugene. "America's Activist Bishops: Examining Capitalism." *New York Times Magazine,* 12 August 1984.

————. *The Now and Future Church*. Garden City, NY: Doubleday, 1984.

Kersten, Lawrence K. *The Lutheran Ethic: The Impact of Religion on Laymen and Clergy*. Detroit: Wayne State University Press, 1970.

King, Martin Luther, Jr. "Letter from Birmingham Jail." In *The Black Church in America*, edited by Hart M. Nelsen, Raytha L. Yokley, and Anne K. Nelsen, 292-98. New York: Basic Books, 1971.

Koch, Adrienne. *Madison's "Advice to My Country."* Princeton: Princeton University Press, 1966.

Koch, Adrienne, and William Peden, eds. *The Life and Selected Writings of Jefferson*. New York: Random House, 1944.

Kotre, John. *The View from the Border.* Chicago: Aldine, 1971.

Kraditor, Aileen S. *The Radical Persuasion, 1890–1917*. Baton Rouge: Louisiana State University Press, 1981.

Krauthammer, Charles. "Perils of the Prophet Motive." In *Challenge and Response: Critiques of the Catholic Bishops' Draft Letter on the U.S. Economy*, edited by Robert Royal, 48-58. Washington, DC: Ethics and Public Policy Center, 1985.

Kristol, Irving. *Reflections of a Neo-Conservative*. New York: Basic Books, 1983.

Kurtz, Harold. "Lobbying—The Opposite of Crusade: How Norman Lear's Group Battles to Keep Religion out of Public Affairs." *Washington Post National Weekly Edition*, 17 February 1986.

Ladd, E. C. *Where Have All the Voters Gone?* New York: Norton, 1982.

Laffin, Art. "The Final Verdict." *Sojourners*, March 1986, 35.

Landess, Thomas, and Richard Quinn. *Jesse Jackson and the Politics of Race*. Ottawa, IL: Green Hill, 1985.

Lawler, Philip F. *How Bishops Decide: An American Catholic Case Study*. Washington, DC: Ethics and Public Policy Center, 1986.

Lee, Robert W. "The Hypocrisy about Religion and Politics." *Conservative Digest*, December 1986, 85-94.

Leege, David C. "The Parish as Community: Developing Community and Commitment." *Notre Dame Study of Catholic Parish Life*, Report No. 10, March 1987.

————. "Parish Organizations: People's Needs, Parish Services, and Leadership." In *Notre Dame Study of Catholic Life*, Report No. 8, July 1986.

Leege, David C., and Joseph Gremillion. "The People, Their Pastors, and the Church: Viewpoints on Church Policies and Positions." In *Notre Dame Study of Catholic Parish Life*, Report No. 7, March 1986, 1-14.

Leege, David C., and Thomas A. Trozzolo. "Participation in Catholic Parish

Life: Religious Rites and Parish Activities in the 1980s." In *Notre Dame Study of Catholic Parish Life*, Report No. 3, April 1983, 1-8.

————. "Religious Values and Parish Participation: The Paradox of Individual Needs in a Communitarian Church." In *Notre Dame Study of Catholic Parish Life*, Report No. 4, June 1985, 1-8.

Lester, Marianne. "Profits, Politics, Power: The Heart of the Controversy." In *Science, Sin and Scholarship: The Politics of Reverend Moon and the Unification Church*, edited by Irving Louis Horowitz, 155-59. Cambridge: M.I.T. Press, 1978.

Liebman, Robert C. "Mobilizing the Moral Majority." In *The New Christian Right: Mobilization and Legitimization*, edited by Robert C. Liebman and Robert Wuthnow, ch. 3. New York: Aldine de Gruyter, 1983.

Liebman, Robert C., and Robert Wuthnow, eds. *The New Christian Right: Mobilization and Legitimization*. New York: Aldine de Gruyter, 1983.

Lincoln, C. Eric. "The Black Muslims as a Protest Movement." In *The Black Church in America*, edited by Hart M. Nelsen, Raytha L. Yokley, and Anne K. Nelsen, 210-24. New York: Basic Books, 1971.

————. *The Black Muslims in America*. Boston: Beacon, 1973.

Littell, Franklin H. *From State Church to Pluralism: A Protestant Interpretation of Religion in American History*. Garden City, NY: Doubleday, 1962.

Litwack, Leon. *Been in the Storm so Long*. New York: Viking, 1980.

Locke, John. *A Letter concerning Toleration*. New York: Bobbs-Merrill, 1955.

————. *The Reasonableness of Christianity*. Palo Alto, CA: Stanford University Press, 1958.

————. *Two Treatises of Government*. Edited by Thomas I. Cook. New York: Hafner, 1959.

Lofland, John. *Doomsday Cult: A Study of Conversion, Proselytization, and Maintenance of Faith*. New York: Irvington, 1977.

Lucas, Lawrence. *Black Priest/White Church*. New York: Random House, 1970.

Luker, Kristin. *Abortion and the Politics of Motherhood*. Berkeley: University of California Press, 1984.

Luthy, Herbert. "Once Again: Calvinism and Capitalism." In *The Protestant Ethic and Modernization: A Comparative View*, edited by S. N. Eisenstadt, 87-108. New York: Basic Books, 1968.

Lyles, Jean Caffrey. "'Military' Psalms Restored to Hymnals." *Washington Post*, 5 July 1986.

McBrien, Richard P. "Roman Catholicism: E. Pluribus Unum." In *Religion and America: Spirituality in a Secular Age,* edited by Mary Douglas and Steven Tipton, 179-89. Boston: Beacon, 1983.

MacIntyre, Alasdair. *After Virtue: A Study in Moral Theory.* Notre Dame, IN: University of Notre Dame Press, 1981.

McKenna, David L. "A Political Strategy for the Local Church." *The Christian as Citizen,* 19-23. Carol Stream, IL: Christianity Today Institute, 1985.

McKinney, William J., Jr. "Performance of United Church of Christ Congregations in Massachusetts and in Pennsylvania." In *Understanding Church Growth and Decline, 1950–1978,* edited by Dean R. Hoge and David A. Roozen, 222-47. New York: Pilgrim Press, 1979.

Macklin, June. "Belief, Ritual, and Healing: New England Spiritualism and Mexican-American Spiritism Compared." In *Religious Movements in Contemporary America,* edited by Irving I. Zaretsky and Mark P. Leone, 383-417. Princeton: Princeton University Press, 1974.

McLoughlin, William G. *Revivals, Awakening, and Reform: An Essay on Religion and Social Change in America, 1607–1977.* Chicago: University of Chicago Press, 1978.

Mahoney, Roger. "The Catholic Conscience and Nuclear War: Becoming a Church of Peace Advocacy." *Commonweal* 109 (23 March 1982): 137-43.

Marcuse, Herbert. *One-Dimensional Man.* Boston: Beacon, 1964.

Marsden, George. "Preachers of Paradox: The Religious New Right in Historical Perspective." In *Religion and America: Spirituality in a Secular Age,* edited by Mary Douglas and Steven Tipton, 150-68. Boston: Beacon, 1982.

Marshall, Gordon. *In Search of the Spirit of Capitalism: An Essay on Max Weber's Protestant Ethic Thesis.* New York: Columbia University Press, 1982.

Martin, Walter. *The Kingdom of the Cults.* Minneapolis: Bethany, 1985.

Marty, Martin E. *A Nation of Behavers.* Chicago: University of Chicago Press, 1976.

———. "Religion in America since Mid-Century." In *Religion and America: Spirituality in a Secular Age,* edited by Mary Douglas and Steven Tipton, 273-87. Boston: Beacon, 1983.

———. *Righteous Empire: The Protestant Experience in America.* New York: Dial Press, 1970.

———. "Two Kinds of Civil Religion." In *American Civil Religion,* edited by Russell E. Richey and Donald G. Jones, 139-157. New York: Harper and Row, 1974.

Martz, Larry. "Trouble on the Far Right: Has Success Spoiled Political Fundamentalism?" *Newsweek,* 14 April 1986, 24-25.

Marx, Gary T. "Religion: Opiate or Inspiration of Civil Rights Militancy among Negroes?" *American Sociological Review* 32 (February 1967): 64-72.

Maust, John. "The NBEA: Striving to Be Both Black and Christian." *Christianity Today*, 27 June 1980, 58-59.

Mead, Sidney. *The Lively Experiment.* New York: Harper and Row, 1963, 1975.

———. *The Nation with the Soul of a Church.* New York: Harper and Row, 1975.

Melton, J. Gordon, and Robert L. Moore. *The Cult Experience: Responding to the New Religious Pluralism.* New York: Pilgrim Press, 1982.

"Members of Congress Hold Ties to 21 Religious Groups." *Christianity Today*, 18 January 1984, 61-64.

Merelman, Richard M. *Making Something of Ourselves: On Culture and Politics in the United States.* Berkeley: University of California Press, 1984.

"Methodists Refuse to 'Wallow in Doom.'" *Religion and Society Report*, July 1986, 2-6.

Míguez Bonino, José. *Doing Theology in a Revolutionary Situation.* Philadelphia: Fortress, 1975.

Mill, John Stuart. "Autobiography." In *Essential Works of John Stuart Mill*, edited by M. Lerner, 11-182. New York: Bantam, 1961.

———. "Three Essays on Religion." In *The Philosophy of J. S. Mill*, edited by Marshall Cohen, 443-524. New York: Modern Library, 1961.

———. "Utilitarianism." In *The Philosophy of J. S. Mill*, edited by Marshall Cohen, 321-98. New York: Modern Library, 1961.

———. "The Utility of Religion." In *Essential Works of John Stuart Mill*, edited by M. Lerner, 402-31. New York: Bantam, 1961.

Miller, James Foyle. *A Study of United Methodists and Social Issues.* New York: United Methodist Church, 1983.

Miller, Perry. *Nature's Nation.* Cambridge: Harvard University Press, 1967.

———. "The Puritan Way of Life." In *Puritanism in Early America*, edited by George M. Waller, 4-22. Boston: D. C. Heath, 1950.

Miller, William Lee. "American Religion and American Political Attitudes." In *Religion in American Life*, vol. 2, edited by James Ward Smith and A. Leland Jamison, 81-118. Princeton: Princeton University Press, 1961.

———. *The First Liberty: Religion and the American Republic.* New York: Knopf, 1986.

Mitzman, Arthur. *The Iron Cage: An Historical Interpretation of Max Weber.* New York: Knopf, 1970.

Monsma, Stephen V. "Windows and Doors in the Wall of Separation." In *The Christian as Citizen*, 14-18. Carol Stream, IL: Christianity Today Institute, 1985.

Moody, Edward J. "Magical Therapy: An Anthropological Investigation of Contemporary Satanism." In *Religious Movements in Contemporary America*, edited by Irving I. Zaretsky and Mark P. Leone, 355-82. Princeton: Princeton University Press, 1974.

Morgan, Edmund S., ed. *Puritan Political Ideas*. Indianapolis: Bobbs-Merrill, 1965.

Myrdal, G. "The Negro Church: Its Weakness, Trends and Outlook." In *The Black Church in America*, edited by Hart M. Nelsen, Raytha L. Yokley and Anne K. Nelsen, 257-64. New York: Basic Books, 1971.

National Conference of Catholic Bishops. *Economic Justice for All: Catholic Social Teaching and the U.S. Economy*. Washington, DC: National Conference of Catholic Bishops, 1986.

National Council of Churches. "Response to *Reader's Digest* Article." 1983.

Needleman, Jacob. *The New Religions*. Garden City, NY: Doubleday, 1970.

Nelsen, Hart M., and Anne K. Nelsen. *The Black Church in the Sixties*. Lexington: University of Kentucky Press, 1975.

Nelsen, Hart M., Raytha L. Kiokley, and Ann K. Nelsen, eds. *The Black Church in America*. New York: Basic Books, 1971.

Neuhaus, Richard John. "Four American Individualisms." *Religion and Society Report* 2 (May 1985): 1-2.

———. *The Naked Public Square: Religion and Democracy in America*. Grand Rapids: Eerdmans, 1984.

———. *What the Fundamentalists Want*. Washington, DC: Ethics and Public Policy Center, 1985.

Niebuhr, H. Richard. *Christ and Culture*. New York: Harper and Row, 1951.

———. "The Protestant Movement and Democracy in the United States." In *Religion in American Life*, vol. 1, edited by James Ward Smith and A. Leland Jamison, 20-71. Princeton: Princeton University Press, 1961.

———. *The Social Sources of Denominationalism*. New York: Meridian, 1929, 1960.

Norton, Will, Jr. "John Perkins, the Prophet." *Christianity Today*, 1 January 1982, 20-22.

———. "John Perkins: The Stature of a Servant." *Christianity Today*, 1 January 1982, 18-19.

Nouwen, Henri J. M. "Creating True Intimacy: Solidarity among the People of God." *Sojourners*, June 1985, 14-18.

O'Connell, John K. "The Catholic Church on Nuclear Arms and Warfare." Unpublished paper, 2 December 1982, 1-11.

"Oh So Sure They're Right." Editorial in *New York Times*, 9 September 1984.

Ostling, Richard N. "A Defeat for Sanctuary." *Time*, 12 May 1986.

———. "Moving into the Mainstream." *Time*, 19 September 1983.

———. "Opting for the Browning Version: The Episcopal Church Picks an Activist Liberal as Its Leader." *Time*, 23 September 1985.

———. "Power, Glory—and Politics: Right-Wing Preachers Dominate the Dial." *Time*, 17 February 1986.

———. "Warring over Where Donations Go." *Time*, 28 March 1983.

Paris, Peter J. *The Social Teaching of the Black Churches*. Philadelphia: Fortress, 1985.

"Peace Pentecost 1985." *Sojourners*, May 1985, 22-23.

"Peace with Justice Week." *Religion and Society Report*, December 1985, 5-7.

Perkins, John. *A Call to Wholistic Ministry*. St. Louis: Open Door, 1980.

———. *Let Justice Roll Down*. Glendale, CA: Regal, 1976.

Peshkin, Alan. *God's Choice: The Total World of the Christian School*. Chicago: University of Chicago Press, 1986.

Pfeffer, Leo. *Church, State and Freedom*. Boston: Beacon, 1953. Revised and enlarged edition, Boston: Beacon, 1967.

Pfeffer, Leo, and Anson Phelps Stokes. *Church and State in the United States*. New York: Harper and Row, 1964.

Pierard, Richard V., and James L. Wright. "No Hoosier Hospitality for Humanism: The Moral Majority in Indiana." In *New Christian Politics*, edited by David G. Bromley and Anson Shupe, 195-212. Macon, GA: Mercer University Press, 1984.

Plasterer, Sue E. "A Study of the 11 United Methodist Churches of Madison, Wisconsin." Unpublished paper, 1982.

Posey, Walter Brownlow. *Religious Strife on the Southern Frontier*. Baton Rouge: Louisiana State University Press, 1965.

"A Prayer of a Chance, Taking Evil Seriously: An Interview with Gordon Cosby." *Sojourners*, June 1986, 15-19.

Pulkingham, Graham. "Interview." *Sojourners*, January 1977, 21-23.

———. "The Shape of the Church to Come." *Sojourners*, November 1976 and December 1976.

Quinley, Harold E. *The Prophetic Clergy: Social Activism among Protestant Ministers*. New York: John Wiley, 1974.

Rauff, Edmund A. *Why People Join the Church*. New York: Pilgrim Press, 1979.

Rawls, John. *A Theory of Justice*. Cambridge: Harvard University Press, 1971.

"Reader's Digest Article Called Half Truths, Hearsay." *Dimensions: The Wisconsin United Methodist Newspaper,* February 1983, 1.

Reapsome, James. "Trends: Black Christians Find Unity in Missions and Evangelism." *Christianity Today,* 15 May 1987, 54 and 57.

Reed, Adolph L., Jr. *The Jesse Jackson Phenomenon*. New Haven, CT: Yale University Press, 1986.

Reeves, Richard. *American Journey*. New York: Simon and Schuster, 1982.

Reichley, A. James. *Religion in American Public Life*. Washington, DC: Brookings, 1985.

"Religion and Education." Special issue of *Daedalus,* Spring 1988.

Religion in America: 50 Years, 1935–1985. Gallup Report No. 236, May 1985.

"Rethinking Evangelization of Black Families." *Our Sunday Visitor,* 24 August 1986.

Reynolds, Barbara A. *Jesse Jackson: The Man, the Movement, the Myth*. Chicago: Nelson-Hall, 1975.

Richardson, James T.; Mary White Stewart; and Robert B. Simmonds. "Conversion to Fundamentalism." In *In Gods We Trust: New Patterns of Religious Pluralism in America,* edited by Thomas Robbins and Dick Anthony, 127-39. New Brunswick, NJ: Transaction Books, 1981.

Richey, Russell E., and Donald Jones, eds. *American Civil Religion*. New York: Harper and Row, 1974.

Riley, Patrick. *Kant's Political Philosophy*. Totowa, NJ: Rowman and Littlefield, 1983.

Robbins, Thomas, and Dick Anthony, eds. *In Gods We Trust: New Patterns of Religious Pluralism in America*. New Brunswick, NJ: Transaction Books, 1981.

Robbins, Thomas; Dick Anthony; Madeline Doucas; and Thomas Curtis. "The Last Civil Religion: Reverend Moon and the Unification Church." In *Science, Sin and Scholarship: The Politics of Reverend Moon and the Unification Church*. Cambridge: M.I.T. Press, 1978.

Robertson, Pat. *America's Date with Destiny*. Nashville: Nelson, 1986.

Roof, Wade Clark. "Alienation and Apostasy." *Society,* May-June 1978, 41-45.

———. "America's Voluntary Establishment: Mainline Religion in Transition." In *Religion and America: Spirituality in a Secular Age,* edited by Mary Douglas and Steven Tipton, 130-49. Boston: Beacon, 1983.

Roof, Wade Clark, and William McKinsey. *American Mainline Religion: Its Changing Shape and Future*. New Brunswick, NJ: Rutgers University Press, 1987.

Roozen, David A. "The Efficacy of Demographic Theories of Religious Change: Protestant Church Attendance, 1952–1968." In *Understanding Church Growth and Decline, 1950–1978,* edited by Dean R. Hoge and David A. Roozen, 123-43. New York: Pilgrim Press, 1979.

Roozen, David A., and Jackson W. Carroll. "Recent Trends in Church Membership and Participation." In *Understanding Church Growth and Decline, 1950–1970,* edited by Dean R. Hoge and David A. Roozen, 21-41. New York: Pilgrim Press, 1979.

Rosenberg, Tina. "How the Media Made the Moral Majority." *Washington Monthly,* May 1982, 26-29, 32-34.

Rothenberg, Stuart R., and Frank Newport. *The Evangelical Voter: Religion and Politics in America.* Washington, DC: Institute for Government and Politics, 1984.

Royal, Robert, ed. *Challenge and Response: Critiques of the Catholic Bishops' Draft Letter on the U.S. Economy.* Washington, DC: Ethics and Public Policy Center, 1985.

Ryan, William C. "The Historical Case for the Right of Sanctuary." *Journal of Church and State* 29 (1987): 209-32.

Sackett, Victoria A. "Between Pro-Life and Pro-Choice." *Public Opinion,* April-May 1985, 53-55.

Sandel, Michael. *Liberalism and the Limits of Justice.* Cambridge: Cambridge University Press, 1982.

Sanford, Charles B. *The Religious Life of Thomas Jefferson.* Charlottesville, VA: University of Virginia Press, 1984.

Scanzoni, John. "Resurgent Fundamentalism." *Christian Century* 97 (10-17 September 1980): 847-49.

Schaeffer, Franky. *Bad News for Modern Man: An Agenda for Christian Activism.* Westchester, IL: Crossway Books, 1984.

———. *A Time for Anger.* Westchester, IL: Crossway Books, 1982.

Schiltz, Timothy D., and R. Lee Rainey. "The Geographic Distribution of Elazar's Political Subcultures among the Mass Population: A Research Note." *Western Political Quarterly* 31 (1978): 410-15.

Seabury, Paul. "Trendier than Thou: The Episcopal Church and the Secular World." Washington, DC: Ethics and Public Policy Center, 1978, 1-7.

Shipp, E. R. "Candidacy of Jackson Highlights Split among Black Muslims." *New York Times,* 27 February 1984.

Shupe, Anson, and William Stacey. "The Moral Majority Constituency." In *The New Christian Right: Mobilization and Legitimization,* edited by Robert C. Liebman and Robert Wuthnow, ch. 5. New York: Aldine de Gruyter, 1983.

Sider, Ronald J. *Rich Christians in an Age of Hunger: A Biblical Study.* Downers Grove, IL: InterVarsity Press, 1977.

Sider, Ronald J., and Richard K. Taylor. *Nuclear Holocaust and Christian Hope.* New York: Paulist, 1982.

Sigmund, Paul. "Christianity, Ideology, and Political Philosophy." In *Essays on Christianity and Political Philosophy,* edited by George W. Carey and James V. Schall, 79-91. Lanham, MD: University Press of America, 1984.

Silberman, Charles E. *A Certain People: American Jews and Their Lives Today.* New York: Summit Books, 1985.

Silk, Leonard. "A Call for Economic Change Based on Moral View." *New York Times,* 12 November 1984.

Simpson, John H. "Moral Issues and Status Politics." In *The New Christian Right: Mobilization and Legitimization,* edited by Robert C. Liebman and Robert Wuthnow, ch. 10. New York: Aldine de Gruyter, 1983.

————. "Support for the Moral Majority and Its Sociomoral Platform." In *New Christian Politics,* edited by David G. Bromley and Anson Shupe, 65-68. Macon, GA: Mercer University Press, 1984.

Skerry, Peter. "The Class Conflict over Abortion." *Public Interest* 52 (Summer 1978).

Skinner, Tom. *Black and Free.* Grand Rapids: Zondervan, 1970.

————. *How Black Is the Gospel?* Philadelphia: Lippincott, 1970.

Smidt, Corwin. "Evangelicals and the 1984 Election: Continuity or Change?" Paper presented at the annual meeting of the Society for the Scientific Study of Religion, 1985.

————. "Evangelicals vs. Fundamentalists: An Analysis of the Political Characteristics and Importance of Two Major Religious Movements within American Politics." Paper presented at the annual meeting of the Midwest Political Science Association, 1983.

Smith, James Ward, and Leland A. Jamison, eds. *Religion in American Life.* 4 vols. Princeton: Princeton University Press, 1961.

Smylie, James H. "Church Growth and Decline in Historical Perspective." In *Understanding Church Growth and Decline, 1950-1978,* edited by Dean R. Hoge and David A. Roozen, 69-93. New York: Pilgrim Press, 1979.

Sojourners Peace Ministry. "The Gospel Compels." *Sojourners,* March 1986, 6.

Solomon, Trudy. "Integrating the 'Moonie' Experience: A Survey of Ex-Members of the Unification Church." In *In Gods We Trust: New Patterns of Religious Pluralism in America,* edited by Thomas Robbins and Dick Anthony, 275-94. New Brunswick, NJ: Transaction Books, 1981.

Speer, James A. "The New Christian Right and Its Parent Company: A Study in Political Contrasts." In *New Christian Politics,* edited by David G. Bromley and Anson Shupe, 19-40. Macon, GA: Mercer University Press, 1984.

The Spiritual Climate in America Today. Princeton: Gallup, 1983.

Stanmeyer, William A. *Clear and Present Danger: Church and State in Post-Christian America.* Ann Arbor: Servant Books, 1983.

Stark, Rodney, and William Sims Bainbridge. *The Future of Religion: Secularization, Revival and Cult Formation.* Berkeley: University of California Press, 1985.

Stein, Ben. "Norman Lear vs. the Moral Majority." *Saturday Review,* February 1981, 23-27.

————. *The View from Sunset Blvd.* New York: Basic Books, 1979.

————. "The War over What We'll See on TV." *Chicago Tribune,* 22 February 1981.

Stockton, Ronald. "The Falwell Core." Paper presented at the annual meeting of the American Political Science Association, 1985.

Stone, Donald. "Social Consciousness in the Human Potential Movement." In *In Gods We Trust: New Patterns of Religious Pluralism in America,* edited by Thomas Robbins and Dick Anthony, 215-27. New Brunswick, NJ: Transaction Books, 1981.

Stringfellow, William. *An Ethic for Christians and Other Aliens in a Strange Land.* Waco, TX: Word, 1976.

"A Tide." *Newsweek,* 15 September 1980.

Tom Skinner Associates 15th Anniversary booklet. 1979.

Torres, Sergio, and John Eagleson, eds. *The Challenge of Basic Christian Communities.* Maryknoll, NY: Orbis, 1981.

Toward the Future: Catholic Social Thought and the U.S. Economy: A Lay Letter. New York: Lay Commission on Catholic Social Teaching and the U.S. Economy, 1984.

Tucker, Robert C., ed. *The Marx-Engels Reader.* 2d ed. New York: Norton, 1978.

"TV: Where the Girls Are Good Looking and the Good Guys Win: But Whose World View Is This?" *Christianity Today,* 4 October 1984, pp. 36-41.

Varenne, Herve. *Americans Together: Structured Diversity in a Midwestern Town.* New York: Columbia University Press, 1977.

Vickers, George. "A Guide to the Sectarian Left." *The Nation,* 17 May 1980, 591-96.

"The Views of American Catholics." *New York Times,* 25 November 1985.

Wald, Kenneth D. *Religion and Politics in the United States.* New York: St. Martin's, 1986.

Wallis, Jim. *Agenda for a Biblical People.* New York: Harper and Row, 1976.

———. *The Call to Conversion.* New York: Harper and Row, 1981.

———. "The New Regime." *Post-American* 3 (1974): 30.

———. "Post-American Christianity." *Post-American* 1 (1971).

———. "Poverty Is a Scandal." *Sojourners,* November 1985, 4-5.

———. "The Rise of Christian Conscience." *Sojourners,* January 1985, 12-16.

———. "What Does Washington Have to Say to Grand Rapids?" *Sojourners,* July 1977, 3-4.

Walrath, Douglas A. "Social Change and Local Churches: 1951–1975." In *Understanding Church Growth and Decline, 1950–1978,* edited by Dean R. Hoge and David A. Roozen, 248-69. New York: Pilgrim Press, 1979.

Walzer, Michael. "Puritanism as a Revolutionary Ideology." In *The Protestant Ethic and Modernization: A Comparative View,* edited by S. M. Eisenstadt, 109-34. New York: Basic Books, 1968.

Weber, Max. *The Protestant Ethic and the Spirit of Capitalism.* New York: Scribner's, 1958.

Weber, Paul J., and Dennis A. Gilbert. *Private Churches and Public Money: Church-Government Fiscal Relations.* Westport, CT: Greenwood, 1981.

Weisman, Steven R. "U.S. and Vatican Restore Full Ties." *New York Times,* 11 January 1984.

"What Does It Mean To Be Pro-Life?" *Sojourners,* November 1980.

Whitehead, John W. *The Second American Revolution.* Elgin, IL: David C. Cook, 1982.

Whitehurst, James Emerson. "The Mainstreaming of the Black Muslims: Healing the Hate." *Christian Century* 97 (27 February 1980): 225-29.

Wilcox, Clyde. "The New Christian Right: Patterns of Political Beliefs." Paper presented at the annual meeting of the Midwest Political Science Association, 1983.

Williams, Peter W. *Popular Religion in America: Symbolic Change and the Modernization Process in Historical Perspective.* Englewood Cliffs, NJ: Prentice-Hall, 1980.

Willimon, William. "A Crisis of Identity: The Struggle of Modern Mainline Protestantism." *Sojourners,* May 1986, 24-28.

Wills, Garry. *Inventing America: Jefferson's Declaration of Independence.* Garden City, NY: Doubleday, 1978.

Wilmore, Gayraud S. *Black Religion and Black Radicalism: An Examination of the Black Experience in Religion.* Garden City, NY: Doubleday, 1972.

Wilson, John. *Public Religion in American Culture.* Philadelphia: Temple University Press, 1979.

———. *Religion in American Society: The Effective Presence.* Englewood Cliffs, NJ: Prentice-Hall, 1978.

Wilson, Robert L., and William H. Willimon. *The Seven Churches of Methodism.* Durham, NC: Duke University Press, 1985.

Wineke, William R. "Social Issues Split Presbyterians." *Wisconsin State Journal,* 23 November 1985.

Woodward, Kenneth. "The Holy Seesaw: Up and Down on Liberation Theology." *Newsweek,* 14 April 1986.

Wright, Louis B. *The Cultural Life of the American Colonies: 1607-1763.* New York: Harper and Row, 1957, 1962.

Yinger, J. Milton, and Stephen J. Cutler. "The Moral Majority Viewed Sociologically." In *New Christian Politics,* edited by David G. Bromley and Anson Shupe, 69-90. Macon, GA: Mercer University Press, 1984.

Yoder, John Howard. "Why I Didn't Pay All My Income Tax." *Sojourners,* March 1977, 11-12.

Zaretsky, Irving I., and Mark P. Leone. "The Common Foundation of Religious Diversity." In *Religious Movements in Contemporary America,* edited by Irving I. Zaretsky and Mark P. Leone, x-xxxvi. Princeton: Princeton University Press, 1974.

Zaretsky, Irving I., and Mark P. Leone, eds. *Religious Movements in Contemporary America.* Princeton: Princeton University Press, 1974.

Ziff, Larzer. *Puritanism in America.* New York: Viking, 1973.

Zwier, Robert. *Born-Again Politics: The New Christian Right in America.* Downers Grove, IL: InterVarsity, 1982.

Index of Names

Kelley, Dean, 16, 19, 20, 23, 28
Kelly, George Armstrong, 81
Kennedy, John F., 77, 98
King, Martin Luther, Jr., 66, 75, 79,
  137, 138, 140, 141, 145
Koop, C. Everett, 119
Kraditor, Aileen S., 157
Krauthammer, Charles, 105
Kristol, Irving, 20

Lear, Norman, 117
Leege, David, 101
Lincoln, Abraham, 77
Locke, John, 8, 9, 10

McBrien, Richard, 101
MacIntyre, Alasdair, 71, 72, 75
McLoughlin, William G., 58, 59, 60
Madison, James, 11, 65
Malcolm X, 144
Marty, Martin, 80
Marx, Karl, 3, 13, 48, 49, 51, 60,
  61, 62, 63, 64, 68, 69, 151
Mead, Sidney, 54, 78
Merelman, Richard, 27
Mill, John Stuart, 10
Mondale, Walter, 100, 133

Neuhaus, Richard John, 72, 73, 74,
  75, 158
Niebuhr, H. Richard, 3, 64
Niebuhr, Reinhold, 75, 85
Nietzsche, Friedrich, 72
Nixon, Richard M., 77, 79
Novak, Michael, 104
Nozick, Robert, 157

Perkins, John, 141, 142
Poling, David, 18, 21, 29
Pulkingham, Graham, 132

Rauff, Edmund A., 21
Rawls, John, 75, 157
Reagan, Ronald, 76, 78, 87, 88, 90,
  100, 103, 118, 119, 120, 126,
  133, 134
Robb, Edmund, 87
Roberts, Oral, 126
Robertson, Pat, 112, 126
Roof, Wade Clark, 20
Roosevelt, Franklin D., 84

Schaeffer, Franky, 107, 115, 124
Skinner, Tom, 141, 142
Smidt, Corwin, 127
Spellman, Cardinal Francis, 82
Stark, Rodney, 1
Stringfellow, William, 130
Swaggart, Jimmy, 126

Tocqueville, Alexis de, 3, 10, 11,
  12, 13, 28, 30, 48, 56, 69, 70,
  71, 72, 74, 75, 82, 155

Varenne, Herve, 41
Voltaire, 9

Wald, Kenneth, 2, 105, 120
Wallis, Jim, 130, 131, 132, 134
Walter, Oliver, 127
Walzer, Michael, 52
Weber, Max, 3, 13, 48, 49, 50, 51,
  52, 53, 60, 69
Whitehead, John, 107, 115
Wilcox, Clyde, 127
Williams, Dorothy L., 119
Wilson, John, 64, 80

Young, Andrew, 145